A Model for Rural Development: An Experiment from Fogo Island, Newfoundland

We are committed to sharing what we know from our Fogo Island work so that others can hold onto the specificity of place that is so crucial to wellbeing.

Zita Cobb, Founder and President, Shorefast Foundation
Joe Batt's Arm, Fogo Island, Newfoundland

Underway today in the region of Fogo Island and Change Islands, Newfoundland is a bold and well-thought out experiment in contemporary rural development. It merits our attention because development intentions are being pursued in a manner that has practical lessons that are useful to those of us with stakes in advancing the prosperity and happiness of people in contemporary rural regions. The Fogo Island case embodies these proactive, strategic and intelligent development qualities that seem to be able to make a difference for attaining an increased measure of influence and control over a rural area's future.

Kenneth E. Corey, Mark I. Wilson with Marie J. Corey
Michigan State University, East Lansing, Michigan

A Model for Rural Development: An Experiment from Fogo Island, Newfoundland

Kenneth E. Corey and Mark I. Wilson
with Marie J. Corey

October 2014

Michigan State University
East Lansing, Michigan USA

Michigan State University Libraries
366 West Circle Drive
East Lansing, Michigan 48824

© 2014 by Kenneth E. Corey, Mark I. Wilson, and Marie J. Corey. All rights reserved.

Printed in the United States of America, on acid-free, SFI-certified paper.
(Sustainable Forestry Initiative, www.sfiprogram.org)

ISBN 10: 1626100349
ISBN-13: 978-1-62610-034-3

Dedication

We dedicate this monograph to ordinary folks everywhere. These are the regular people, who too often do not have their voice heard by the decision makers and the powerful.

We are grateful to Professor John Friedmann for reminding all of us that ordinary folks need to be at the table so that they can be involved in expressing their stake in the development of their local place and its region. The lessons discussed from the Fogo Island and Change Islands region are offered here in support of getting ordinary people to the table; staying at the table, and once included there to practice informed and intelligent decision making in planning that ensures that their regional development priorities attract the respect and resources needed to bring satisfaction from having contributed to the advancement of the social well-being and happiness of their community.

Contents

Figures and Photo Credits xi

Preface xv

Acknowledgements xvii

Part I: Introduction

The General Pathway of the Monograph 3
Why Read This? 4

Part II: Background and Method

Background 9
Origins of the Monograph 10
Why the Fogo Island Rural Development Work Seems to Resonate 11
Methodology 11
    A Role for Islands in Modeling? 12
    Effective Modeling 13
    Place, Place, Place and Specificity, Specificity, Specificity!!! 14
Our Job 15

Part III: Pre-Existing Conditions to the Model: Merchant System and The Fogo Process

Early European Contact 19
Merchant Credit System 20
The Fogo Process 22
    Background at the Provincial Level 22
    What Happened at the Fogo Island Level 24

Part IV: The Shorefast Foundation Model for Rural Development

Development and a Participatory Process 32
Specificity of Operations 33

Part V: Rural Development-Planning Elements

Business Structure, Logistics and Distribution 37
Fostering Connectedness 39
Recognizing Our True Assets 41
    Ocean, Land and People 42
    Geotourism 42
Building on Inherent Assets of a Place – Optimizing for Place/ Community 43
    Fogo Island Arts Program 44
    Business Assistance Fund and Regional Economic Development 45
    Fogo Island Inn 48

Building Culture into the Fabric of a Business 53
Community Ownership of Capital 55
Holding on to Ways of Knowing 57

Part VI: Next Stages in the Fogo Island Rural Development Model

Fogo Island Dialogues... 63
New Ocean Ethic 65
Marketing and Business Development 70

Part VII: Team Shorefast: Leader, Champion, Innkeeper, Teacher, Learner and Local Economy Diversifier – the Invention of a New Social Entrepreneurship Model

Team Shorefast.. 77
Board Chair and Ocean Advisor Gordon Slade 79
Gordon Slade and Battle Harbor as Proof-of-Concept 79
Founding Brothers of the Foundation: Anthony Cobb and Alan Cobb 81
Other Members of the Shorefast Board of Directors 81
Other Key Team Shorefast Members... 81
Founder and President Zita Cobb 82
    Leader and the Team 82
    Principal Face of the Foundation 82
    How Useful is the Fogo Island Model Elsewhere Without a Zita Cobb? 83
    Zita Cobb and Inn keeping 84
    Zita Cobb and the Unconscious Conspiracy 85

Part VIII: The Model Interpreted and Imagined

Imagining and Extending Our Interpretations... 89
A Metaphor to Frame Our Conclusions 90
Historical Baseline 90
Early Stage Resuscitation... 91
Geology At The Edge 92
Next Steps... 94
    Importance of Early Measurement and Monitoring 94
    Importance of Vertical Policy and Program Alignment 95
Maturing... 96
    Initial Indications of Modeling Potential 97
    Infrastructure, Regulation and Learning/Training.. 99
    Institutions, Information Infrastructure, Information Accumulation, Affinity
        Networking and Training.. 101
End States 103
    The Fishery 105
    Fogo Island Arts 105
    Business Assistance Fund 106
    Fogo Island Inn and Spin-Off Scenarios 107
    New Ocean Ethic, Literacy and Responsible Practice 111
    Fogo Island Dialogues 114
    Economic Development...115

Social Entrepreneurship 117
Now It Is Up To You 120

Part IX: Concluding Comments: A Model of Informed Actionable Rural Intelligent Development

Transparency 126
    Surplus Allocation 126
    Preliminary Metrics for the Fogo Island Model for Rural Development 128
Understanding 132
Inform Action 133
First Principle 134
Ordinary Folks: Another First Principle 135
Role Models: From the Ordinary to the Extraordinary 136
A Reminder for Would-Be Users of the Fogo Island Model: Place-Making is
    Everyone's Job 137
Our Final Comments on the Model's Roots and a Vision for Its Future 138
    A Model for Rural Development: An Experiment from Fogo Island, Newfoundland 138
    Activating the Model Elsewhere: From Pilot to Demonstration To Worldwide
        Implementation 140
    Theory and Method 142
    Empirical 143
    Fund-Raising, Resources Generation and Investment Partnering For Model
        Activation 144
    Deep Explication Combined with Our Intended Value Added 145
Why Are Some of Us Doing This Work? 146

Appendixes

1 Geotourism Elaborated 151
2 Connected Community Engagement Program of Connect Michigan 153
3 Product Business Outline (Excerpt From Proposal): A Project to Kick-start the Cottage
   Industry for Handmade Goods 155
4 Economic Cost-Benefit Assessment: 2012 Fogo Island Partridgeberry Harvest
   Festival 157
5 The Seven Seasons of Fogo Island and the Change Islands Region 159
6 A Shorefast Foundation Reading List 161
7 Some More Principal Components of the Fogo Island Model for Rural Development 163

Figures 171

References 201

Index 215

Figures and Photo Credits

Figures begin on page 173.

Figure 1: Map of the Fogo Island and the Change Islands Region (Photo courtesy of the Shorefast Foundation) First mention in text: page 9.

Figure 2: Landscape of Fogo Island Region Countryside (Photo: Paddy Barry) First mention in text: page 9.

Figure 3: Seascape of Fogo Island Region Countryside (Photo: Alex Fradkin) First mention in text: page 9.

Figure 4: Iceberg Near the Fogo Island Shore (Photo: Paddy Barry) First mention in text: page 9.

Figure 5: Diving Whale off Fogo Island (Photo: Paddy Barry) First mention in text: page 9.

Figure 6: A Traditional Newfoundland Cod Trap with Shorefast Cable (Photo courtesy of the Shorefast Foundation) First mention in text: page 11.

Figure 7. View of Cod Face (Photo: Paddy Barry) First mention in text: page 20.

Figure 8. Full View of Cod Fish (Photo: Paddy Barry) First mention in text: page 20.

Figure 9. Cinema Located in the Fogo Island Inn (Photo: Alex Fradkin) First mention in text: page 25.

Figure 10. Carpenter Working on a Fogo Island Punt Boat (Photo: Jamie Lewis) First mention in text: page 44.

Figure 11: Close-Up View of Mural in the Guest Elevator of the Fogo Island Inn (Photo: Eric Ratkowski) First mention in text: page 49.

Figure 12. Fogo Island Inn Guest Room: View and Sound of Sea from Open Window (Photo: Alex Fradkin) First mention in text: page 49.

Figure 13: Fogo Island Inn Guest Room: Note Bath Tub and Hand-Made Furnishings (Photo: Alex Fradkin) First mention in text: page 49.

Figure 14: Fogo Island Inn Suite with Wood-Burning Stove and Punt Boat Rocker (Photo: Alex Fradkin) First mention in text: page 49.

Figure 15: Dining Room of the Fogo Island Inn (Photo: Alex Fradkin) First mention in text: page 49.

Figure 16: Food Presentation # 1 (Photo: Alex Fradkin) First mention in text: page 49.

Figure 17: Food Presentation #2 (Photo: Alex Fradkin) First mention in text: page 49.

Figure 18: Murray McDonald, Executive Chef of the Fogo Island Inn with a Mummer (Photo: Paddy Barry) First mention in text: page 50.

Figure 19: Nicole's Café for Modern Interpretations of Newfoundland Regional Cuisine (Photo: Paddy Barry) First mention in text: page 50.

Figure 20: A Garden-to-Table Source for Some of the Produce for the Fogo Island Inn (Photo: Joe Ip) First mention in text: page 50.

Figure 21: One of a Number of Gardens that Source the Fogo Island Inn Kitchens (Photo: Paddy Barry) First mention in text: page 50

Figure 22: Local Garden Carrots on Their Way to the Fogo Island Inn's Dining Tables (Photo: Jamie Lewis) First mention in text: page 50

Figure 23: The Bar of the Fogo Island Inn: Its Signature Cocktail is the "Rockin Fogo" (Photo: Paddy Barry) First mention in text: page 51.

Figure 24: Profile of the Long Studio (Photo: Paddy Barry) First mention in text: page 54.

Figure 25: End View of the Long Studio (Photo: Bent René Synnevåg) First mention in text: page 54.

Figure 26: Tower Studio with Colored Rock in Foregraound (Photo: Bent René Synnevåg) First mention in text: page 54.

Figure 27: Tower Studio: View of the Dark Side (Photo: Bent René Synnevåg) First mention in text: page 54.

Figure 28: Bridge Studio (Photo: Bent René Synnevåg) First mention in text: page 54.

Figure 29: Squish Studio: With Blue Sea and Blue Sky (Photo: Bent René Synnevåg) First mention in text: page 54.

Figure 30: Squish Studio: With Iceberg, Growlers (pieces of floating ice) First mention in text: page and Waves (Photo: Paddy Barry) First mention in text: page 54.

Figure 31: Squish Studio: At Sunset (Photo: Bent René Synnevåg) First mention in text: page 54.

Figure 32: Wells House: Refurbished and Modernized Residence for Artists-in-Residence (Photo: Joe Ip) First mention in text: page 54.

Figure 33: View of the Fogo Island Inn from the Sea (Photo: Alex Fradkin) First mention in text: page 54.

Figure 34: Fogo Island Inn: A View on the Diagonal (Photo: Alex Fradkin) First mention in text: page 54.

Figure 35: An End View of the Fogo Island Inn (Photo: Alex Fradkin) First mention in text: page 54.

Figure 36: A Night View on the Angle of the Fogo Island Inn (Photo: Alex Fradkin) First mention in text: page 54.

Figure 37: Social Enterprise: Business Minded Ways that Serve Social Ends (Photo courtesy of the Shorefast Foundation) First mention in text: page 56.

Figure 38: Barr'd Islands Church has Been Re-Purposed as a Space for Performance (Photo: Paddy Barry) First mention in text: page 59.

Figure 39: The Dr. Leslie A. Harris Heritage Library is Located in the Fogo Island Inn (Photo: Alex Fradkin) First mention in text: page 70.

Figure 40: A Cozy Spot to Read in the Harris Library of the Fogo Island inn (Photo: Alex Fradkin) First mention in text: page 70.

Figure 41: Close-Up of a Mummer in the Fogo Island Inn during the Christmas Season (Photo: Paddy Barry) First mention in text: page 72.

Figure 42: Two Mummers at the Fogo Island Inn at Christmas Time (Photo: Paddy Barry) First mention in text: page 72.

Figure 43: Gordon Slade, Chair and Ocean Advisor of the Shorefast Foundation (Photo: Jamie Lewis) First mention in text: page 80.

Figure 44: Zita Cobb, President and Founder of the Shorefast Foundation (Photo: Luther Caverly) First mention in text: page 83.

Figure 45: Fishers Hauling in the a New Cod Pot that Enables Higher Price Points (Photo: Paddy Barry) First mention in text: page 129.

Figure 46: The New Cod Pot on the Deck of the Fishing Boat, it Enables Sustainability (Photo: Paddy Barry) First mention in text: page 129.

Figure 47: A View of the Motor Vessel Ketanja Near an Iceberg (Photo: Alex Fradkin) First mention in text: page 130.

Figure 48: Visitors Taking The Ketanja Boat Tours to See Icebergs, Seabirds and Whales (Photo: Alex Fradkin) First mention in text: page 130.

Figure 49: The Punt Chair was Built by Carpenters with Punt Boat Skills (Photo: Steffen Jaggenberg) First mention in text: page 133.

Preface

After first learning of the innovative regional development work on Fogo Island, we were enthused. In large part, our enthusiasm stemmed from what sounded like a fresh and creative approach for rural revival that was underway there. Dramatic architecture; the siting of artist studios perched on North Atlantic Ocean cliff edges; the advancement of art; the use of business both to generate income for the local communities and to design business to serve social ends; and to accomplish these intentions by means of the promotion and interfacing of these isolated localities with the development potential and opportunities of the global marketplace.

After preliminary investigation from a distance, we knew that we had to do some direct observation in the field. After seeing for ourselves what was happening on the ground on Fogo Island, we were more intrigued than ever. A small inn was partially constructed at the time of our initial visit to the island; its unique shape and the blending of traditional vernacular building design with imaginative contemporary design told us that we would have to return someday to see the finished project. More follow-up investigation and the initial field experience combined to compel us to want to document and make available our interpretations of the exciting work on Fogo Island. After working with planners, residents and business people in the rural regions and isolated places of Michigan's Upper Peninsula and northern Lower Peninsula, we knew that many others would appreciate and could learn from the development innovation underway on Fogo Island. We also believed that a wider readership with an interest in the future development of rural and small town regions might respond to the Fogo Island case.

We want the Fogo Island development lessons, in particular, to be considered by practitioners who are engaged in and committed to the planned and strategic development of rural places, especially in North America, but elsewhere as well. The practitioners who are foremost in our intentions are the regional development professionals and the local development citizen volunteers who work with, advise and support these professionals to improve the rural areas where they live and work.

We also are interested in having our findings used by scholars. Those scholars are the researchers and teachers and their students who are pursuing, and intend to engage in, careers focused on small town and rural regional development.

We have in mind that the lessons that we have derived from the Fogo Island development experiment might be used by these intended readers to catalyze and inspire innovation in local civic engagement and empowerment. Based on our years of working with and observing rural-area stakeholders, we are sensitive to the routine neglect and marginalization of rural and small town regions, especially when compared to society's dominant worldview and behavior toward city-regions. Thus, rural stakeholders may benefit particularly by being proactive and better informed by taking up local development tasks on their own initiative rather than waiting for others to take the lead or help out initially. Once a bottom-up self-determination mindset and resulting collective behavior has begun to show actual development results, there is a greater likelihood of others joining in and collaborating, especially in a rural regional development effort.

The Fogo Island case embodies these proactive, strategic and intelligent development qualities that seem to be able to make a difference in attaining an increased measure of influence and control over a rural area's future. With additional cases of rural development innovation in diverse locations and economic ecosystems from around the world, a broader movement in support of rural renewal can be set in motion. This too is part of our motivation in documenting the intelligent development that we have discovered to be underway on Newfoundland's Fogo Island and the Change Islands.

Initially, we had thought to document our findings in a peer-reviewed journal article targeted to a joint readership of regional development practitioners and scholars. However, as we delved deeper and learned more about the specifics of the emerging Fogo Island Rural Development Model, it was determined, at least initially, to document our interpretations in much more detail than usually is accommodated in an article. For now, we have opted for this format of a monograph so that the specificities of the Fogo Island region's place and processes might be seen in enough detail, with accompanying operational explications, that others elsewhere might use the model to inform effective strategic analyses and actions in their own rural regions. Further, in the spirit of the Shorefast Foundation President, Zita Cobb's vision of having Fogo Island serve as a model for rural development, we have prepared this monograph for maximum accessibility in both a free online edition and low-cost print edition options.

Kenneth E. Corey
Michigan State University
East Lansing, Michigan, USA

Mark I. Wilson
Michigan State University
East Lansing, Michigan, USA

with

Marie J. Corey
Michigan State University
East Lansing, Michigan, USA

October 2014

Acknowledgements

Our appreciation is extended to the following individuals. Without their support and the sharing of their knowledge our research into the Fogo Island Model for Rural Development would not have been possible: Mandy Applin; Paddy Barry; Jonathan Briggs; Stephane Beausoleil; Mona Brown; Rex Brown; Melanie Coates; Zita Cobb; Alexander (Sandy) Crawford; Kathleen Crotty; Sandra Cull; Eric Frederick; Leslie Grimm; Carolyn Hatch; Diane Hodgins; Liz Keefe; Rex LaMore; Jacob Luksic; Murray McDonald; John Melcher; Pauline Payne; Dona Penton; Sean Penton; Brian Pollet; Jerry Ropson; Vida Simon; Gordon Slade; J.D. Snyder; Jack Stanley; and Kevin van Vuren.

The authors are indebted to the Chicago Regional Office staff of the U.S. Economic Development Administration (EDA) for the grant support over the years to the Center for Community and Economic Development (CCED) of Michigan State University that prepared us to conduct this rural and small town development research. This work was directly informed by the EDA project entitled, "Creating Innovative Regional Infrastructure to Support Export Market Entry and Expansion for Small and Medium Businesses." This multi-year project was directed by CCED's J.D. Snyder.

We pursued this case study of Fogo Island's development as part of our quest to identify good practices and benchmarks for regional planning professionals and their citizen and business stakeholders who were the primary clients of the EDA-grant project in exporting noted above. When we initiated the Fogo Island research, our principal external professional planner practitioner colleagues on the exporting project were Jane Fitzpatrick regional planner for the East Michigan Council of Governments, and Jeff Hagan regional planner and executive director for the Eastern Upper Peninsula Regional Planning and Development Commission. We appreciate their feedback as we engaged in the translational research that stimulated and encouraged the initial stage of this work on Fogo Island.

Michigan State University is a land-grant university. It is an institution of higher education in the United States that was founded in 1855. It was chartered then by the state of Michigan under state law as an agricultural land-grant college. At that time, in the U.S., the dominant university education was what was called "a traditional classical curriculum;" higher education then was not widely available to many ordinary people whose principal work options were farms and factories. The land-grant mission as pursued by Michigan State University offered both a practical and a traditional higher education for ordinary people. As the University evolved its programming it extended its research expertise beyond the classroom and into the communities of the state and the world. Consequently, our research of the Fogo Island case in particular is inspired by and in the tradition of land-grant values to extend knowledge to ordinary people so that they may have opportunities to advance themselves and to engage and advance their communities.

We are particularly grateful to the Department of Geography of Michigan State University especially for supporting the field research in Fogo Island. And thanks too go to the School of Planning, Design and Construction of Michigan State University for enabling the production of the initial draft and distribution of this monograph. The critique and feedback obtained from this phase have been invaluable to the completion of this project.

Michigan State University Libraries and its dedicated staff deserve special appreciation. Without their support and suggestions we would not have been able to produce this monograph in a timely and widely accessible and affordable form. Such accessibility is at the heart of the objective of getting the information about the Fogo Island Rural Development Model available at no cost and low cost to readers. The MSU Libraries were essential to enabling us to bring this monograph to fruition; special thanks are due to: Ruth Ann Jones, Marketing and Public Relations Coordinator; Jonah Magar, Expresso Book Machine Coordinator; and Cliff Haka, Director of Libraries.

Finally, our traveling companions and co-explorers in the field, Clare and Bob Banks made our initial Newfoundland and later Fogo Island discoveries possible and such a joy. World travelers Valda and Ian Wilson were the first trailblazers among our family and friends to visit Newfoundland and Labrador. It was their initial experience in the field and subsequent reporting back to us that stimulated our exploration of Newfoundland so long ago. They described: the special nature of the province; the vastness of Newfoundland; a selection of rugged places and the most compelling assets of those places; and the attractiveness and warm hospitality of the people. It was this rich cultural and natural mix that first whetted our appetite to travel to and observe "The Rock" as Newfoundland is known locally. Therefore, these geographic travel and field pioneers too deserve our fond acknowledgement and appreciation.

Part I

Introduction

◖◗

We are attracted to this case of rural regional development because it demonstrates a contemporary way to stimulate new, additional inward-flowing revenues from beyond its local territory. It therefore is a case in building a local exporting strategy based on delivering services to niche consumers from the global marketplace whose spending brings income from outside the subject region into its local regional economy. Such initiatives are important for regions of small towns and rural places because successful exporting can enable increased levels of self-reliance, by empowering rural communities to revive their local economies. In doing so, communities can enliven local society, retain the best of local culture and contribute to informed and responsible use of natural resources thereby bringing about the sustainability of a healthy natural environment.

Importantly, such a model of rural development is a source for provoking fresh thinking and thoughtful action in other rural places. The Fogo Island, Newfoundland case discussed here is offered to readers who are seeking solution pathways to the empowerment and intelligent development of their own rural regions. The level of discussion offered here is highly specific and sufficiently detailed in order to provide working insight into the formulation of entrepreneurial rural development strategies and operational insight into the early stages of planned strategy execution. From these interpretations and understandings, readers may be able to better illuminate, devise and follow more effective planned pathways toward renewed development of their own rural and small town localities. Our final conclusion here is that the Fogo Island Rural Development Model, even in its early stages is an innovative experimental case that deserves our study and should be monitored into the future as an on-going source of valuable rural development lessons and inspiration.

The General Pathway of the Monograph

The monograph is organized by introducing the purpose, context, background, method and notion of the Fogo Island Model for Rural Development. The core of the monograph is two-fold: (1) the rural development-planning elements, seven in all; and (2) the next stages in the Fogo Island Rural Development Model; including both actually planned and imagined future scenarios. The leadership role of Zita Cobb, President of the Shorefast Foundation, is elaborated with particular attention to the working details of her and her team's creation of a social business or social entrepreneurship model for guiding development and investment for Fogo Island. The monograph continues with an in-depth framing of the life-cycle phases of the Fogo Island Model for Rural Development; some phases are actual and empirical, other stages are our imagined likely normative scenarios resulting in end-states that follow from earlier development stages. The monograph concludes by challenging the reader to model and customize the lessons derived from the Fogo Island development approach and by participating in the initiation of a re-development process for her/his own home rural region.

By taking the lead from Zita Cobb's admonition to be specific, the monograph's narrative emphasizes our interpretations of the operations of the Fogo Island development process in some detail. Throughout the narrative of these working details explicit references are offered to concepts, e.g., life-cycle stages and methods from the literature to frame the empirical issues under discussion with the appropriate intellectual context thereby demonstrating intelligent development which aids in the modeling or the transferability of more universal ideas to the particularities of a place for a certain phase in a development cycle (Wilson, Kellerman and Corey, 2013).

Why Read This?

Underway today in the region of Fogo Island and Change Islands, Newfoundland, is a bold and well-thought out experiment in contemporary rural development. It merits our attention because development intentions are being pursued in a manner that has practical lessons that are useful to advancing the prosperity and happiness of people in contemporary rural regions. Importantly, this experiment is engaging the new development opportunities in social that have evolved as a result of the globalized information society and networked economy.

These happenings are underway in a seemingly unlikely place: Fogo Island, Newfoundland, Canada. The island is remote, small in area and population, but its leadership and people have begun to plant the seeds of development, renewal and sustainability in this place. It is a case worth our inspection because its leaders are aspiring to harness some of the macro forces of globalization, while simultaneously working at preserving some of the most cherished qualities of its local past. Having instigated these development actions, the leadership and people of the Fogo Island and Change Islands region also want to share what is being learned there with the rest of us. They want this development activity to be a model for rural development elsewhere. This write-up therefore seeks to capture some of the operational specifics of the Fogo Island rural development work so that development professionals and development citizen volunteers in other rural places might have a model of how the people and its leadership have approached the challenging business of local rural renewal.

The Fogo Island rural development model is emerging during a particularly interesting and challenging period for regional development in North America. As the inexorable move of people and increasingly limited economic opportunities continue to migrate from the countryside to city-regions, small towns and rural regions are routinely neglected and marginalized more than ever by government -- and the marketplace. As national and sub-national governments have drifted into a seemingly permanent state of stalemate and inaction, and as global and national economies continue to struggle with extricating themselves from the aftermath of the Great Recession, there are discernible signs of sub-provincial and sub-state level city-regions and metropolitan areas taking up development initiatives on their own (Katz and Bradley, 2013). As part of the effort to stimulate greater revenue and inward income flows to sub-state regions, since 2010 the Obama Administration has been encouraging these places to ramp up exporting activities. In Newfoundland, the sub-provincial regional Economic Development Boards were closed down in 2012. Collectively, all of these dynamics were influencing our perceptions and mindsets when, by chance, we came upon Fogo Island's innovative actions in rural regional development. These were the factors that compelled us to share our rural development journey of discovery and learning with you.

Part II

Background and Method

☙

The Fogo Island and Change Islands region geologically is nearly 500 million years old. Fogo Island is about 25 km long and 14 km wide, with a total area of 237.71 square km (91.78 square miles). The 2006 census documented a population of 2,706 people, with the 2011 population of the neighbor Change Islands of 257. In the 1960s some 5,000 people were living in ten communities (Nemtin and Low, May 1968; Clarke, 2012: 130-177), or separate village outports (Harris, 2008) distributed around the coastal rim of Fogo Island. The local perspective then was seaward, not landward. (See Figure 1 Map of the Fogo Island and the Change Islands region.) Because these outport villages based their livelihood on the resources of the sea, their orientation was to the ocean. Thus, interior land connections by road were underdeveloped resulting in most of the Fogo Island communities being isolated except by marine access. About 60% of the island's population was on welfare in the 1960s.

Background

Our interest in rural Newfoundland began in the summer of 2001 when we traveled throughout western Newfoundland and crossed over into Labrador to explore the Red Bay National Historic Site. We were struck by the extraordinary warmth and hospitality of the people and the rugged and stunning beauty of nature there. The seascapes and landscapes, for us, were remarkably, yet simply attractive and remote. They evoked by-gone days of struggle and survival (See Figure 2 and Figure 3 for representative views of the region's countryside). On top of all these features there were icebergs being transported along the northern coast of Newfoundland and Fogo Island by the Labrador Current of the North Atlantic Ocean. As a result of this initial and memorable field experience, we vowed that we would return after retirement when we would have the time to explore and examine much of the remainder of central and eastern Newfoundland. The heart of our compulsion to return to Newfoundland was driven primarily by our quest to view more icebergs and maybe to see some whales also (See Figure 4 view of iceberg and Figure 5 view of whale). Plus we wanted to confirm whether the other regions of Newfoundland were as charming and the people as welcoming and gracious in the parts of this huge island that we had yet to view and engage more fully. We also wanted to assess whether the level of underdevelopment had changed noticeably over the longer than a decade period before our return to Newfoundland in the spring of 2012.

In the interim period between the early 2000s and the present time, we conducted policy and development planning translational research in the rural and small town regions of Michigan's northern Lower Peninsula and the Upper Peninsula. A major practical learning from this rural-region development work in Michigan was that local development professionals and citizen development volunteers wanted and learned best when they are able to see and experience comparable good practice regional development models from elsewhere. Consequently, we prepared two books during that period that principally were for sub-provincial and sub-state level regional development practitioners and civil society volunteer stakeholders. We used good practice benchmarking and model cases from elsewhere to make critical points for more intelligent development planning by regional planner practitioners and their local citizen stakeholders (Vettoretto, 2009; Corey and Wilson, 2006; and Wilson, Kellerman and Corey, 2013).

Origins of the Monograph

In the spring of 2012, we returned to Newfoundland, although at that time we knew little more about Fogo Island than the existence of some recently completed artist studios and their eye-catching contemporary architectural design and dramatic sitings. As a result, we made a point of including Fogo Island on our overall field exploration itinerary. From this return trip to Newfoundland and our field observations, especially on Fogo Island, we made a presentation in northern Michigan to the Regional Economic Development (RED) Team and the Export Strategies Steering Committee of the East Michigan Council of Governments (EMCOG). The presentation introduced the recent Fogo Island rural development approach that had been initiated by the local Shorefast Foundation.

Our discussion in the northern Michigan meeting emphasized and compared the similarities between Fogo Island's economic ecosystem and northern Michigan's regional ecosystems. Strategically, the primary message of this presentation was to emphasize that the relatively fresh (to us) concept of geotourism was being used on Fogo Island and the Change Islands region to attract wealthy tourists from around the world to the islands. The geotourism concept is defined and elaborated below as part of the discussion on "Recognizing Our True Assets. Also, refer to Appendix 1. Conceptually, the geotourism approach was important for the eastern Michigan region because it was part of an economic development planning project to develop a strategy for the region for using the exportation of goods and services (such as tourism services) to generate inward-flowing income and increased revenues to the local region. To our presentation, the EMCOG group responded readily to the many similar development issues between rural Fogo Island and rural northern Michigan. The Fogo Island case was ideal for demonstrating that an external tourist attraction approach is an example of exporting services. In the Fogo Island case, tourism is the means to bring external revenues into the local economy, and in the process over time, it is intended to diversify the economy of the Fogo Island region. This illustrates the application of economic-base theory (Chan, 2011: 18-20).

Encouraged by the success of our Fogo Island presentation to local development practitioners and citizen volunteers in Michigan, we presented an academic paper on the Fogo Island development strategy to development researchers and scholars at the 2013 Annual Meeting of the Western Regional Science Association, in Santa Barbara, California. Again, the presentation and discussion elicited a great deal of positive response and interest principally because of the innovative nature of the Fogo Island's development strategy which is being implemented by the Fogo Island-based Shorefast Foundation. Note: a shorefast is the line and mooring cable used to attach a cod trap to the shore -- a metaphor for being bound to place and community (Refer to Figure 6 for a drawing of A Traditional Newfoundland Cod Trap).

Why the Fogo Island Rural Development Work Seems to Resonate

Why the more enthusiastic than usual responses to both our development practitioner and scholarly presentations? In today's fast-paced and information overloaded metropolitan and urbanized worlds around the globe, our rural places generally are neglected and as a result are emptying their futures as their youth beat inexorable paths to cities and the greater work opportunities of the urban regions. We, and our audiences in rural Michigan and elsewhere, found the Fogo Island rural development case, even in its present early stages, to be quite compatible with the felt need to have an actual understandable and comprehensible example – or model – to inspire and motivate ourselves and our rural client stakeholders and regional planning partners to develop productive local economies and happier small towns and rural regions.

Methodology

The method that we have employed in preparing this monograph was to make observations in the field and to conduct in-depth interviews with selected stakeholders. We also have devoured every bit and snippet of empirical documentation that we were able to access over the last several years so that we might catch-up with and try to stay somewhat abreast of the rapidly changing development implementation scene that is underway there. We, of course, have brought to this work our own conceptual frameworks and cultural filters. In part, we are motivated to use and test our own regional planning development mindsets as means to analyze Fogo Island's past and contemporary realities and to assess the actions being planned there and the investment priorities being made there.

After several field-research visits to Fogo Island, we wrote up our initial findings and understandings. We circulated the draft to a selection of Shorefast Foundation principals and a selection of development experts external to Fogo Island who were not part of the Fogo Island work. With that feedback, we have responded by filling in the gaps that were revealed and elaborating on those parts of the draft that needed greater depth and explication.

The narrative that has resulted from this process is intentionally detailed and loaded with operational specifics. This is in response to the Shorefast Foundation leadership's goal for translating their development work in the Fogo Island and Change Islands region into a model for rural development elsewhere. For development stakeholders beyond the islands to be able to consider using Fogo Island planned development processes and learnings to influence and shape their own rural development strategies and tactics, the work from Fogo Island needs to be detailed and specific.

A Role for Islands in Modeling?

Our prior research and practice work in regional development has taught us that, islands, especially small islands, can be particularly useful in deriving development lessons, and in the process, enable us to become aware of operational level issues and contexts and thereby acquire better understandings of the empirical. By definition, the physical separation and discreteness of an island can offer the incubator-like protection needed for experimentation and proof-of-concept explication. For example, we acquired these island-advantage insights from career-long investigations in and on Singapore (Corey and Wilson, 2010). In addition to mining these empirical insights, islands and their relatively simplistic, isotropic-plane clarity, can sharpen and focus the conceptualizing and theory-informing activities that are needed to move beyond a particular case of idiographic research to the search for more abstract generalizable principles or nomothetic research contributions. This, of course, is at the heart of creating a model for others to consider and use.

This "islandness" may be considered, in some respects, an inherent comparative advantage for constructing and experimenting with the Fogo Island Model for Rural Development. For example, because of the physically bounded nature of an isolated rural island some of its characteristics may be clearly identified and more plainly and evidently used in demonstrating the fundamental similarities with other rural places and regions. As a consequence, islands may bring particular value in the early-stage periods of an experiment in regional development. As we examined the initial development strategies, operations and practices underway in the Fogo Island and the Change Islands region, we kept in mind the pilot nature and learning potential of this work for others. Further, there is a modest literature on the role of islands as useful in cases of experimental regional development work and in having institutions that account for relatively better economic performance (Feyrer and Sacerdote, 2009; Congdon Fors, 2014). Delving more deeply into such research and practice literature may reveal additional insight into the comparative and modeling power of islands in deriving development lessons. The island factor is noted several more times in the discourse of the monograph.

Effective Modeling

The discussion that follows is informed by our conceptual framing and interpretation of: (1) intelligent development; and (2) guidelines for effective model building for the use of local and regional development practitioners. By intelligent development simply, we mean informed decision making. This can occur through the marriage of the conceptual and the empirical, with the result being that the Fogo Island regional development case examined here is conceptually framed by us both in operational knowledge of the specific assets and challenges of a place, and in part by the philosophy, theory and strategy that flow from and inform the conditions on the ground (Corey and Wilson, 2006: 37-38; Wilson, Kellerman and Corey, 2013: 191-211). Applying economic-base theory and the geotourist strategy noted above illustrate our application of intelligent development planning.

By an effective model, we mean that it should have transparency, be understandable, have an impact on decision making and action taking; and by attending to these attributes, ownership (Lachapell, 2008) in regional development goals and particular approaches can be more readily realized by the principal stakeholders of the regional community (Lee, Jr., 1973). Doug Lee's key and overarching guideline is to keep the model simple. It should be widely understandable and clearly able to inform planned action. He observed that complicated models in community planning situations do not work well, if at all. Because highly complex models will not be understood especially by community volunteer stakeholders and the practitioners whose assignment it is to execute a model, such complicated frameworks do not make for effective and compelling models. We intend here to keep these guidelines in mind as each element of the Fogo Island Rural Development Model is discussed below. The facts of the case are many and intentionally intertwined, but we will do our best to explicate the relationships; so, that from this unpacking, the reader might acquire an operational grasp of the cause and effect dynamics and be positioned to conceive how they might inform their own local strategizing.

For whom did we prepare this monograph? The state of regional planning, i.e. development planning at the sub-state or sub-provincial scale varies widely around the world. In North America, U.S. regional planning generally is not central to the national government's set of policy priorities and funding; in any case, it is the state-level governments that may or may not place priority on the development strategies of their regions. In Canada, such regional planning has had more attention and recognition, but in Newfoundland in 2012, all of the Regional Economic Development Boards were closed; cost cutting and tight budgets were the reasons given (Briggs, June 25, 2013). Consequently, we are sharing our findings and interpretations here especially for the consideration of regional planners, development practitioners and citizen stakeholders of those small town and rural regions in both Canada, the U.S. and elsewhere who might benefit from and be inspired by the regional development innovations underway in the Fogo Island and Change Islands region.

Among other characteristics, even though federal and provincial governments have invested and partnered with the institutions, communities and people of a region (in this case, Fogo Island), thereby forming a "private-public partnership," the development effort here principally is a bottom-up grassroots effort that owes its impetus largely to non-governmental initiative. Given the generally undistinguished record of governmental performance and partisan stalemate that predominates today, more places and localities are taking it upon themselves to move forward with development initiatives without depending on governmental partners (Katz and Bradley, 2013). While this has much to be commended, it is important that government be held accountable to meet its responsibilities in providing and maintaining basic infrastructural requirements for contemporary development of the places and regions under its jurisdiction.

Place, Place, Place and Specificity, Specificity, Specificity!!!

Canadian Alice Munro was awarded the Nobel Prize for Literature in 2013. The citation from the Svenska Academien reads in part:

> Munro is acclaimed for her finely tuned storytelling, which is characterized by clarity and psychological realism. ... Her stories are often set in small town environments, where the struggle for a socially acceptable existence often results in strained relationships and moral conflicts – problems that stem from generational differences and colliding life ambitions (Svenska Academien, 2013).

Much of her fictional imaginings takes the reader deep inside the rural and small town households and families of rural southwestern Ontario. She was born in Wingham, Ontario; she grew up in the local countryside; and resides in nearby Clinton, Ontario. Her second husband was a cartographer and geographer. Her place-centric worldview contextualizes clearly the specifics of contemporary rural life and its realities – especially at the level of the individual person.

Today's and tomorrow's rural persons too often are struggling to accommodate the buffeting winds of change, including the external forces of technological and globalization forces. These forces, of course, cut both ways. They cause challenges to these rural localities, but they also represent opportunity.

As a person experienced in working in and charting a highly successful career course in the business environments of the global economy, and as a person who also has come from a deeply rooted localized place-centric early life, Shorefast Foundation President Zita Cobb is well-positioned, not unlike Alice Munro, to draw on both legs of her background. As she too constructs rural imaginings, her visions are at the scale of place and its regional context. Boldly, she has charted a new life course; with the team support of the Shorefast Foundation, her family, her neighbors, her friends, both local and from away, she is engaging rural revival work at the seam of the local and the global. She and her team of colleagues are passionate about their work, because she believes that: "All rural places are in trouble" (Cobb, February 13, 2014). She has opined that rural communities around the world are being unnecessarily "flattened."

Taking a page from Zita Cobb's mantra of the strategic importance of focusing on the specificity of place, the discussion that follows throughout the monograph takes up her mandate by detailing, as much as space permits, the operational workings and specificities of the emerging Fogo Island Model for Rural Development – even as it currently is being created and perfected by means of mid-course corrections. These details are central to the goal of having rural development stakeholders around the world benefit from the experience and findings that are underway on remote rural Fogo Island. Without detailed, operational explication of the intended means and ends that comprise the Fogo Island Rural Development Model, it is difficult and abstract for non-participants to translate distant activities into near and place-relevant local actions. The reader might consider the Fogo Island regional case as a benchmark and early-stage good practice illustration and use its experience to date to inspire analogous strategizing and planned action-informing for the advancement of one's own small town and rural place (Vettoretto, 2009).

Our Job

We have determined that our role here is to interpret the findings and to translate those understandings and that knowledge into comments on and suggestions for planned action and process improvements – for the use of the intended readers, i.e., those persons who are considering the Fogo Island Model to inform strategic planning in their home regions. We are not concerned with critiquing the work currently underway in the Fogo Island region. Rather, we seek to comment in ways that the reader can derive learnings for taking an alternative path or extending the action for possible longer term benefits.

We see our value-added contribution to bring our outsider perspectives to bear and to identify lessons to be taken from the Fogo Island and the Change Islands region and in the that context become aware of how those learnings may be considered for shaping development in places and regions beyond the islands. Given the heavy working commitments of the members of Team Shorefast another of our intended contributions is the pulling together, compiling and documenting the many development activities that are being planned and executed in the Fogo Island region. A holistic integration of the many interrelated development activities underway on the islands can be helpful in maintaining a strategic focus for the work.

In response to her conclusion that rural areas globally are being "unnecessarily flattened:"

> Zita Cobb has stated, "I am convinced that there are ways to be part of the world that are much kinder to the dignity of our human spirit – ways to reach out while holding on. We are committed to sharing what we know from our Fogo Island work so that others can hold onto the specificity of place that is so crucial to wellbeing (Cobb, April 2, 2014).

In sum then, the targeted audience for the monograph especially is for rural development stakeholders – both development professionals and development volunteers – whose goals are to advance the economies and societies of their home regions and places. In the end, their primary task in engaging the monograph therefore is to use the kinds of processes and content discussed here and translate that material to their own locality in ways that are congruent with and appropriate to the specifics and context of home.

Part III

Pre-Existing Conditions to the Model: Merchant System and The Fogo Process

☙

Before drilling down into the specificities of the Shorefast Foundation's construction of its Fogo Island Model for Rural Development it is necessary to lay down the general historical foundation upon which Shorefast has built its development model. These happenings have influenced and informed the future. These are comprised of the sweep of events from the deep past through to the past of only two generations ago. They are framed here as: (1) early European contact; (2) the merchant credit system; and (3) The Fogo Process. These are some of the forces that have formed the place and people of Newfoundland, Labrador and Fogo Island and the Change Islands. Simply, these dynamics have shaped the conditions and mindsets of today's Fogo Island residents as they participate in the current, largely Shorefast Foundation-led, programs to lay in a new course of local development for a better future. These pre-existing conditions have and are shaping and influencing the what and the how of the Model for Rural Development on Fogo Island that is currently evolving.

Early European Contact

Newfoundland's history includes some of the earliest documented human contact and interaction with North America by Europeans. The L'Anse aux Meadows National Historic Site of Canada on the Northern Peninsula of the far northwest of Newfoundland was the first authenticated European (Norse) presence on the continent. It is dated circa 1000 AD. This short-lived Viking settlement region was preceded by native peoples for thousands of years before this. The native Dorsets (Paleo-Eskimos) and the native Beothuks are the vanished peoples of Newfoundland (Such, 1978). On commission from King Henry VII, in 1497, Giovanni Cabato (aka John Cabot), originally of Venice, Italy, claimed Newfoundland for England and he reported that the Grand Banks of the North Atlantic waters south and east of the island had rich stocks of cod fish. Cabato, sailed from Bristol, England; he:

> followed Erik the Red's route to Greenland, he rediscovered the island of Newfoundland. Soon Newfoundland's abundant fisheries were being robustly exploited by Europeans, especially the Basques, the Old World's most intrepid fishermen (Fischer, 2012: 106).

Queen Elizabeth I granted a patent to Humphrey Gilbert in 1578. Subsequently, in 1583, he declared Newfoundland to be one of England's earliest colonies. Thereafter, migratory fishers from France, Portugal, and Spain (the Basques), in addition to those from England, began fishing the waters of Newfoundland, especially for then-plentiful cod fish (Clarke, 2012). Thus, began the colonial era of Newfoundland's history; its land area ranks it as the fifteenth largest island on earth at 111,390 square kilometers (Fischer, 2012: 12). One should keep in mind that this land area principally has served as the platform from which visitors, and later, residents pursued profit and economic advantage from the sea's natural resources (For images of cod fish, see Figure 7 of a cod's face and Figure 8 of cod in full view).

David J. Clarke, in his history of the northern Newfoundland region called "The Isles of Notre Dame" Bay, an area that encompasses Fogo Island and the Change Islands, he included this quotation:

> As early as 1612 colonizer John Guy (d. 1629) wrote that 'the Newfoundland [cod] fish, being so acceptable in France, Spain and Italy, may ... yearly return great quantities of money.' This was true for nearly 500 years. Like most Newfoundland coastal communities, those on the Isles owe their existence to the sea's bounty (Clarke, 2012: 1).

As to Fogo Island's geographical position and early advantage, the island:

> Lies on [the] shallow Fogo Shelf, which attracts salmon, cod and other species. ... Until the late 1700s Fogo was a summer home of the Beothuks. European fishermen visited its waters from the early 1500s and summer residences began at Fogo Harbour (now Fogo), an outpost of Devon and Dorset businesses, in the 1680s, with permanent settlement beginning in 1728 (The Canadian Encyclopedia, January 23, 2014).

After commercial fishing shifted from being conducted by migratory workers to fishers who were permanent residents of coastal Newfoundland, then a local merchant credit became rooted in Newfoundland.

Merchant Credit System

From the 16th through the 18th centuries, the practice of fishing by Europeans in the waters of Newfoundland and Labrador was seasonal and migratory in nature. Cod fishing took place from spring until early autumn when the majority of these fisher-worker "servants" returned home to Britain and Europe for the winter (Newfoundland and Labrador Heritage, n.d.). In the Fogo Island region there were some English permanent settlers, but until the French fishery preserve known as the French Shore moved its boundary westward in 1783, European settlement had not taken off.

> By 1857 Notre Dame Bay was home to over 7,000 permanent residents, the vast majority living east of Exploits. Almost all of these people were English West Country Protestants. The only large concentrations of Irish Roman Catholics in Notre Dame Bay settled in Tilting, on eastern Fogo Island, and at Fortune Harbour (Clarke, 2012: 2).

Of the sedentary fishery in Newfoundland, the *Dictionary of Newfoundland English* has discussed the early condition of the sedentary fisheries of Newfoundland. Using the phrasing of the day, the entry stated that three classes of actors comprised the system of merchant credit; also known as the "truck" system: (1) the merchant, who supplied the capital; he was an entrepreneur who purchased and exported "salt cod-fish, and the financing of the fishing operation through the advance of supplies and credit" (refer to page 326); (2) the "planter or resident boatkeeper, who supplied the skill;" and (3) "the servant who contributed labour" (refer to page 459). In order to try to make ends meets, the "servant role" usually engaged the entire outport worker's family of husband, wife and the children (Story, Kirwin, and Widdowson, 1990).

Truck means "payment other than in money" (Story, Kirwin, and Widdowson, 1990: 585). Again, the Dictionary of Newfoundland English provides us with a vivid explication of the merchant credit or truck system; and in the language of the time.

> Every merchant, and master of a fishery, is the huckster of his whole establishment; and the servants are compelled to purchase their supplies of food, raiment, and every trifling necessary, of the person in whose service they may chance to be engaged. No money passes between them; but the account of every article that is supplied to the fisherman is entered in the books of their masters ... The merchant finds the ship or vessel, the nets and the provisions, in fact, the means of carrying on the fishery which he supplies to the planter. ... The various firms agreed at one time not to buy fish from another merchant's planters (Story, Kirwin, and Widdowson, 1990: 326-327).

The truck system was a form of indenture (Rose, 2007: 271). In the spring of each fishing season the merchants advanced to the fisher the supplies for fishing and living; at the end of the fishing season in the autumn the fishers repaid the merchants with the results of their dried and salted fish catch for the entire season. The risk to the fishers was they were provided with the supplies, gear and food in the spring without knowing the price of these materials. In the autumn the merchant sets the price for those goods after he has received from the fishers the fish catch for the season and learned what price the fish earned from the often fluctuating international markets. The setting of the value of the fish catch in this way too often was seen as benefitting the merchant at the expense of the fisher and his family members who also worked in processing the fish catch. Even though the credit or truck system had benefits and risks both for the merchant and the fisher, the rub is that the fishers and their families did not have effective control while the merchants are perceived as having relatively more control despite their vulnerability in the international marketplace. Under this system of interdependencies many merchants went bankrupt and many fishers and their families went into debt and became destitute. In his book on *Cod: The Ecological History of the North Atlantic Fisheries*, George Rose provides the reader with a balanced and fair discussion of both sides of this debate (Rose, 2007: 271-272).

The system came to the then British colony of Newfoundland when the English migratory fishery was replaced by the resident fishery. Such credit-based economies occurred routinely in some places of Britain where "cash was scarce and where only a very limited variety of locally produced goods existed to meet residents' needs ... these locations typically were in rural mining, fishing, farming and logging communities" (Newfoundland and Labrador Heritage, n.d.: 1-2).

The struggle to rid Newfoundland of the merchant credit system continued on into the late 1930s and 1940s (Neis, 1981; NL Interactive, Fall 1998; Dawe, 2006). The legacy of the various meanings that are derived from the realities and myths of that system for today's regional development decisions resides in the experience and passed-down memories of the great grandparents, the grandparents and the parents of people in Fogo Island and the province. These memories influence contemporary mindsets and world views. They affect the ways the new and additional contemporary opportunities and traumas influence the local and provincial societies (Douglas, 1986). Our discussion here now can turn to the game-changing and highly influential Fogo Process. This process too is influencing the world view and meanings that affect Newfoundland and Fogo Island individuals and social behavior.

The Fogo Process

In setting the stage for understanding the impetus for the evolution of today's Fogo Island Model for Rural Development work, one must be aware of events from the 1960s that came to be known as The Fogo Process. These events were instrumental in shaping the course of history that followed for Fogo Island, and in turn the Shorefast Foundation. Essentially the leading actors of the Foundation perceive their current work as "The Fogo Process: Phase 2."

Background at the Provincial Level

Newfoundland and Labrador has been called 'Britain's Oldest Colony and now is Canada's newest province' (Clarke, 2012). This is more than merely a cleaver phrase. On March 31, 1949, Newfoundland joined Canada. Having been a long-standing and typically under-invested colony, it brought colonial problems into the Confederation. For example, this vast island area had only 150 kilometers of paved highways; the economy depended on an inshore fishery that operated with low levels of technology; and nearly "two-thirds of its then-population of 350,000 lived in communities with fewer than 1,000 residents" (Hoggart, 1979: 215). To address Newfoundland's widespread underdevelopment, the then-new provincial government moved to address these conditions by means of industrial expansion and upgrading transportation infrastructure. A program of resettlement grants to families was implemented in 1953.

Keith Hoggart's (1979) analysis and explication of resettlement in Newfoundland provides useful insight and context for the seminal Fogo Process. The story requires elaboration here for an operational grasp of the societal disarray and natural resources destruction, which were set in motion during the early days of the province.

Initial resettlement grants were for up to $150 per family. As stated, this resettlement program was intended to help the residents of the province to benefit from the above economic development and infrastructure investments. This version of resettlement resulted in 697 families being resettled. By 1960, the objectives of the resettlement program had changed; this was merely the beginning of an additional three-phase cycle of resettlement trial and error programs by government (Hoggart, 1979: 215). Operating with a weak economy and a huge number of tiny widely scattered coastal fishing communities, the province attributed subsequent poor industrial growth to the high cost of providing basic community services to the 1,200 or so settlements dispersed across its territory.

The response to this situation was for government to "encourage" evacuation of small communities. However, the means to accomplish this end consisted merely of publicity about the potential benefits of resettlement, such as improved community facilities, and an increase in the resettlement grants from $150 to $600 per family.

> By 1965, in a further effort to gain traction on resettlement, the federal government of Canada joined with the province. Grants for the resettling of families from the small isolated settlements were increased while simultaneously prodding such residents to evacuate by not improving community facilities.

The prime objective of federal involvement was to foster the development of Newfoundland's offshore fishing industry, which needed labour in larger urban centres for trawlers and processing plants. To encourage resettlers to relocate into these centres, additional housing grants were given to households that moved to government designated "fishery growth centres" (up to $3,000 per family) (Hoggart, 1979: 216).

However, Hoggart reported that the 1965 to 1971 period generated increasing criticism and partisan party political opposition. Now resettlement was widely perceived as forcing relocation against the wishes of residents. Social disruption, combined with "modest" economic benefits precipitated an electoral overthrow of the incumbent political party in the 1972 provincial election.

The new provincial government allocated resettlement funds to pursue a new objective of helping "workers move to available jobs." This shift resulted in various alterations in resettlement patterns, however "the employment prospects and incomes of resettlers showed little overall improvement after moving." Hoggart notes also the improved community facilities resulted -- "although this must be viewed in the context of a deliberate governmental neglect of small communities and the fact that many communities were evacuated because their school was closed" (Hoggart, 1979: 218).

For the province, this fourth and last phase of resettlement brought only marginal gains. Specifically, (1) the number of communities evacuated was 261; (2) only marginally were the number of people living in communities over 1,000 persons increased, i.e., by 11,175 persons; and (3) in hope of avoiding being forced to resettle, the number of settlements incorporating as local governments increased from 67 to 223 from 1960 to 1971; this was thought to demonstrate "vitality and initiative." In the end, the resettlement program, over its total of four phases produced little of its intended objectives and it stirred up enough opposition to hasten its own demise (Hoggart, 1979: 218).

Note: Fogo Island did not incorporate its local government as a municipality until March 1, 2011. What else differentiated Fogo Islanders' reactions to, and behavior toward the long 1953-1975 period and the various phases of resettlement turmoil at the provincial level?

What Happened at the Fogo Island Level?

Unlike in many other Newfoundland communities, its resistance to resettlement was successful in the Fogo Island case. This success is attributable to a series of experiments conducted by Memorial University of Newfoundland and the National Film Board of Canada in the late 1960s. The experiments involved using interactive film and video in the island's remote economically distressed locations. These experiments became widely known as the Fogo Process and adopted in developing country around the world (Williamson, 1989).

> The idea was to train isolated populations with little exposure to media in the use of film (and later video) so that they could create a collective image of themselves and their social problems, which they might exchange with distant decision makers, such as in governments and financial institutions. This early experiment in participatory media became known as the 'Fogo Process' because it was first developed on Fogo Island, Newfoundland. The experiments on Fogo stand out as an early example of a community island project that used innovative media practices to resist what seemed to be an otherwise unstoppable movement toward resettlement of their community and an imposed, top-down 'modernization' of the island's way of life. Villagers on Fogo eventually resisted government plans to resettle them and formed a cooperative to run their fish plant (Crocker, 2008: 59).

The visually recorded stories also were instrumental in facilitating internal organizing and solidarity among the island's residents and neighbors. The stories stimulated feelings of shared challenges, empathy and were instrumental in enabling the Fogo Islanders to present their case with a united front to external and distant authorities and decision makers thereby being successful in avoiding resettlement.

In order to obtain a visual impression of the conditions and state of development on Fogo Island in the 1960s, the reader should view some of the footage that is available over the internet. These images are quite insightful and useful in providing context for the motivation of the islanders to resist resettlement (National Film Board of Canada, 1968).

Because of the industrial scale and the overfishing-induced collapse of the commercial cod fishery, in 1992 the federal government of Canada imposed a moratorium on fishing for the northern cod fish. The moratorium resulted in an immediate loss of employment, the closing of processing plants and the often-permanent docking of cod fishing boats. It also caused the further loss of population and abandonment of some outport communities across Newfoundland (Harris, 2008).

"The Fogo Process" that more than a generation ago used film and video for community organizing and political intervention activities functioned as stimulants for the Film House and the eCinema project that the Shorefast Foundation supported and hosts. The Fogo Island e-Cinema initiative was part of a limited number of pilot projects by the National Film Board (NFB) of Canada to deliver unique cultural offerings – documentaries, animation and alternative dramas – to underserviced communities. When the e-Cinema project was initiated on Fogo Island, the films could be delivered overnight via high-speed Internet line or via hard drives. Digital cinema allows an enormous flexibility to establish or modify programming to suit the needs of audiences. The National Film Board of Canada always has explored ways to make its rich video and film collection available to the regions of Canada. This Fogo Island project was NFB's first English-language e-Cinema partnership in Canada. Quebec was the location for an earlier French-language initiative by NFB. The e-Cinema facility has been moved from its original nearby location and incorporated into the new Fogo Island Inn as one of its attractions (Refer to Figure 9 for the new cinema in the Fogo Island Inn).

The legacy assets of the film-based Fogo Process and the importation of the e-Cinema can serve as benchmarks and good practices for contemporary technology-enabled creativity in remote rural regions. With this heritage of bold innovation and independence of community action, today's generation of islanders would seem to be better positioned to build on these past communication and technology inspired ways of connecting over long distances to take advantage of today's and tomorrow's information, communications and networking technologies to succeed in the global marketplace with all of its new demands for effective connectedness.

A key part of the Foundation's and Town of Fogo Island's early-stage regional development action requires addressing fundamental infrastructure provision. This is needed to operationalize the harnessing and engagement of global and local business opportunities. The challenge here is to have the needed digital and information communications technologies infrastructure and services equitably distributed, accessible, and affordable to all of the island's households and businesses and institutions. Then implementation of individual business enterprise development plans can be pursued more widely, especially in complementarity to the economic spillovers of the Fogo Island Inn. Refer to Appendix 2 entitled, "Connected Community Engagement Program of Connect Michigan." It discusses and elaborates how rural localities and regions in Michigan have addressed these challenges. These are self-help good practices (Vettoretto, 2009) for today's Fogo Islanders to consider adapting and shaping to the specifics of their information technologies and communications conditions and vision for social business development expansion and wider spatial and locational distribution.

The Fogo Process served to reveal the islanders' resilience, their discovery of commonalities across the various communities, their ability to overcome internal locational separation of the island's settlements and religious differences to come together around the implementation of a strategy to resist government programs for resettlement. The Fogo Process documented on film and video the fundamental intelligence and capacity of local individual ordinary people to take collective action based on newly-recognized common ground discovered by means of the film-based interviews that were recorded in the small communities distributed across the island (Clarke, 2012: 180-183). The social capital created by its people in the 1960s is an invaluable innovation asset for development of the region. Thereby, drawing on their historical resilience, the islanders already have demonstrated an ability to discover, learn and mobilize themselves as they did in the 1960s to resist resettlement. From that resistance they formed the Fogo Island Co-operative Society Ltd. The Co-op and the fishery industry of Fogo Island survived and, functioning at a smaller scale, the local fishery has thrived for nearly two generations. The following statement from the Web site of the Fogo Island Co-operative Society Ltd. captures the inherent passion and determination of Fogo Islanders to take control of their own destiny by mobilizing their collective strengths that were drawn from the social capital development assets that were based on the specific blend of local culture and nature that was created there over the last four hundred years or so.

> In 1967, we had to make a life-altering decision on Fogo Island. Leave our beloved island home and resettle on the mainland of Newfoundland and Labrador, or stay and find a way to make it on our own. We stayed and we made it our own. To ensure our survival, we turned to what we knew best for hundreds of years…the sea.

> Following a process of community self-discovery now known worldwide as the Fogo Process, our fishers formed the Fogo Island Co-operative Society, a community based enterprise on which we built the economy of our island. We built more boats. We built bigger boats. We took over processing facilities abandoned by private enterprise. We built more plants. We sought new markets.

The Fogo Island Co-op has not only survived, it has thrived now for over forty years. When giants in this industry failed, some merged, some sought government interventions the Fogo Island Co-op has remained resilient and continues to focus on the future (Fogo Island Co-operative Society Ltd, n.d.).

In addition to founding the fisher's cooperative, resisting resettlement permitted other initiatives thanks to The Fogo Process; these include: the development of a near-shore, long-liner fishery; educational facilities were integrated; and from the early 1990s the promotion of highly localized conventional and quaint tourist attractions received attention. These included:

> museums, hiking trails to abandoned settlements, icebergs, whales and the outport way of life. Brimstone Head, a prominent landmark in the town of Fogo has been proclaimed by the Flat Earth Society one of the four corners of the earth (The Canadian Encyclopedia, January 23, 2014).

Despite the extraordinary tradition of remote-island style hospitality of Newfoundlanders, including Fogo Islanders, the lodgings options on the island have been limited. There have been some bed and breakfasts in houses distributed sparsely across the island, but no hotel or inn with quality accommodations have been available until 2013.

The Shorefast Foundation leadership has attributed the Fogo Process as being instrumental in shaping the course of history that followed the disruptions of the resettlement period, and in turn, stimulated the creation of the Foundation. "We see [the] current work essentially as 'The Fogo Process: Phase 2.'" (Cobb, January 28, 2014).

Part IV

The Shorefast Foundation Model for Rural Development

The Shorefast Foundation was founded in 2003 by Zita Cobb and her brothers Anthony and Alan. It is a registered Canadian charity. "We use business minded ways to achieve social ends. … We use a new model for economic and cultural resilience that may hold learnings for small communities everywhere. Our model is based on social engagement, strategic investment in community capital, and inclusive local economies" (Shorefast Foundation, Our Foundation, n.d.)

This monograph has been prepared for the use of planners – both professional and volunteer citizen planners – who want to invest their energy and intellect into the planned betterment of rural communities everywhere. This goal drives one of the often-mentioned spin-offs of the Shorefast Foundation and Zita Cobb's development work on remote Fogo Island. It is the hope that recent development results there will serve as a model for people in other rural areas who wish to resuscitate their own places. The purpose of this monograph is to capture and translate some of the essential development particulars that have been created and are being used in the Fogo Island and Change Islands region of Newfoundland toward the ends of: (1) interpreting these Fogo Island development concepts and actions; and (2) assessing the body of this development work to date as exemplary for possible inspiration and motivation for other rural regions and their development stakeholders.

In Zita Cobb's various presentations about the Shorefast Foundation's vision and strategy for Fogo Island's resurrection, she uses the seven planning elements discussed below for organizing planned actions to obtain that vision for the region's intended more diverse and sustainable economic future. These are the means by which she, the Shorefast Foundation and the people of the Fogo Island and Change Islands region are pursuing the ends of creating jobs and instilling the worldview needed to ensure the community's sustainability in the global economy while also retaining the essence of Fogo Island's unique culture.

The reader should note that in the next section of the monograph we employ Cobb's seven planning elements for modeling rural development. However, throughout the narrative of the paper, we are intentionally avoiding being slavish about keeping the discussion only within these seven categories. The strategy underpinning the model requires a great deal of complementarity and interdependence therefore; we apply relational theory explicitly in this case because it does not put sharp edges on concepts. "Rather, it accommodates and explains the complicated relationships of the knowledge economy in realistic terms, i.e., terms that reflect well the empirical complexities of today's networked world" (Corey and Wilson, 2006: 214).

Development and a Participatory Process

Below, as we identify and analyze the ingredients that have been conceptualized and used to construct this Fogo Island model for rural development, the working definition for the nature of "development" here should be recognized as rooted in a philosophy of the region's people gaining more "ownership" and therefore control over the assets of their local environment (Lachapelle, 2008). This operational definition also requires social and material advancement in order to generate economic prosperity. Greater equality, freedom of choice and happiness are some of the aspirational qualities that can be expected from this mix of "what has been" toward a vision of a local economy that is diverse and sustainably linked to the global economy and all the technological challenges and opportunities that such connectedness entails. This development definition draws on a range of multiple sectors from the past as well as those of the present and the future that hold promise for local economic diversity and a globalized mindset of future prosperity stimulated by innovation and entrepreneurship. The end-state results from this concept of development are in the framework of "what should be." It is the willed planned intended outcome that the development process seeks to produce. Many attributes of this definition are congruent with and inspired by the one initially framed by communication scholar Everett Rogers. He defined development as:

> A widely participatory process of social change in a society intended to bring about both social and material advancement (including greater equality, freedom, and other valued qualities) for the majority of the people through their gaining greater control over their environment (Rogers, 1976: 225).

Shorefast Foundation is a registered Canadian charity established in 2003. It is governed by a Board of Directors composed mostly of local neighbors, friends and relatives along with some representation of people "from away" who have experience and knowledge of development. The board membership is as follows. Refer to the web site of the Shorefast Foundation for brief biographical information on each (Shorefast Foundation, n.d., Board of Directors):

- Zita Cobb - President
- Anthony Cobb - Treasurer
- Alan Cobb - Secretary
- Gordon Slade - Chair
- Glen Best
- Cathy Duke
- Lillian Dwyer
- Barb McInnes
- Robert Nelson

Specificity of Operations

Throughout the discussion that follows, there is a conscious attempt to document and to follow the lead of the Shorefast Foundation regarding the criticality of knowing in detail the distinguishing assets of one's locality and thereby being positioned to act on the potential development opportunity and advantages that are offered by that knowledge. Foundation President Zita Cobb has been quoted as saying:

> The hardest part is for people [in] rural communities to understand what they have of value. That means getting a better understanding of what could have an economic value to others. It's that inventory taking. The landscapes and spirits of places are being taken away as it becomes harder to distinguish the look of one place from another. It is the specificity [emphasis added] that matters and the rural is being flattened (Ross, October 3, 2013).

Such operational asset awareness enables local rural development actors to take informed planned action. Such intelligent development can empower rural development stakeholders to avoid the all too conventional recent reactions of rural people to give up on the rural and to wait for others to save them (Ross, October 3, 2013).

In discussing the Fogo Island development work, Foundation leadership routinely draws on the community capital framework of Mark Roseland (2012) to assess local assets to prioritize investment among the various forms of capital. See more discussion on this at the beginning of the section below entitled, "Community Ownership of Capital." The Foundation also is guided by the specificity of place as an essential imperative in assessing a region's assets as well as positioning and aligning those assets in planning and implementing the Shorefast Foundation's development strategy for the region of Fogo Island and the Change Islands.

Part V

Rural Development-Planning Elements

When the Shorefast Foundation began to re-prioritize its programming from an earlier scholarship-centric strategy to an initial strategy of economic diversification and job creation for the local economy, several important preparatory supportive initiatives were being executed and produced complementary results. A government-led strategic planning effort already was underway and produced the "Socio-Economic Strategic Plan" for the Fogo Island and Change Islands region (Kittiwake Economic Development Corporation and D.W. Knight Associates, July 2008). Additionally, as part of the region's strategy development, the Town of Fogo Island was officially created effective March 1, 2011. This involved the amalgamation of four existing Towns and one Regional Council (Town of Fogo Island, "Home Page," n.d.). The Town of Change Islands located west of Fogo Island was incorporated in 1951 (Town of Change Islands, "Home Page," n.d.).

To organize and frame the development that is currently active in the Fogo Island and Change Islands region, we have adopted the Shorefast Foundation's seven planning elements for modeling rural development. These include:

- Business Structure, Logistics and Distribution
- Fostering Connectedness
- Recognizing Our True Assets
- Building on Inherent Assets of Place – Optimizing for Place/Community
- Building Culture into the Fabric of a Business
- Community Ownership of Capital
- Holding on to Ways of Knowing

Business Structure, Logistics and Distribution

The structure of business planning is based on the principal economic sectors that have been selected for development. Embedded in this particular mix of sectors is the dynamic of job creation that builds on the past and seeks to make sustainable the economic future, while at the same time intends to seed in economic functions that are in demand globally and an entrepreneurial business mindset and related behavioral processes that will be self-generating and responsive to changing conditions so as to achieve economic sustainability in future.

Drawing on the historical foundation of the region's economy, the fishing industries sector should be invested, modernized and its business processes organized for competing even more effectively in the regional and global marketplace. Tapping into the opportunities and potential of today's and tomorrow's global economy, the Shorefast Foundation has initiated: the Fogo

Island Arts Program; the Business Assistance Fund Program; and the Fogo Island Inn. These three economic domains represent the on-going and early-stage development activities that are intended to mobilize and diversify the region's economy by means of job creation and the upgrading of the local workforce to enable it to compete and succeed in the global economy.

Next stage initiatives and programs include: the Fogo Island Dialogues; and the New Ocean Ethic. These two more recent programs are interdependent with and complement the above three economic sectors and domains that existed or recently have been initiated.

The overarching function that supports and is intended to advance the diversification of the region's economy is connectivity. Connection will bind together these various programmatic initiatives. Longer-term future initiatives, yet to be determined, also will depend on connection. Connection is a fundamental and essential requirement for doing business and economic development in today's and tomorrow's globalized and networked economy.

In general, connection is operationalized by means of logistics and, in contemporary good business practice, the more comprehensive and encompassing concept of supply chain management. To define supply chain management (SCM), it includes the flow of goods and services as traditionally included under logistics, and SCM further includes information flows, as well as multiple and inter-enterprise relations. Generally logistics is conceived as practiced within one firm and its logistics function manages flows between the subject enterprise, its suppliers and its customers. In the early development stages of today's Fogo Island economic resurrection, the Business Assistance Fund Program and the Fogo Island Inn are functioning mostly as individual enterprises and are relying principally on logistics concepts in their business behavior.

Particularly, the success of the Fogo Island Inn also will depend importantly on effective public relations, media relations and marketing globally. These business functions must rely on information flows via robust networked information and communications technologies and an effective World Wide Web presence. Given the global nature of the Inn's strategy to attract affluent geotourists and the possibilities of building corporate alliances for business meetings, and given the complex relations of the Inn's business producers, suppliers, supplier's suppliers, consumers, distribution, and transportation to and from remote Fogo Island, a supply chain management capacity needs to be evolved and perfected (Lummus, Krumwiede and Vokurka, 2001; Marien, 2003). For an elaboration refer to the food sourcing challenges of the Inn's restaurant discussed below. These logistics and supply chain management challenges are magnified by the Shorefast Foundation's philosophy of not doing business with corporations and countries whose business practices are antithetical to the principles of community empowerment, community ownership and social justice and ethics.

Fostering Connectedness

In order to have the capacity to execute the kinds of internet-facilitated networking discussed above, local Fogo Island and Change Islands region's enterprises and households need the investment and education to achieve full operationality in its digital connectedness. Such capacity will require the investments needed in infrastructure for electric power provision and the widespread spatial distribution of internet connectivity and internet services provision. Even with these outcomes actions need to be planned and taken to maintain such electronic connectedness during winter conditions of service disruption due to heavy ice and winds.

In addition to these electronic connectedness issues, the current insecurity of transportation linkages for passengers and freight require action. Connections between the islands of the region and the Newfoundland mainland are concerns for the full realization of the region's development goals. The principal problems include: ferry service, air strip infrastructure and air service, especially when the ferry breaks down or when there is no back up ferry to replace the primary ferry when it needs to be maintained and repaired.

During the height of the tourist summer season in 2013, the ferry was out of service for two separate periods because of equipment failures and resultant repairs; and in a third event in August, 300 people were stranded overnight at the Fogo Island ferry terminus because there was insufficient automobile and truck vehicle ferry capacity to accommodate the heavy demand on a Tuesday after the weekend of the Brimstone Head Folk Festival.

A visitor stranded by the August 2013 ferry problem was quoted as follows in a local newspaper:

> "There were some kindhearted islanders who responded to the plight of the stranded travelers and went from car to car offering water, pop, sandwiches and whatever they had to spare." (Wells, August 21, 2013).

> Further, there was a lack of effective communication and notification of the public for this lapse in ferry service. This further complicated the situation and added to the inconvenience of the ferry users.

This was however an opportunity for visitors to the island to experience directly the extraordinary hospitality and warmth of Fogo Island's residents. This behavior is representative of one of the island's most attractive cultural assets. However, these recent logistics failures call attention to the depth of the long standing problems with the region's ferry services. Provincial governments seem to have been particularly behind the curve in anticipating and acting in producing solutions to the ferry long-standing problems. In October 2013, two smaller-capacity ferries were substituted for the larger-capacity Captain Earl W. Winsor ferry. This patchwork solution was scheduled to be in effect for four months (CBC

News, October 14, 2013). Actual new-ferry construction and significantly improved service remains several years into the future; see the last paragraph of this section below.

It should be noted that these problems impact local interests and visitors alike. From the visitors, the ferry problems generate poor touristic reviews. But even more significant are the negative impacts locally – especially during the peak tourist summer season. The greater volume of visitor vehicles using the finite space on the ferry, results in significantly limiting the ferry space, logistics opportunities, and timing issues for the fishery and construction sectors, as well as the already noted negative impacts on the growing tourist sector. The Fogo Island Town Council has been calling for two vessels with adequate vehicle capacity to operate during the high-demand season. There is not a spare ferry available for this route for about two years. Late in 2013, the Province issued a call for bids to build a new ferry. A contract for a new ferry was completed, but it will be September 2015 before a new replacement ferry is scheduled to go into service.

During these 2013 breaks in ferry service, residents of the region had the option, at a small charge, to fly to Gander International Airport on the mainland of Newfoundland via small fixed-wing aircraft from the Fogo Island airstrip; and Change Islanders had the same destination option, but via helicopter. Shorefast Foundation principals have been in discussion with provincial officials about enhancing the airstrip on Fogo Island. The objective is to lengthen the current 3,000-foot runway to a 5,700 foot runway.

Given the region's long history of living from and working on the sea, the orientation of the communities is toward the ocean. Its outport communities had little need for land connections between the various small settlements (Harris, 2008). When there was a need for inter-village connectivity, it could be satisfied by boat transportation. Currently, there are just 50 miles of paved roads on Fogo Island.

So, another internal-to-the-region connectivity need is for more of the region's roads to be paved. The residents have called for the paving of more roads to meet today's different and changing economic and social requirements. Connectedness, both within the Fogo Island and Change Islands region, and between the local region and the external world, is central to the goal of transitioning from the old economy that was almost totally dependent on the fishery sector to the networked multi-sector new economy that increasingly depends on linkages to the global knowledge economy and the global information society. Given the discussion above on the connectivity assets of the region, it seems that high priority needs to be assigned for enhance the various connectivity infrastructures of the region.

Electrical power provision and broadband networking also need to be assessed and strategies planned for making the businesses and households of the region able to compete in the global marketplace. Without significant progress on fostering reliable and ubiquitous connectedness, many of the region's development aspirations are at risk. Taking inspiration from past communication and technology-based initiatives, e.g. the Fogo Process and the e-Cinema Film House that are described elsewhere in the monograph, enhanced contemporary internal and external digital connectedness are needed to advance and support each of the programs that have been initiated to diversify and modernize the local economy.

In November 2013 Transportation and Works Minister Nick McGrath announced that by September 2015 a new 80 meter vessel would replace the current ferry, the Captain Earl W. Winsor.

> The new ferry is no bigger than [the] current ferry, so the problem of excess demand in the summer is not solved, but it has much better ability to deal with ice in winter which will serve the Islands communities well (Briggs, December 2013).

The new ferry's capacity is able to carry 200 passengers and 60 vehicles; and it is designed to sail in ice. The contract to build the new ferry, worth $51 million, was awarded to Damen Shipyards located in The Netherlands [the location later became Romania] (CBC News, November 13, 2013). While this long-awaited announcement was welcomed locally, it also attracted commentary that the commissioning of a new ferry for Fogo Island and the Change Islands was an opportunity for realizing larger ferry capacity and for having the new ferry constructed in the Province.

Recognizing Our True Assets

Most places in the world have regional or local development assets; at least at some level of value. If one wants to engage in development, especially for the purposes of the economic development of a region, then one must recognize directly and indirectly the "true" assets of a place. These are assets from which value-added and advantage may be derived. Doing development studies of the Fogo Island and Change Islands region shows that it is a particularly rich place for regional development experimentation from which development strategists elsewhere may derive lessons for consideration in their own development planning. In the process of analyzing such development, one may learn about and be better positioned to recognize the strategic development potential of another area. The Fogo Island region, a place with some four hundred years of human history, provides a deep and special source of inspiration for just such asset recognition-learning and practice. In leading the development of the region, the Shorefast Foundation has worked from the proposition that the past holds the key to the future. Ask the Foundation leadership where to begin development and they will say, "You need to know who you are and what you have."

Ocean, Land and People

The Foundation has perceived the ecosystem of its home region and its past principally as ocean, land and people. Analysis of and living in the region plus extensive studying, working and traveling globally has led Foundation leaders to formulate a development vision and a well-considered program of action that is intended to be responsive to the specific development needs and aspirations of the region. The Foundation's end-state vision for the future is a local economy that importantly continues to be based on the fishery sector, but the envisaged economy also is intended to be diversified so that there is no longer sole dependence on the fishery, which is an already-vulnerable means of economic production that is highly localized and has functioned fundamentally from a culture and orientation that is inward looking.

Specifically, the initial future-vision pathway toward economic diversification consists of three legs: (1) the Fogo Island Arts program; (2) the Business Assistance Fund and its microfinance loan program; and (3) the Fogo Island Inn. Each of these programs springs from past and current assets of the island region and for the intended creation of new assets and economic capital spin-offs and revenue generation for the future of Fogo Island and the Change Islands region.

For this region, the ocean and its resources are the assets of nature. The land is largely barren and it has the constant companionship of powerful weather; it is windswept, i.e. it has a windscape; land here functions principally as the platform from which the resources of the sea have been and continue to be the primary source of value-added for the local regional economy. People, of course, function as the key dynamic in this three sub-system ecosystem; for it is the local people, with all of their cultural heritage, traditions and ingenuity, who have responded to and striven to make a living from the bounty and the uncertainties especially of the maritime and terrestrial environments. The economic diversification for the future relates to an additional critical people component to this equation; it is the people from beyond the islands. It is the external people that are critical to the strategy of attracting geotourists, global consumers and external investment partners from the global society willing to match their interests with those local interests of Fogo Island and the Change Islands. This internal and external people relationship is a supportive asset because, as has been observed, Fogo Islanders have a "love of strangers" (Cobb, May 31, 2013).

Geotourism

This concept has been framed as foundational and an intended competitive advantage for the Fogo Island and Change Islands region's future. What is geotourism? Jonathan Tourtellot of the National Geographic Society (2013) coined the term "geotourism." In his words, "geotourism is tourism that sustains or enhances the geographical character of a place – the environment, heritage, aesthetics, food, culture and well-being of a local people" (Center for Sustainable Destinations, n.d.) The Shorefast Foundation states further:

> We believe that these geographically and culturally unique islands are extremely well suited to visitors wanting to experience this. We plan to add the necessary infrastructure to catalyze this industry on Fogo Island and Change Islands and to do so in a manner that engages the local people as masters of their own destinies (Shorefast Foundation, Home Page, n.d.).

Early framing and the practice of geotourism, especially in Europe, was geology centric. An early purpose was "to fund the preservation and then conservation of geosites and geomorphosites" (Hose, et. al, 2011: 339).

The working definition of geotourism that the Shorefast Foundation has framed and adopted includes the nature and the environment, culture, art, architecture, and economic history especially the exploration of the responsible utilization of natural resources including the local fishery. However, the Foundation has included particularly strategic comparative advantage by emphasizing the marketing to and attraction of geotourists of means. Such targeting is intended to enhance revenue generation and in the process minimize the impact of relatively low numbers of tourists on the environment. Refer to Appendix 1 for an elaboration of the kinds and evolution of geotourism.

To support the goal of having Fogo Island become a global-leading geotourism destination, the Shorefast Foundation has created The Fogo Island Inn. The Fogo Island Arts Program and the Business Assistance Fund program function in complementary support of this place-specific goal.

Building on Inherent Assets of a Place – Optimizing for Place/Community

Each of these first three early-stage programs of the Shorefast Foundation is designed to build on the assets of the region. These include: the Fogo Island Arts Program; the Business Assistance Program and its micro-finance loan program; and the luxury Fogo Island Inn. But why give priority to the arts? Because art is a way of knowing, both from local and from distant original sources, art and design merit attention when spurring regional development. Zita Cobb "is passionate about the power of arts as an economic and social engine;" she has stated:

> My belief is that our society hasn't quite figured out how to give arts and artists their due. ... I think they should be at the table for discussions on a variety of things. I really see the interdependence of things, and business is not separate from the arts. It really needs to come together (Bartlett, 2008: 116).

Consequently, one of the early bundles of interdependent initiatives that formed the vision and action of the Shorefast Foundation was based on architecture, design and art. These initiatives ranged from traditional boat (punt) building projects (to re-purposing rehabilitation of selected houses and churches to planning and constructing from scratch a stunning architectural Fogo Island Inn that integrates contemporary and traditional design inspirations. Nurturing the original sources of art, i.e., the artists, also is encompassed with the residencies programming for artists.

Fogo Island Arts Program

The strategy for resurrecting and diversifying the local economy depends on infusing external influences and having local mindsets and behaviors appreciate and market to the development potentialities for consumption of the local region's services and products by global economic environments beyond the islands. In the arts sector, for example, the Shorefast Foundation's Fogo Island Arts artists-in-residence program brings in creative practitioners from around the world to do their work, learn from and live in the local region. This program was established in 2008. These contemporary artists may include painters, sculptors, filmmakers, writers, curators, designers and thinkers, among others. In turn, local residents are able to get exposed to and learn from these artists "from away." These interactions can occur via immersion of the external artists in the communities, and by means of exhibitions, presentations and discussions. In the process, the external artists are able to take back home their unique and rich Fogo Island lessons and experience, while local residents are able to learn new artistic technique and method, plus experience the opportunities, demands, standards and challenges of the global marketplace.

The principal assets of the local people's creativity and imagination are being tapped into and showcased from such traditional talents as: boat building and design; vernacular architecture; quilting; and folk art, among other art forms, e.g. food innovation and furniture crafting (See Appendix 3 on Product Business for Homemade Goods; and refer to Figure 10 to view a local carpenter working on the crafting of a part for a Fogo Island punt boat). The exchange and cross-fertilization between the local and the global intends to plant the seeds of new creative business worldviews built on the foundation of the long-standing Fogo Island tradition of self-reliance and re-cycling of the use of materials necessitated by remoteness. For more about Fogo Island Arts and its rich range of programming, refer to Fogo Island Arts, n.d.; these programs include: the residencies; the Fogo Island Dialogues; exhibitions; publications; cinema; design initiatives and education.

The Fogo Island Arts residency program generally issues annual calls for proposals. Numbers of artists in residence by year at the time of this writing have included: 2014 – 14; 2013 – 20; 2012 – 18; 2011 – 10; and 2010 – 6.

Jonathan Briggs of the Shorefast Foundation's Business Assistance Fund has observed that the Arts Program functions as a financial engine in other ways:

> In addition to the community effects listed above, the Arts Program that draws leading contemporary artists to the Artist Residency program is intended to attract to Fogo Island the affluent art patrons that follow these artists. These arts patrons - wanting to know/see/experience what influenced the artist - will stay at the Fogo Island Inn, thus initiating the direct monetary transaction on Fogo Island (December 16, 2013).

Business Assistance Fund and Regional Economic Development

The Shorefast Business Assistance Fund was established through a $1 million donation from Dr. Jozef Straus and his wife Vera. The amounts of the loans average $25,000. Typically, these loans are at an interest rate of 2% for a term of five years.

The Business Assistance Fund Program of the Shorefast Foundation is a one-million dollar microfinance low interest loan fund. It is:

> designed to kickstart or expand business ideas that support the vision of Fogo Island and Change Islands as world renowned geotourism destinations. The purpose is to stimulate the economy of Fogo Island and Change Islands. ... We need to encourage business activities on Fogo Island and Change Islands that are built on the special qualities of the place and the people. These activities will become drivers for our local economy. We also need to create additional goods and services to engage and attract visitors to our islands (Shorefast Foundation, "Home Page," n.d.)

Shorefast's microfinance fund was inspired by the Grameen Bank that was founded by Professor Muhammad Yunus of Bangladesh. Its origins date back to 1976. It was an effort "to create economic and social development from below." Micro-credit was a principal means to enable poor people, especially rural village women, to break out of poverty. The documented success of the Bank was so effective and such a model for poor around the world, that Professor Yunus and the Grameen Bank were awarded and shared The Nobel Peace Prize in 2006 (Grameen Bank, n.d.).

The Business Assistance Fund Program of the Shorefast Foundation solicits the submission of "a business idea that lends itself to the unique attractions of the islands and speaks to the culture and history of these places ..." Each business idea is assessed individually. Business ideas may be supported with the Foundation by these types of assistance: business plan guidance; funding option advice; training via workshops on setting up and operating a small business; and loans to business idea submitters. Successful applicants are offered a loan at a preferred interest rate.

To explicate the details of the Fund's operations, they are paraphrased here. To be able to access the Fund, people must: execute the business according to the Fund's purpose; operate the business on the islands; and demonstrate the likelihood of becoming profitable within a reasonable time period. Additional funding criteria include:

- Access or leverage additional funding
- Attract visitors and tourists to the islands
- Reduce the islands' dependency on imported goods
- Use locally-available products
- Promote the creation of high quality and traditional crafts
- Respect the environment
- Promote healthy living and good nutrition
- Provide locally produced foods
- Expand activities and products for our visitors, especially as they relate to culture and ecotourism

The Business Assistance Fund became available in May 2009; by June 2013, fifteen businesses had been awarded loans. These are the types of businesses and the number of loans that have been made: Accommodation, 3; Traditional Foods, Fabrics and Clothing, 2; Marine Cultural Adventures, 2; Daycare Facility, 1; Traditional Irish Bar, 1; Artisan Guild, 1; Agricultural Co-op, 1; Greenhouses, 2; Bakery, 1; and Taxi service, 1.

These data and most of the information provided here are from correspondence with Jonathan Briggs of the Shorefast Foundation in the summer of 2013. He led the operation of the Business Assistance Fund Program of the Shorefast Foundation and functions as the non-resident in-house business assistance consultant for the Foundation. During the loan program period noted above, he reported that he has consulted with more people than those interested only about funding their business plans. "Many were not seeking funding – they wanted a discussion about options and realistic advice and then went on [to] make their own plans" (Briggs, June 19, 2013).

For guidance as to the types of business to be funded, Jonathan Briggs notes that the Foundation draws on its vision of geotourism and the tourism recommendations of the region's Socio-Economic Strategic Plan. As introduced above, this plan was published in 2008 "as a socio-economic snapshot/map prior to serious progress on municipal amalgamation" (Kittiwake Economic Development Corporation and D.W. Knight Associates, July 2008). Later, the Town of Fogo Island government was officially created on March 1, 2011 by the amalgamation of four existing Towns and one Regional Council (Town of Fogo Island, n.d.). The Town of Change Islands was not part of this amalgamation; it had been incorporated much earlier in 1951 (Town of Change Islands, n.d.).

Based on these Business Assistance Fund activities and experiences over these last four to five years, Jonathan Briggs was asked to assess the Program to June of 2013:

> Being a positive advocate, listening, and encouraging confidence are where I feel I've added the most value to people to date. There is no Chamber of Commerce or other resource where people can go to have a frank discussion about their business ideas. Banks and government services are seen as intimidating. The people of Fogo Island and Change Islands are resilient, tenacious and cautious. Many are of an age where they do not want to start a new business. They have experienced over 200 years of people from away telling what is best for them, and it often has not been. Once the Fogo Island Inn is fully operational and clearly demonstrates it can draw an affluent customer base I believe a younger generation of new business owners may be encouraged to return home. Moving forward the Business Assistance Fund needs to evolve to reflect past experience and be more active in the area of business coaching, and training as complements to the micro loan activity (Briggs, June 19, 2013).

From the funding criteria for the Business Assistance Fund listed above and from the results so far of the types of business and the numbers involved, one may logically conclude that there has been congruence and supportive complementarities between the stated intentions of the Business Assistance Fund Program in seeking to build on the inherent assets of the place and optimizing these assets for the community.

In 2008, Shorefast's Jonathan Briggs and his wife started a community festival. "The Partridgeberry Harvest Festival is the only local festival that is expressly designed to benefit, and bring together, all the communities of Fogo Island and Change Islands in a celebration of local talent and culture" (Fogo Island Partridgeberry Harvest Festival, n.d.). The purpose of the Festival is "to provide a marketplace for people to sell their crafts and by doing so develop pride in their abilities. A positive response by customers has led to several businesses growing considerably once they were connected to a market place" (Briggs, June 21, 2013). The festival has become an opportunity to keep and renew the island's cultural capital by enlivening traditional crafts, recipes, oral history, music and the spirit of community. It has been celebrated as the Sixth Annual Fogo Island Partridgeberry Harvest. It was last held on October 12-13, 2013; this was the Canadian Thanksgiving Weekend. What is a partridgeberry? Outside of Newfoundland and Labrador it is known as lingonberry or cowberry. This is an important event for assisting the local community to be aware of and to reinforce its growing enterprise-development mindset.

The 2012 Festival attracted 1,200 paid ($3.00) admissions. Additionally, there were 200 complimentary admissions which included volunteering, vendors, staff, committee members and presenters. This community asset showcase attracts a significant number of visitors from throughout the province of Newfoundland and Labrador, especially from Gander, Twillingate and Lewisporte. "Almost 75% of tickets sold at the Entertainment night were to visitors to Fogo

Island. That brings new money to the economy, which stays on the Islands" (Fogo Island Partridgeberry Harvest Festival, n.d.: 3). This is an illustration of an export-based inward income flow into the local economy that was noted above. Refer to Appendix 4 for the costs and benefits of the 2012 Fogo Island Partridgeberry Harvest Festival. Lastly, the Festival, being held in October, serves touristically to bridge the end of summer and the beginning of the late fall period, i.e. before the Northwesterlies signal that winter is approaching; i.e. this is part of the goal of tapping into the seven seasons of Fogo Island (Refer to Appendix 5 for an outline of the principal weather expectations for the region's seven seasons).

Fogo Island Inn

The last of the three early-stage planned programs of the Shorefast Foundation recently was completed and opened, i.e. the Fogo Island Inn in May 2013. This timing was able to take advantage of the 2013 summer tourist season. The Toronto-based Sustainable EDGE design and engineering consultant for the Inn's green design has described the project of follows:

> The Fogo Island Inn is a 29-room high-end eco-tourism facility on the island of Fogo, off the north-east coast of Newfoundland. In addition to providing accommodations the Inn also houses a community library and art gallery, an e-Cinema and a five-star restaurant. The project is an initiative for community economic development by the Shorefast Foundation, a social enterprise.

> A goal of the project was to make the Inn as energy and cost efficient as possible so that maximum revenues could accrue to support the community and be re-invested in "Finding new ways for an old continuity," as noted by Zita Cobb, founder of the Shorefast Foundation. Sustainable EDGE provided sustainable engineering consulting which included facilitating an Integrated Designpilot Charrette, high performance building envelope design and consulting on high-efficiency mechanical systems. Systems include radiant heating from solar thermal and wood boilers, solar domestic hot water for rooms and laundry, displacement ventilation with heat recovery, demand ventilation and summer outdoor air cooling with dehumidified outdoor air and kitchen exhaust air cleaning to avoid cooking odors.

> Sustainable EDGE provided green building consulting throughout the project's design and construction phase (Sustainable EDGE, n.d.).

There are additional features to the ones noted above; the Inn has conference and event facilities to accommodate such activities as corporate retreats, weddings and gatherings. There are roof top wood-fired sauna and hot tubs with stunning views of the ocean and the Little Fogo Islands on the horizon. There also is an exercise room. The e-Cinema seats 42 persons in comfortable theater seats. The Inn's guest elevator's three fixed walls are floor-to-ceiling exquisite maps; they are hand-painted cartographic murals depicting in great detail the names (some of which have been assigned to the guest rooms) and locations of the islands positioned around the northern rim of Fogo Island. (See Figure 11 for a close-up of the map mural depicting the geography of the Fogo Island and the Change Islands region) These are the special kind of place optimizing detailed touches that serve to deepen the geotouristic experience.

The Fogo Island Inn provides an extensive range of guest services. For example, assistance is available for entering one's vehicle in the ferry queue to enable timely departure from the island to the mainland. The number of staff working in the Inn at the time of its opening was approximately 100. These investments, combined with close attention to the localization of the guest experience, gives one a sense of the high quality and personalization of the Inn's services.

Fogo Island Arts works with the Fogo Island Inn's the Community Host Program which offers a wide range of arts, fishery, cultural, out-of-doors and other customized activities that enable guests to interact with local residents for enriching exposures to the islands' unique traditional, material and natural assets. Every guest room has floor to ceiling windows providing sea views all the way to the Little Fogo Islands. The guest rooms are furnished with binoculars and a selection of half a dozen or so books on and from Fogo Island and Newfoundland topics and authors. One may keep the TV in the guest room or have it removed. Many guests prefer the sound of the sea and luxuriate in the ability to reflect on the island's natural and cultural environments and its remoteness (See Figures 12, 13 and 14 for views of a selection of the Inn's guest rooms).

The keystone asset of the Inn is its world-class restaurant, with its special place-specific local and Newfoundland food signature for the dining room (See Figures 15, 16 and 17). There are logistics and accessibility challenges in food sourcing, and of course the harsh seasonal weather and climactic conditions require extraordinary effort for the production and localization of the Inn's culinary offerings. In keeping with contemporary eco-dining practices, Executive Chef Murray McDonald's goal is to keep the source of foods prepared for the Inn's restaurant as local and culturally relevant as possible. (See Figure 18 of Chef McDonald and a mummer at Christmas time in the Fogo Island Inn) Such farm-to-table cuisine intends to lessen human impact on the earth. So, when local sourcing is not possible, a next fallback position for Chef McDonald is to seek products that traditionally were part of Newfoundland's history and heritage. For example, if certain items during the triangular trade period of the 18th and 19th centuries arrived on the shores of and were consumed in Newfoundland, then these would be acceptable to serve in the Inn. These might include: cheeses from France; chutney from England; and rum from the Caribbean, among many others.

Adding to these food sourcing limitations and challenges of Chef McDonald is the already-constrained nature of the suppliers available for the general Newfoundland market as well as the even more remote location of the Fogo Island region. The ways that the large food and food services suppliers bring their mass-market mindset and business behaviors to the Atlantic Canada market do not match well to the high-end geotourism and eco-dining values of the Fogo Island Inn and other such restaurants in Newfoundland. Large, global-mindset food services corporations have sales and service relationships that run counter to the Inn's values of local investment, local control and community-based capacity building in food production. These big-business corporations often force exclusive deals and dictate pricing. The operating business philosophy of the Fogo Island Inn and the Shorefast Foundation is not to use their own financial resources to buy goods and services from firms, countries and places where basic labor laws and environmental protection laws are ignored and dominant neoliberal business practices are pursued. Based on the long history of exploitation by non-resident and distant fishery merchants in the province, one should not be surprised that predatory corporate relationships are being avoided as part of the Shorefast Foundation's ethos.

The food sourcing challenges are multiple. For the tastes of the affluent guests of the Inn and other discriminating geotourist customers, whose numbers reasonably can be expected to increase over time, the food sourcing and supply-chain linkages need upgrading especially to be responsive to the selective requirements of the Fogo Island Inn and Nicole's Café for example. Refer to Figure 19. Current provincial food service supply patterns are and have been targeted at institutions, such as hospitals, and at older customers. Further, new-generation suppliers are not on the horizon.

Again, the Inn's Chef McDonald strives to keep procurement as local as possible. While he can buy produce from farmers, regulations prohibit him from buying fish directly from a fisher. Proteins, such as meats, are difficult to source; any meat produced locally on the island, e.g. lamb, has to be certified in Comfort Cove, on the mainland of Newfoundland and shipped back to Fogo Island. The four local cultivators do not plant until May 24; so, green tops come up in June; carrots in July. The chef tries to wild forage every day; July and August is blueberry time; September and October are partridgeberry months. In addition, the Chef and staff of the Inn maintain nearby garden plots for the restaurant. (Refer to Figures 20, 21 and 22) "We have 15 varieties of potatoes alone. It's been interesting to experiment with local produce. Last week we served four different preparations of turnips. The other week I tried cooking with caribou moss." Chef McDonald is no stranger to the weather and seasonal issues of growing one's own produce in Newfoundland. He is a native Newfoundlander, who also is highly and widely experienced having acquired his food planning, sourcing, design, preparation and presentation expertise from around the world's top hotels and resorts. "We believe that food is the perfect way to share Fogo Island's seven seasons" (Appendix 5). Chef McDonald has infused time-honored local recipes with leading edge culinary practices to produce food that is regional, local and creative. Regarding the struggles noted above, Chef McDonald said that they have been a blessing in disguise; they have made me be more self-reliant and find solutions myself" (McDonald, May 30, 2013).

The efforts of Chef McDonald to date have demonstrated that his experiments have paid off. A globally food-knowledgeable dining guest to the Inn within days of opening in May 2013 wrote this about the Inn's food product:

> We stayed at the Inn for three nights and every meal was a gourmet treat. I even had goat cheese ice cream with beet gelatin ... a must try once. Other wonderful meals included grilled halibut, cod, scallops, and duck. For lunch a lobster steam bun ... chock full of fresh lobster and delicious. Another lunch favorite was the pasta with short ribs ... amazing. The meringue shell filled with luscious fruit was delicious (Corey, June 13, 2013).

In addition to implementing the Inn's intensely local food products and services, the chef's practice draws explicitly on contemporary and traditional influences, the result is that the kitchen provides world class eco-dining for its discriminating geotourist clientele. The beverage and spirits staff of the Inn also are investing their imaginations in their services and presentations. They are deepening their wine cellar and spirits inventory. They will continue to give guests the option of having ice from icebergs in their drinks. During the early days of the Inn's opening the staff were devoted to inventing and naming a "signature cocktail" as a branded product to be associated particularly with the Fogo Island Inn, similar to the long-standing association of the Singapore Sling and Raffles Hotel in Singapore. Later, we learned that the new signature cocktail for the Fogo Island Inn consists of these ingredients: spruce vodka; lemon juice; and simple syrup. This concoction has been christened the "Rockin' Fogo" (See Figure 23 for a view of the bar in the Fogo Island Inn).

Regional development practitioners and scholars around the world are recognizing that regional food products and preparations are increasing in strategic importance for advancing rural tourism. In late September-early October, 2013, Linnaeus University, School of Business and Economics, Kalmar, Sweden organized and hosted a significant food event – a conference entitled "Tourism, Local Foods and Regional Development" -- that brought "Researchers from all over the world ... to present high quality papers on these topics":

> The place of food in rural tourism, current trends in regional food consumption, consumer perspectives on regional foods, perceptions of restaurant owners and chefs, the promotion of local food supply chains, willingness-to-pay for regional foods, food festivals and events, second homes, regional foods, food related entrepreneurship, food product development, regional food and carbon management, IT and food networks, regional food policy, the promotion of food localization, fair trade and regional development, the role of local food in ethical consumption, the development of intellectual property protection for regional food products, and the branding of regional foods as well as broader issues regarding regional food networks and regional development (Linnaeus University, n.d.)

The conference was held in conjunction with the regional Harvest Festival (Ölands Skördefest) on the island of Öland near Kalmar, Sweden. The 17th Ölands Skördefest took place September 26-29, 2013. It has grown in such popularity over the years that over 100,000 people attend. Villagers open their doors and invite visitors to participate in some 900 activities; events include fairs, markets, festivals, art shows, and hot air balloons (Ölands Skördefest, n.d.).

Analogously, as Fogo Island Inn Chef Murray McDonald planned for the Inn's first Canadian Thanksgiving weekend, a get together of a selection of Newfoundland's most innovative chefs was convened at the Inn. They were helpful and forthcoming when he first returned to Newfoundland to take up his post as the Executive Chef of the Fogo Island Inn. He referred to the five invited visiting chefs as "almost like a culinary family" (Wells, October 8, 2013: 2). This gathering of the chefs was timed to coincide with the Sixth Annual Fogo Island Partridgeberry Harvest Festival as well as the Thanksgiving celebration.

In creating the menu for the seven-course gourmet dinner for the Inn's Canadian Thanksgiving weekend, the family of chefs decided to each prepare something different and to focus on "something that is a Newfoundland ingredient." Chef McDonald's approach was to innovate and be informed by localization in the process of inventing and practicing culinary ingenuity.

> Don't expect to sit down to a traditional Thanksgiving dinner with all the trimmings. There will be a traditional feel and vibe, but the food is a bit out there. ... A lot of my dishes are slightly out there, but I bring it back to the ground and make it a dish that is of this place and of Newfoundland and of Fogo Island. I always try to have that effect to the dish. It is a bit abstract — the new Newfoundland cuisine — that's my motto on it all (Wells, October 8, 2013: 2).

He planned on using local ubiquitous lichen, i.e. caribou moss. The chef chose it for its earthy, mushroom-like taste. Because of its extremely high acidity, it requires a two-day process to neutralize the pH balance. He took his inspiration from the ancient local Beothuk people and their use of this ingredient that always has been on the rocks of Fogo Island. Indeed, the acidity is so strong that the moss burns holes in the rocks. This level of imagination drives the quest for authenticity that is in keeping with the values of geotourism that have formed the core of the Fogo Island Inn's and the Shorefast Foundation's strategic core concept in seeking to diversify the local economy.

The gathering of the chefs for the Thanksgiving and Partridgeberry Festival weekend on Fogo Island also featured at the Inn:

> a dialogue about Newfoundland cuisine, similar to dialogues that have been taking place on the arts at the Inn. Cooking as these chefs will be doing over the weekend would certainly be considered an art form (Wells, October 8, 2013: 3).

This kind of complementary, meticulous and nuanced business and organizational behavior has "method to its madness," so to speak. The convening of these innovative chefs of Newfoundland has the basis for enabling the formation of networks of affinity among peer and like-minded contemporary food-industry professionals of the province. This might be elevated in future to address the systems-level requirements of supply-chain gaps, as well as marketing issues that currently challenge the special needs of the new eco-dining and geotourist investments that are being made at a number of locations across the vast space of the large mainland island of Newfoundland.

Based on our interviews some interesting seeds are being sown. Into the future therefore, one may expect the Fogo Island Inn food and beverage staff to continue to innovate, improvise, create, and in the process, seek gradually to address some of the regulatory and supply-chain hurdles of sourcing food, and in the process further enrich the islands' cultural capital by means of distinctive local food production and possibly by means of philosophical changes in local corporate logistics and business process improvements that are respectful of local development values that depend on community awareness, ownership/buy in and empowerment as a means to realize more healthy local economies and sustainable natural resources ecosystems.

In many ways, the Fogo Island Inn is the economic engine and integrative means for connecting the Fogo Island Arts Program as well as being something of a larger scale business development exemplar and source of learning for participants in the Business Assistance Fund Program. With the Inn now in place and thereby being able to work out the kinks of starting up a new niche business with a sizable staff, the functional links with the other two initial programs (the Arts and the micro loan fund) can begin to function fully in a complementary, supportive and inter-locking manner, with resulting more productive outcomes being the result.

These dynamics over time may be expected to generate synergies that will benefit visitors to the Inn specifically and to the islands more generally. As this organizational and business maturation continues, more gaps and needed improvements will be revealed. For example, a critical link that demonstrated a system weakness for the region several times over the summer of 2013 was the inconsistency, dependability and capacity of the ferry service to and from Fogo Island and the mainland of Newfoundland.

Building Culture into the Fabric of a Business

The examination above of the early-stage development programs of the arts, business development and the Inn has introduced and documented explicit cultural content throughout each of the three initial programs of the Foundation. Chronologically, the Fogo Island Arts Program was the lead initiative with the Fogo Island Arts Residencies. Fogo Island offers "a residency-based contemporary art venue for artists, filmmakers, writers, musicians, curators, designers, and thinkers from around the world." These residencies are at the core of building both cultural heritage and contemporary culture into the material and the imaginative realms of shared knowledge. Embedded in both these physical and cultural domains is the expectation that innovation and creativity will be nurtured in the unique natural and human ecosystem of the islands.

The four artist studios and the residences where the artists work and live respectively are icons and metaphors for innovation and creativity. Designed by contemporary architect Todd Saunders, the studios are visually bold and dramatic. The drama is accentuated by most being sited on the edge of and overlooking the North Atlantic Ocean. The studios were constructed during the 2009-2011 period. Long Studio (Joe Batt's Arm location) was completed in 2010; the other three studios were completed in 2011; they are: Tower Studio (Shoal Bay); Bridge Studio (Deep Bay); and Squish Studio (Tilting). Refer to Figures 24 through 31; i.e., eight photos). Nearby vernacular residential structures that house the visiting international artists-in-residence have been rehabilitated and brought up to modern living standards, and their traditional design has been maintained (Refer to Figure 32 Wells House).

Architect Todd Saunders is a native of Newfoundland and founded his architecture practice in Bergen, Norway in 1996. He also is the architect for the dramatic new Fogo Island Inn which opened in May 2013. It too perches over the rocky edge of the sea; its contemporary architectural design incorporates the look and shape and wooden material of traditional fish processing structures (Refer to Figures 33 through 36 four views). Thus both the new and the old structures are thoughtful and imaginative representations of building local culture and contemporary culture into their forms and functions. Important strategically, the use of contemporary architecture sends the bold eye-catching message that a new culture of business entrepreneurship is being planted and nurtured as a critical contribution toward the realization of a diverse and sustainable economic future for the Fogo Island and Change Islands region. Further, this new enterprising culture is being built on the envisaged foundation of a thriving competitive seafood industry and a strong culture of cooperation across the region and of high quality seafood products and effective business initiatives. The cumulative result during this early stage of the Fogo Island regional development strategy is to resurrect the local economy by means of diversification is a viable fishery sector with emergent sectors in the arts, small business formation and growth, and geotourism – all to be sustainable into the future.

These development actions are grounded conceptually. Incorporating culture throughout these initiatives is a good fit with the "development from tradition" pathway of development anthropologist Denis Goulet. This approach is "a form of development suited to a particular society [and] should be sought from within the latent dynamism of that society's value system: its traditional beliefs, its meaning system, its local institutions and popular practices (Goulet, 1983: 19). Such cultural, intellectual and business grounding may be an important strategic planning stimulant for other rural places as stakeholders there process the lessons being generated in the execution of the Fogo Islands rural development model.

Community Ownership of Capital

Every day Zita Cobb says that she focuses on the most important thing; i.e., "what can we [the Shorefast Foundation] do for the community?" Focusing on the types of community capital as framed by Mark Roseland helps her answer and be responsive to this most important thing. Roseland's concepts for community capital consist of six forms of capital that represent the assets of a community: (1) natural capital, e.g. non-renewable resources, fossil fuels and renewable resources, fishery; (2) physical capital, e.g. infrastructure; (3) economic capital, e.g. finance and business; (4) human capital, e.g. knowledge, skills; (5) social capital, e.g. connectedness, ethics; and (6) cultural capital, e.g., tradition, values, food. According to Roseland, these types of capital are the backbone of his Community Capital Sustainability Framework (Roseland, 2012: 12-19).

From Zita Cobb's experience in business and finance, she embraces the teachings of learning organization and systems management authority Peter Senge that there must be a strong commitment to truth, "it means a relentless willingness to root out the ways we limit or deceive ourselves from seeing what is, and to continually challenge our theories of why things are the way they are" (Senge, 2006: 148). Using some of the forms of capital introduced above for example, she sees business practice as it should be rather than continuing to follow the natural capital and social capital destructive practices that have prevailed in so many places throughout the industrial age. Many business executives today still see economic capital as the dominant system with environmental or natural capital and social capital serving as handmaidens to the demands of the economic capital system. Rather, fresh eyes focused on the "real" world would compel a reflective business person to conclude that the role of business should recognize that there cannot be a healthy economy without a vital and renewing environment and a stable and dynamic social order. Senge has written, "fortunately, many smart organizations understand the importance of this shift in perspective and practice, and are acting accordingly" (Senge, et al, 2008: 103).

As a consequence of these conceptual and philosophic influences integrated with the historical and empirical realities of the Fogo Island and Change Islands region, the Shorefast Foundation, in conjunction with community involvement, assessment and feedback, has initiated a program of actions designed and intended to catalyze stakes and ownership by the people and businesses of the islands.

> The [Fogo Island] Inn's operations are housed in a Business Trust, managed by a group of trustees. The Business Trust's sole beneficiary is the Shorefast Foundation, thus no other entity can receive any amount of surplus from operations. The Shorefast Foundation, a registered Canadian charity, has a mandate to provide economic and cultural resilience to the local residents through its programming and funding of other non-profit agents. Inn surpluses will move through the Foundation and be invested in many projects which in turn help support the local economy (Hodgins, May 16, 2013).

Zita Cobb refers to this organizational relationship as "not-just-for-profit." This is an example of social enterprise, whereby business minded ways serve social ends (See Figure 37, Social Enterprise). Owned by the Shorefast Foundation, the charity; the investment decisions for the surpluses generated from the Inn and other business initiatives are relegated by the Foundation for priority setting by the community. Again, these business initiatives include the arts, the business assistance fund, the Fogo Island Inn, other heritage and preservation efforts, and emergent ocean awareness, literacy and the ocean ethic program. Also, a program of Dialogues with knowledgeable persons in these sectors has been initiated. With venues planned for Fogo Island and other global locations, the Fogo Island Dialogues will ensure a constant flow of fresh issues and perspectives from diverse sources that should illuminate relevant trends and patterns that may inform Shorefast's priorities and investments (Fogo Island Arts, September 27, 2013; Shorefast Foundation, 2013 and 2014).

The community ownership of capital is intended to be realized by means of a range of capital development approaches. A high priority objective is that the community generates income in the form of economic capital and the income stays in the community to build up the local place. The Shorefast Foundation supports associated businesses through a business trust. After expenses have been paid, the profits from the business of the Fogo Island Inn are reinvested in the community by means of community decision making. This source of economic capital and other opportunities for investment and stakeholder engagement result in various partnering relationships with the people of Fogo Island and Change Islands and the Foundation. Thereby, they are influenced to invest in the revitalization of their local economy to help make it more economically diverse, vibrant, stable and self-sufficient.

Micro loan recipients from the Business Assistance Fund form investment partners with small business owners by means of economic capital. Fogo Island Arts is part of a social enterprise-based business model that will support the economic viability of the Fogo Island Inn and the growth of tourism on Fogo Island. For example, local persons and households who have benefitted from interaction with and creative stimulation from the international artists to Fogo Island under the residency program are owners of human capital, social capital and cultural capital. Residents, fishers and other business persons and volunteers who have provided services to geotourists to the Fogo Island Inn's Community Host program and its extensive guest experiences and activities will have invested or gifted energy, time and emotion with return on those investments yielding benefits across the range of natural capital, physical capital, economic capital, human capital, social capital and cultural capital. Each of these forms of direct and indirect capital investment, over time, likely will have the cumulative effect of building and spreading various levels of ownership and stakeholding across the islands (Lachapelle, 2008).

An expected outcome will be that the community's people increasingly will have greater control and influence over their work, quality of life and their place in and contribution to the community as a whole. These critical feelings of self-determination, empowerment and investment in the locality may be expected to deepen and may be reinforced by such policies as the Fogo Island Inn's luxurious facilities being open and welcoming to island residents for their patronage; these facilities include the contemporary art gallery, the e-Cinema, the meeting space and the five-star restaurant.

Holding on to Ways of Knowing

Coming from a family and a community that by and large did not read and write, Zita Cobb learned that "knowing" came from sources other than the written word. She is an eighth generation Fogo Islander, but she is among the first generation that can read and write. Having gone away to university, she learned that word-of-mouth experience-based knowledge acquisition and formal scholarly-based knowledge acquisition both are critical ways of knowing. As a consequence, she says that she has been preoccupied with ways of knowing which respects all knowledge sources. Traditionally, Fogo Islanders had a purity of knowing; they operated from first principles; i.e., they knew fish. Over time however, Cobb has observed, "the rest of the world began to skyrocket past us."

The Foundation is not engaged in antiquarianism. When envisioning Fogo Island's future pathway toward a more diverse and sustainable local economy, her world view has compelled her to value and retain active respect for the local heritage and cultural capital of past ways of knowing while simultaneously incorporating new ways of knowing that preserve natural capital and physical capital while also generating new economic capital by means of new human capital development and social capital development.

The three early-stage programs of the Shorefast Foundation are richly embedded with the remembrance and preservation of ways of knowing that are relevant to today as well as having the power to remind local and visitor alike how significant it is to appreciate the past roots of authenticity, ingenuity and perseverance that should inform the future. It is through the interdependent relationships of past and future ways of knowing that the emerging Fogo Island model for rural development ultimately may demonstrate its power and potentiality for utility elsewhere.

For example, the Fogo Island Inn and its deep offering of experiences and local knowledge acquisition activities for guests are designed explicitly to bring together direct and active interaction with islanders and the local environment for mutual learning and reciprocal discovery and awareness. These engagements can be particularly rewarding because of the extraordinary hospitality and warm forthcoming hosting environment that is so pervasive and comes so naturally from nearly every Fogo Islander that one meets. This indeed is an idiosyncratic social and human asset of the region. Each of the human-nature or human-culture or human-physical experiential options made available by the Inn offers varying degrees of exertion and intimacy of exposure; they are likely to satisfy the range of expected geotourists in search of unique place encounters or even whimsy -- at the "edge of the world."

Fogo Island is said to be one of the four corners of the earth by members of the Flat Earth Society (Candice Does the World, n.d.). A small sampling of guest experiences that are organized by the Fogo Island Inn's Community Host Program include: five different drawing and sketching opportunities – some out in the landscape and some indoors; three different exposures to marine and ocean assets, ranging from exploring cod culture to a lobster harvesting and dining picnic and to sea bird watching aboard an ocean-outfitted vessel in the Little Fogo Islands; explore the Island's natural ecosystem including rocks, natural history, wild botany and tailored trail trekking; and several introductory overview and introductory experiences to Fogo Island itself (Geology At The Edge Organization, n.d.).

Beyond the activities organized by Fogo Island Inn programming, the physical design and visual representation of the Inn manifest yesterday's and today's building and structural design ways of knowing. The use of stilts for example, was a building tactic used historically to adapt construction to the uneven rocky surfaces at the edge of the sea for original structures such as fish processing stages. Both the Inn and three artist studios, i.e., Long, Squish and Bridge, use the uneven stilting method. As a general principle the physical capital commissioned by the Shorefast Foundation has sought to hold on to ways of knowing by:

- Translating what 'was' into something new
- Creating a Fogo Island contemporary design
- Harnessing the power of the specific
- Telling about Fogo Island's life and culture.

Contemporary building and contemporary conservation work on the Inn, re-purposed buildings such as former churches and restored houses for visiting artist residencies have valued and used wood (Refer to Figure 38 Barr'd Islands Church). In order to protect the natural capital of its spectacular site, the design of the five-star Fogo Island Inn operated from these heritage-inspired guiding principles for contemporary construction (See DesignalmiC, n.d.; Sustainable EDGE, n.d.):

- Landscape undisturbed to the fullest extent possible
- Preserved footpath
- No wires
- Solar thermal heating
- Local sourcing of materials
- Recapturing heat
- Rainwater cistern

Holding on to ways of knowing has been a pervasive working priority throughout the run up to the preparation and the launch of the geotourist strategy. Foraging for naturally bent wood from nature to aid in the building of punts or small wooden boats has spurred renewed interest and application by the island's boat builders. Using local craftspersons and carpenters to apply their imaginations to the design and building of furniture for the Inn provided work and resuscitated these local and disappearing skill sets. A similar revitalization process occurred with the commissioning and production of 250 unique quilts for use in the Inn.

The interior design and product of the Fogo Island Inn is a best practice (Vettoretto, 2009) and benchmark for reminding the guest of the priority for explicating the reasons for and value of holding on to ways of knowing and how such practice reinforces one's perception of the island's place identity. Refer to the Web page of the Fogo Island Inn, browse the images there while taking in the following features of the blending of past and contemporary cultural-capital rooted ways of knowing and doing (See DesignalmiC, n.d.; Sustainable EDGE, n.d.):

Each guest room is a contemporary expression of traditional outport design and décor; i.e. "handmade modern."

Every object that the guest touches, sees and experiences fortifies Fogo Island culture. That is because homes here are not just constructed, they are created from what is inside the people. Custom made, organic, natural fiber beds are a feature of the Inn's guest rooms.

The Inn's rooms and spaces have full wireless access, complemented by discreetly hidden technology.

Heated towel racks, and heated toilet seats with built-in bidet complement each room's heating sources.

The guest rooms have natural wood floors with in-floor heating. Wood burning stoves are in many rooms including the lobby area.

The guest rooms are named after the mysterious and sacred islets of the Little Fogo Islands and their rocks and shoals that lie just north and can be seen from each guest room window.

All guest rooms have floor-to-ceiling windows with swing open sections for listening to the sounds of the sea.

The Inn's guest rooms and other common spaces are furnished with custom designed, locally crafted furniture and textiles.

Covering a bench in an alcove just outside the e-Cinema theater of the Inn is a long needlepoint pillow cover that depicts the social history of Fogo Island including the film-based Fogo Process, the formation of the Fogo Island Co-operative Society and a great deal more, such as images of individual islanders who were instrumental in advancing the development of the island's community. Several of these individuals depicted on the pillow cover are members of the Inn's staff.

Every textile and piece of furniture is handcrafted and made of the island's people – from the quilts to the chairs and wallpaper patterns.

It is said that this is the only place in the world where one can soak up contemporary outport (Harris, 2008) design, simply by spending time in one's own room.

When we arrived at the Inn, we were met by the two Newfoundland dogs. This is a living, warm and pleasurable way of underscoring the island's local place identity. The dogs are named Make and Break.

Part VI

Next Stages in the Fogo Island Rural Development Model

Beyond the initial three early-stage programs of Fogo Island Arts, Business Assistance Fund and the Fogo Island Inn, two additional programs are underway recently: (1) the Fogo Island Dialogues; and (2) the New Ocean Ethic. Both of these more recent efforts are logical extensions from the early-stage activities that are underway.

Fogo Island Dialogues

An initiative of Fogo Island Arts, the Fogo Island Dialogues has inaugurated a new phase of Fogo Island Arts' evolution" (Fogo Island Dialogues, Home Page, n.d.). With the opening of the Fogo Island Inn in May 2013 the vocational and organizational place for new complementary and spin-off activities has been set by the Shorefast Foundation. The Fogo Island Dialogues is one of these next-stage programs. The following description captures an early working concept for the Dialogues.

> The Fogo Island Dialogues will be a roving series of conferences, held on Fogo Island and other locations (such as St. John's, Montreal and Vienna). Featuring leading thinkers in their respective fields, the Dialogues will address important questions faced by the global community in the 21st century. The initial series of conferences, scheduled for spring 2013, will look at the topic of 'the livelihood and renewal of remote communities.'

> The Fogo Island Dialogues exemplify how all Fogo Island Arts initiatives are framed by an engagement with the Island's local communities. While the conferences will provide an opportunity to reflect on the circumstances of rural and remote communities, such as those found on Fogo Island and Change Islands, the Fogo Island Arts' project as a whole will function as a business initiative for the Islands. Fogo Island Arts plans to partner with a number of institutions globally to stage these conferences and to produce the series of publications that will accompany the Dialogues (Shorefast Foundation, n.d., Arts).

Strategic planning method and strategy implementation experience inform us that strategic processes are effective when internal local organizational settings are infused with fresh ideas, generic conceptual frameworks and problem solutions from external experts that are new to the thinking of local strategists. The Fogo Island Dialogues represent just such external enrichment when it is related to the empirical specifics of the local setting (Corey and Wilson, 2006: 238). Debate and the mutual learnings that result can generate a value-added dimension to the strategic reflection that grounds intended actions both in local needs and aspirations as well as in global theory and practice.

> The Dialogues bring together key thinkers from the international and local communities – arts professionals, academics, economists, geographers, planners, architects whose knowledge and experience bring value to these discussions of issues related to the livelihood and renewal of rural locations (Fogo Island Arts, September 27, 2013).

Various editions and discussion themes for the Dialogues have been offered or planned for 2013 and 2014: (1) in July 2013 at the Fogo Island Inn, the topic discussed among 25 professionals was "Belonging to Place;" (2) in November 2013 "Culture as Destination" is the overarching theme and the venue is the MAK, the Austrian Museum of Applied Arts and Contemporary Art in Vienna; this Dialogue considers the realm of the digital as a destination and as a mode of knowledge consumption; and (3) for 2014, the Dialogues will be held in different locations and hosted by various international institutions. For an update and a current understanding of the Dialogues, refer to the Shorefast Foundation, 2013 and 2014.

With the specificity of the Fogo Island and Change Islands region as the empirical focus, each edition of the Dialogues will explore the role of art in influencing social change. The organizing concept for the Dialogues is premised on using this particular island region "as a metaphor for any rural locale, the concept of the island as laboratory is tested through dialogue." This approach should advance the Shorefast Foundation's goal of having the Fogo Island case serve as a Model for Rural Development.

Fogo Island Arts was an early stage program of the Foundation that has begun to mature sufficiently to demonstrate its organizational culture of learning and dynamic responsiveness. For example, in order to better position the Arts program ultimately to have a presence and influence in the international marketplace of cosmopolitan contemporary art, a strategy role was created and staffed by Nicolaus Schafhausen. He is artistic director of Kunsthalle Wien. The Kunsthalle Wien is the exhibition hall of the City of Vienna for international contemporary art and discourse.

Schafhausen's talents and extensive European and global experience as curator, artistic director, and manager is the profile needed to facilitate the taking of Fogo Island Arts into the world of contemporary institutionalized art, wherein Fogo Island Arts can realize its income generating role as part of the overall Foundation economic development strategy to develop a more diverse local economy for the Fogo Island and Change Islands region. Schafhausen now is serving in the role as strategic director of Fogo Island Arts. His curatorial (Rosenbaum, 2011) and leadership skills will be critical in the planning and execution of the Fogo Island Dialogues. His international network and rich social capital assets are expected to be instrumental in enabling Fogo Island Arts to build off and complement the continuing innovative resident artists program. For a demonstration of Nicolaus Schafhasen's attributes as a principal in the implementation of Fogo Island Dialogues and for some insight into the kind of style and approach of the invitational Fogo Island Dialogues, refer to the video at Kunsthalle Wien, May 26, 2013.

The Fogo Island Dialogues should be expected to benefit Fogo Island Arts in particular and the Shorefast Foundation range of programs in general. This should be the case because the Dialogues will provide an ongoing flow of valuable diverse external expert knowledge and experience designed to inform and connect to the specific development issues of Fogo Island, and all by means of a selection of world class authoritative knowledge holders. This is an intelligent implementation tactic for keeping the overall development strategy responsive to shifting and dynamic global societal and environmental forces and market demands.

Earlier in 2014, a Dialogue was held in Toronto. Among other activities, the event staged an auction. One of the Fogo Island Arts initiatives announced that evening was the creation of a young curator award program. It was said to be an investment in the future by means of the award program for youth.

In the spirit of dialogue and conversation, these questions were posed, "why bring contemporary artists from around the world to Fogo Island by means of a residency-based art venue?" The response was that it is a way to bring international attention to Fogo Island and to Canada. The program provides opportunities to make significant contributions in artistic practice that is "local in context and global in scope." Such creation in film, music, thinking and reflection, writing and curation as well as art and design can enrich culture as well as to economic goals. Why art? What does it bring to development? Art is a way of knowing; and it can generate innovation for design; plus it comes from original sources. An additional reply emphasized the complementary role of search. Exploration in the search for understanding can enable deriving meaning of and for the world. Further, artistic search and engagement can facilitate comparative creation and discovery between comparable rural places. Such artistic exchange can lead to social exchange; thereby groundwork may be laid to create "a global network of localized places." Such probing and interaction as described here illustrate the nature, function and value of the Fogo Island Dialogues. They represent valuable opportunities to educate and to acquire fresh new external insights for virtually all of the programs of the Shorefast Foundation.

New Ocean Ethic

For hundreds of years, the economic base of the Fogo Island and Change Islands region has been the ocean fishery. This has been the source of the islanders' livelihood as well as their cultural capital. Only the most recent generations have come to a realization that the resources of the ocean located just off these shores are finite. During this recent period, both local boats and factory fishing boats from many countries of the world depleted the commercial cod fish stocks so severely that the government of Canada enforced a moratorium on the cod fishery in 1992. As a consequence, the foreign factory fishing ships have departed the local waters. The local fishers were left with only two options, either leave fishing altogether or shift to other species in the hope of maintaining a livelihood. Many left the region and some who remained were able to make the costly shift to other species, especially to snow crab and northern shrimp. The Fogo Island Co-operative Society reports that it "has not only survived, it has thrived" (Fogo Island Co-operative Society Ltd, n.d.). However, it is clear that informed science-based natural resources management practices are essential if some level of commercial fishery sustainability is to be an integral part of the Fogo Island future.

The New Ocean Ethic program therefore is a complement to this traditional economic base of the islands. Other forces, such as climate change, also threaten the already vulnerable marine ecosystem of the local region. For example, climate change has been cited as contributing to: warmer ocean bottom temperature, influx of sea ice and change in species. So, the challenges are daunting if the health of the ocean is to be protected locally and globally. The solution to these problems is to affect pervasive mindset change and resulting practices so that, over time, a balanced and sustainable mindset-to-effective-stewardship-behavior is the dominant human practice and a new natural resource utilization culture becomes imprinted.

This will not be a quick fix; these over-exploitation practices have prevailed for hundreds of years. It is deeply ingrained in the Atlantic fishing, sealing, whaling and sea birding cultures. The Europeans brought this culture and behavior with them as they extended their fishing practices to North America (Bolster, 2012).

The Shorefast Foundation consequently has conceived the New Ocean Ethic program as its strategic response to the above contemporary ocean issues. Similar to the Fogo Island Dialogues, the Foundation's ocean agenda essentially is a next stage set of action activities.

What is the envisaged New Ocean Ethic concept? It is to induce incrementally, "changes in thinking, leading to new approaches to ocean use [these] are the ultimate goals of the concept ... The underlying principle is that we must learn more, understand more and do more" (Shorefast Foundation, 2013: 1-2). As a consequence of the just-noted history and factors, the New Ocean Ethic:

> is an essential component of the Foundation's planning for the transformation of the Fogo Island and the Change Islands region into a 21st century geotourism destination. The vision for this program therefore is to position the islands as a leading model community in its harmonious and sustainable relationships with the ocean (Slade, June 14, 2013).

To begin the ocean awareness and intelligent development-based process and to lend support to such a local, national and global change effort, the Shorefast Foundation is initiating a program for a New Ocean Ethic (Shorefast Foundation, 2013). In 2005, Gordon Slade, Shorefast Foundation Chair and Ocean Advisor, founded the Canada Ocean Lecture Series. It is a partnership between Simon Fraser University and the Foundation. "The aim of the series is to create awareness of Canada's vast marine environment and its importance to Canadians. Lectures to date have been held on the Atlantic and Pacific coasts and in central Canada" (Simon Fraser University, n.d.)

There are some representative sentiments gathered from our interviews and research into the Foundation's ocean programming. To operationalize the New Ocean Ethic activities as part of the Fogo Island Rural Development Model, the strategy is to facilitate moving the local fishery squarely into the 21st century. This means capitalizing on recent trends that have begun to emerge in the region; nearly a generation after the shock and reaction to the 1992 commercial cod fishing moratorium: there seems to be more interest in the ocean; there may be greater respect for the creatures of the sea; and there is an explicit interest in treating and framing the produce of the region's ecosystem as a high-priced food item – that is one of the cleanest in the world. The implementation of the Foundation's New Ocean Ethic seeks to have fishers, and people more broadly, become "literate" of the ocean and not just fishing in it. In future thereby, there will be more widespread knowledge of and appreciation for the biodiversity issues and the sustainability requirements of the regional ocean ecosystem.

A range of different, but ocean-related actions are planned by the Foundation as community activities to create and support the development of a local model New Ocean Ethic:

> For promoting and educating an ocean literate society, establish an Ocean Literacy Center on Fogo Island; the Center is to include a state-of-the-art touch tank; including a selection of Change Islanders trained in ocean literacy.

> Conduct citizen science projects, e.g.: develop a real-time community owned data base and social media in partnership with the Fisheries and Marine Institute of Memorial University of Newfoundland (MUN); conduct community-wide meetings sharing marine environment and ecosystem information.

> Create a Fogo Island Ocean Atlas with assistance from MUN's Marine Institute: map underwater geographic features; by placing equipment and a technology platform on their boats; fishers are positioned to collect and archive data on fish stocks and to seek better understanding for improving productivity and sustainability. The fishers and their boats are regularly at sea, yet traditionally little data and precise information has been brought back to advance scientific knowledge. For example, the water can be analyzed systematically, sea ice may be studied, changes in tides can be monitored and other information may be sensed and recorded for date, hour and location with Geographic Positioning Systems (GPS). Citizen science work can improve our collective awareness and understanding of unknown issues that would alert or benefit us.

Conduct Marine Research: establish a nearby Marine Environmental Observation Prediction and Response (MEOPAR) Network buoy with MUN. With the provincial Department of Fisheries and Oceans: research on capelin, continuation of multi-beam sonar work; and tagging of cod pot cod.

Extend the 2008 Cod Potting Experiment to every fisher in Newfoundland to: 15 cod pots per fisher and unprocessed cod pot cod licensed for supply to the Fogo Island Inn. According to the Foundation's Web page, "The cod pot is ocean and habitat friendly and the method produces a top quality product which, in turn, leads to higher prices."

Pilot a Fisheries Project: whereby the fishers and tourists go out to fish together in order to learn about the fishery on Fogo Island.

Conduct ongoing research on Little Fogo Islands Sea Birds with MUN.

Complete the training to provide oil spill protection to protect the sea birds of the Fogo Island archipelago; training provided by MUN's Marine Institute and the Canadian Coast Guard.

Develop seafood value chain services to bring product from conception to final consumer, i.e. in: processing, distribution and marketing. Discussions are ongoing with the Fogo Island Co-operative Society to explore new markets and production options.

Use songs and stories of the sea for: cultural and entertainment development featuring local songs, stories and poems performed by the people of Fogo Island. This demonstrates the value of the New Ocean Ethic by means of entertainment and draws on local cultural capital.

Implement an active program of investment partnerships and supportive networking in order to fund, advance and complement the activities above

Continue the Canada Ocean Lecture Series (Slade, June 14, 2013).

Refer to the Foundation's working paper on the New Ocean Ethic for elaboration on some of these community activities (Shorefast Foundation, 2013). The vision of the Foundation's intended beneficiaries are: the ocean and marine life; the province, Atlantic Canada and the nation; visitors to the region of Fogo Island and the Change Islands; the existing Fogo Island Marine Interpretation Center; the Fogo Island Inn Guest Programming; pre-school through university students, and fishers and other fishery practitioners.

The shorter-term role of the New Ocean Ethic program in the context of maturation of the whole Fogo Island Rural Development Model is to support and complement the principal economic capital asset of the region, i.e., the fishery. The ocean program also is intended to provide a complement to the geotourism strategy of the overarching model for rural development. There is an expectation that the ocean programming on the islands will be an attraction especially via geotourism visitors to the Fogo Island Inn and family visitors to the future Ocean Literacy Center. Shorefast ocean leadership sees the ocean programming as a model that any coastal community, especially one that depends on the sea might consider for emulation and tailoring to its own particulars. In situations where government support for such concerns is not forthcoming or a shared priority, then localities have to rely on their own citizens and local institutions. If issues are seen as relevant to them, then real change and initiative may be led by the citizens. Locally organized events, such as regular World Ocean Day events or community beach clean-ups can be helpful in initiating, maintaining and mobilizing citizen ocean respect, awareness and action. The Shorefast Foundation's Chair Gordon Slade opined:

> Everybody can and should be doing something for the world. I don't hear many people talking about what a community can do on its own. Often there seems to be a general need or desire for direction and to be content to rely on government. Historically, we on Fogo Island did not rely on government. Instead, motivation came from within, i.e. from within ourselves (Slade, June 14, 2013).

Longer-term, the New Ocean Ethic program should provide continuous impetus to mindset change locally and globally toward behavioral change that ideally results in ubiquitous responsible and sustainable use of the ocean's resources. The Shorefast Foundation's New Ocean Ethic represents a knowledge niche role by the Foundation and contribution to the other ocean and marine centers around the world in maritime and ocean research, science, education and policy. This may suggest an ocean community-organizing role in the possible formation of a global marine and ocean network for citizen science and public education. Today's globalized information and communications technologies and networking capabilities begs the question, is it desirable and feasible to consider the formation of such a network?

A major benefit for the Shorefast Foundation's ocean agenda would be that it might be able to selectively draw on many of the existing science and public education programmatic assets of the world's other ocean centers – electronically – while contributing and sharing its own local and regional growing experience and expertise in the advancement of ocean ethics and sustainable natural resources utilization. In the end, the Shorefast Foundation has stated, "Through this New Ocean Ethic we hope that Fogo Island and the Change Islands can be models for the rest of the world" (Shorefast Foundation, Home Page, n.d.).

Marketing and Business Development

The geotourism-based strategy being pursued on Fogo Island is so foundational to the goal-realization of the region's development, and in turn, to the construction of the Fogo Island Model for Rural Development that it merits its own attention here. With the Fogo Island Inn as the income-generating centerpiece of the Foundation's geotouristic strategy, marketing to the up-market global geotourist is critical and challenging. Why? Because there are geotourists and there are geotourists. In designing the Fogo Island Inn, architect Todd Saunders used the design criteria listed immediately below to address this focused market segment of persons, their families and friends with the wherewithal needed to make the expensive and time-consuming journey to come to the remote location of the Inn and to pay the relatively stiff tariff for being accommodated and hosted by and in the five-star Fogo Island Inn. These then are the kind of geotourist guests and their likely demands for which the Inn was designed.

> The Fogo Island Inn is an architectural gem that was born of Fogo Island, Newfoundland. It is a home for intrepid, curious and discerning high-comfort explorers from the global market place. Designed and crafted as a cultural and ecological hub, the Inn is a place to experience the old and the new — through exposure to the fishery, through art, through architecture and design and through food.
>
> Embracing the emotional resonance and quiet beauty of everyday life in Newfoundland's outport communities, the Inn is a venue for dialogue between guests and the island's people, places and things. In this way, it acts as a direct conduit to the culture, traditions and stunning beauty of this unexpected place at the edge of the world.
>
> All twenty-nine of the Inn's spacious guest rooms and suites have stunning panoramic views of the North Atlantic from floor-to-ceiling windows. The custom-made king-size beds are designed to be separated into two super twins; all rooms are individually decorated with bespoke locally hand-crafted furnishings and textiles, and most have wood-burning stoves.
>
> Northern European-style wood-fired saunas and hot tubs are located on the roof of the Inn — a perfect place for stargazing and a brilliant way to restore after a long, happy day of adventure on the island.
>
> The Fogo Island Contemporary Art Gallery, the Inn's fine dining restaurant, lounge and bar, and the Dr. Leslie A. Harris Heritage Library, specializing in literature of the region are all located on the ground floor, while the Fogo Island Cinema, a partnership with the National Film Board of Canada, conference facilities and the gym are located on the second floor (DesignalumiC, n.d.) (Refer to Figures 39 and 40 for views of the Dr. Leslie A. Harris Heritage Library).

In order to keep the Inn green, ecologically unobtrusive and not disturb the experientially rich special natural and social environment and characteristics of this special place, the guest-room capacity of the Fogo Island Inn was set at twenty-nine. Approximately 35 diners can be seated in the fine-dining restaurant. These small scales and capacities are intended to achieve and maintain the balance needed to preserve the Island's touristic comparative and competitive advantages of remoteness, striking and quiet beauty, authentic cultural heritage, and social intimacy among some of the world's most hospitable people. Were the Fogo Island and Change Islands region to be inundated with mass touristic numbers, and that applies also to the Inn, this special place would be diminished and the islands' environment put in jeopardy.

Identifying and motivating these kinds of well-heeled geotourists necessitates marketing that is sophisticated, highly targeted, nuanced and cosmopolitan in tone and means of delivery. Mass marketing is unlikely to meet the need for attracting the intended clientele and for sustaining the authentic remoteness of the natural and cultural environments. Indeed, mass marketing likely would undercut the Inn's very existence. Monitoring the marketing of the Inn's approaches and results to meet this challenge is likely to generate valuable lessons for the Fogo Island Inn, the Shorefast Foundation and those with stakes in having robust models available to assist in strategic development planning for our own home rural regions.

The launch of the Fogo Island Inn in the late spring season, and therefore in time for the 2013 summer season, catalyzed a great deal of initial interest in the Inn. This interest resulted in important recognition and publicity. For example, The Air Canada inflight magazine, enRoute, published the results of its 12th annual people's choice (The Canadian Press, October 24, 2013). The restaurant of the Fogo Island Inn was rated third among the top ten national finalists. It ranked only behind two Toronto city-region restaurants; Chef McDonald's Fogo Island Inn restaurant was the only rural kitchen to be so honored; the other nine kitchens were in cosmopolitan urban and metropolitan locations. The Inn's launch and resulting early recognition suggests the criticality of quality of product -- and timing in general, and the timing and focusing of targeted marketing initiatives in particular.

In the meantime, as the 2013-2014 winter months approached, the Fogo Island Inn launched a personalized marketing initiative that would seem to have some attractiveness for such targeted earliest guests to the Inn. By way of background on timing, in interviews and presentations, Zita Cobb has mentioned that Fogo Island has seven seasons. Refer to Appendix 5 for a description of all seven seasons, their months and principal environmental and cultural characteristics.

Probably, the most difficult months to fill the rooms of the Fogo Island Inn is the period from late fall until the beginning of April. By placing this three-season period within the context of all seven seasons, this framing suggests that one ought to give some serious thought to paying return visits to the Inn, especially with relatives and friends in tow. Room prices were reduced a bit, and the enticement is that one can share the unique Fogo Island experience and in the cozy winter, holiday season and luxury atmosphere of the Inn's exquisite contemporary architectural design after being out in the island's bracing winds, snow and glitter. One might even be able to cuddle the Inn's two Newfoundland-breed greeter dogs, named Make and Break.

These are the celebration days and activities that the Inn suggests for five months of the three seasons of late fall, winter and ice season: Halloween; Guy Fawkes Night; anniversaries; executive retreats; Gales of November; company party; Christmas; New Year's; Valentines; artists retreats; and hiking. Refer to Appendix 5.

Using the place-specific and local culture-specific frame of "seven seasons" is an innovative way of framing the marketing for some of the fascinating qualities of Fogo Island. For rural region and urban-region developers elsewhere, such similarly original creative and appropriate, highly particular marketing tactics might be used to attract touristic interest to one's home region? Turning the challenge of harsh weather periods into truly interesting and unique experiences is worth more study and thoughtful reflection in planning and marketing strategies (Gappert, 1987). Another season related spin-off might suggest marketing to targeted Southern Hemisphere markets using opposite seasons as a possible point of attraction.

Further, the seven seasons frame can be used to highlight special local cultural practices and traditions that otherwise might remain unknown to people from beyond Fogo Island and Newfoundland. For example, the twelve days of the Christmas season is an ideal time to introduce mummering, a seasonal house-visiting custom originating from Britain and Ireland, to the visiting geotourist. Historically, pre-Newfoundland mummering had two forms, a play and the house visit; the former is little practiced in Newfoundland today.

> The house visit, unlike the play, took place among social equals, and its main purpose was the visiting of neighbors, the reaffirmation of social bonds and the sharing of 'Christmas cheer.'
>
> Mummers in Newfoundland, moving in groups of various sizes, did their rounds during the twelve days of Christmas. Central to the visit was the guessing game, where the hosts attempted to work out the identity of the visitor. Disguise was of the utmost importance, because in such small tight-knit communities individuals could be recognized just as easily by their hands or gait as by their faces. Therefore, hands were kept covered, voices disguised, clothing was stuffed to try to hide body shape, and many mummers even attempted to alter their gait (Lochnan, 2011: 100).

Covering the face with a veil of a piece of net curtain or lace and secured by head gear of some kind was a way of disguising the visiting neighbor (Refer to Figures 41 and 42 to view mummers in the Fogo Island Inn at Christmas time). Mummers coming to the home and knocking on the door for entry represented the stranger, the figure from the outside. "The stranger – was a fearful character who brought with him the unfamiliar and the unknown. In these intimate [outport] communities the behavior of neighbors was predictable and the behavior of strangers, as mummers was not" (Lochnan, 2011: 103).

Such place-specific cultural practices in other places may have counterparts, and represent the kind of idiosyncratic tradition that might stimulate analogous touristic interest and new marketing opportunities. Many other places might advertise Christmas activities, but mummering at Christmas is likely to represent a comparative advantage in holiday tourist attraction. Thereby the Fogo Island Model for Rural Development can demonstrate tactical level emulation development practices as well as the strategic level modeling that has been noted here throughout.

Further, other geotouristic opportunities and spill-overs are suggested by the mummering example. Keying off the Irish roots of seasonal visitations noted above, the outport of Tilting, to the east of the Fogo Island Inn which is located in Joe Batt's Arm, is known for its Irish culture and dialect (Enright, September 25, 2013). It has been designated (1) a National Historic Site of Canada, and (2) a Registered Heritage District by the Heritage Foundation of Newfoundland and Labrador. Practicing architect Robert Mellin has published a highly-regarded book on Tilting's unique cultural capital and physical material capital (Mellin, 2003). Being introduced to mummering, Tilting makes for an interesting complementary exposure to an important segment of Fogo Island history for any geotourist who would travel to the region to acquire some in-depth knowledge about some of the traditions and heritage of the place. Learning from such relationships represents rich sources of new ideas for visitors and rural development practitioners elsewhere (Canada's Historic Places, n.d.).

Part VII

Team Shorefast: Leader, Champion, Innkeeper, Teacher, Learner and Local Economy Diversifier – the Invention of a New Social Entrepreneurship Model

Within the context of being an illustration of contemporary rural development modeling, the Fogo Island case can be perceived as so unusual, that it may raise some concern for readers here. The principal one is the role played by a great deal of private not-for-profit philanthropic money and by the lead actor of the cast, Zita Cobb. Her special, seemingly singular ability to motivate, lead, set and champion the island region's development agenda fills the Shorefast stage. So, the concern is that the Fogo Island case is likely to be perceived as too special and particular because few other places have such idiosyncratic and propulsive assets as a Zita Cobb to draw on.

But the readers too should follow Zita Cobb's values and practice. Intelligent development is a team enterprise. It is more like baseball and not like golf or tennis. Zita Cobb plays a starring role, but could not do her job without the full and active support of her cast, i.e., the team support from those discussed below and the community of which she is a member, a neighbor a relative and a stakeholder like each and every resident of the island region. However, for applicability to other regions, if one recognizes that development funding and other supportive resources can and should come directly from other sources beyond philanthropy such as, government and or business for example. Why? Because cross-sector partnerships are critical to successful regional development. Also, when considering the modeling potential of the Fogo Island case for other rural areas, it must be recognized and acknowledged that place-making is a collective undertaking (Friedmann, 2010: 159). Such an enterprise demands a cast of critical and facilitative and collaborative roles to be played out under intelligent, informed and effective direction and leadership that is arrived at by means of "the team." The full drama of intelligent regional development must be played out by all components of this and every development drama.

Thus all community development efforts require resources and leadership, but how those assets are conceived, framed and mobilized to the particulars of each place are the critical factors. Thereafter, for purposes of modeling elsewhere from the Fogo Island case, one can focus on the place-specific content or subject matter and the processes to be created irrespective of the nature of the funding source or even the amount of funding and the composition of the leadership function to be played out.

Team Shorefast

We have conferred here the label of "Team Shorefast" to encompass the assembly of diverse Foundation actors, their roles and the production/direction functions that are underway on Fogo Island. This label, we believe, embodies the organizational ethos and the required collective undertaking that is propelling this drama in rural community resurrection that is being produced there.

Analogous to a drama or an opera being staged in the theater (Peattie, 1970), the cast and initial investors are bringing this new social entrepreneurial model on Fogo Island to fruition. The production is composed of: lead actors; their immediate co-star performers; the broader body of support actors, the chorus, orchestra, local and external investors and physical props – among other "dramatic" necessaries such as promotion, advertising, business functions, and among additional support functions, an audience is essential; we the readers here can perform that role.

Just as the complexities of staging and producing plays and operas require structure and organization, so too does the development of a place and its region. How are the various functions of the Shorefast Foundation as producer of the rural development model organized and structured? Legal requirements have resulted in the following organizational structure for the full set of activities and functions that comprise the Shorefast Foundation organizational entities:

> The Inn's operations are housed in a Business Trust, managed by a group of trustees. The Business Trust's sole beneficiary is the Shorefast Foundation, thus no other entity can receive any amount of surplus from operations. The Shorefast Foundation, a registered Canadian charity, has a mandate to provide economic and cultural resilience to the local residents through its programming and funding of other non-profit agents. Inn surpluses will move through the Foundation and be invested in many projects which in turn help support the local economy (Hodgins, August 21, 2014).
>
> Shorefast operates a social enterprise where surpluses from business activity flow thru the Charity and are reinvested in community programs. Entities under this unique corporate structure include Shorefast Foundation (federally registered Canadian charity, The Fogo Island Inn and the Fogo Island Shop (for-profit economic engines housed in a Business Trust which holds operations of the Inn) and Fogo Island Arts (non-profit arts institution) (Shorefast Foundation, Shorefast Controller Position, July 31, 2014; Hodgins, August 18, 2014).

How are the characters' roles and actors for this production cast? Below is discussed a selection of the lead actors and other members of the Shorefast cast. As noted above, the leadership role is executed by the Shorefast Foundation's board of Directors (Shorefast Foundation, n.d., Board of Directors). Even in the early formative days, when created in 2003, the Foundation and its Board of Directors took the lead by means of collective decisions, e.g., such as shifting from a scholarship-centric enterprise to a job creating and economic revitalization enterprise, the Board of Directors performed the key strategic and investment decisions. So that the reader might acquire an understanding of the issues and nuanced inter-relationships that go into constructing a productive governance and advisory resource such as a team of volunteer board of directors and staff actors for effective regional development, we next discuss some of the Shorefast Foundation's cast of characters and their respective roles. The Shorefast Foundation has evolved a list of readings. The readings draw importantly on the "next generation of economists" and others (Cobb, March 2, 2014); a result is that the Foundation actors can "stay on the same page of the institution's script," so to speak, as they all contribute to and perfect the production – of the experimental Model for Rural Development for the Fogo Island and the Change Islands region (Refer to Appendix 6 for the Shorefast Foundation's Reading List).

Board Chairman Gordon Slade

It is useful to illustrate some of the individual attributes that the Board of Directors bring to Team Shorefast. Board Chairman Gordon Slade provides a great deal of relevant experience and development credibility to the Team (Refer to Figure 43 for a photo of Gordon Slade). In his special expert role as Ocean Advisor, he brings a particularly strategic contribution to the Board; he not only has knowledge of the island's base economy--the fishery--he performs the principal lead role for the New Ocean Ethic programming of the Shorefast Foundation (Shorefast Foundation, n.d., New Ocean Ethic). His knowledge and operational experience of ocean relationships with business, science and policy environments beyond the Fogo Island and the Change Islands region have equipped him well to advocate for an informed and intelligent utilization of natural resources, such as the Newfoundland fishery, that is at the same time responsive to market forces and respectful of the scientifically-determined limits of capture so that sustainable natural conditions will prevail. Additionally, he operates with an appreciative stance relative to the ordinary person; his support of citizen science for example, illustrates the value of routine data collection of marine conditions from working fishers as they go about their normal business routines (Wells, August 6, 2014). He respects and taps into such indigenous knowledge sources as well as findings from scientists.

Gordon Slade and Battle Harbour as Proof-of-Concept

Another significant contribution to Team Shorefast by Gordon Slade is his pioneering work in saving and putting on an operational footing the Battle Harbour National Historic District and Heritage Properties. Battle Harbour is a pre-Confederation Newfoundland settlement located on the remote southeastern coast of Labrador (Battle Harbour National Historic District National Historic Site of Canada, n.d.). It is an example of an early traditional outport fishing community. It evokes the merchant-dominated history of the province by means of a mercantile complex composed of salt fish premises, wharves, large wooden stores and former homes, that today's geotourists may rent during their exploratory visits to the island. In addition to its marine assets, the place is rich in geological and other natural resources. Mike Earle, one of twenty former fishers "retrained as heritage carpenters to faithfully restore the buildings to their original state," commented that for Battle Harbour's preservation:

> Gordon Slade almost single handedly raised most of the money himself ... Slade worked to have Battle Harbour designated a National Historic District, and little by little, the heritage carpenters painstakingly restored 22 of the buildings, some of which date back to the 1700s (Kobalenko, April 2008).

With Gordon Slade on the Shorefast Board of Directors his prior early Battle Harbour development planning and implementation experience and learnings can be represented in the Foundation's on-going program of monitoring and strategizing; thereby, Battle Harbour can serve as a proof-of-concept model for Newfoundland's Fogo Island Model for Rural Development. Like Fogo Island, forced resettlement and later formulating a goal of diversifying the settlement's contemporary economy are at issue in the earlier pilot case of Battle Harbour and they are key factors also in the revival of Fogo Island. Gordon Slade founded the Battle Harbour Historic Trust In 1990. We asked him to update us on his perception of how Battle Harbour has performed and has been received to date. He wrote:

> Battle Harbour was up and running in 1997. From 2000 to 2013 the number of visitors varied from 1200 to 2000. The variation in visitors per year seemed to relate to road conditions from Red Bay to Mary's Harbour, cruise ship visits, other events happening on the island of Newfoundland and zero marketing budget. Battle Harbour has been successful as it has diversified the small local economy. Trained heritage carpenters who are working across Canada, provided youth summer employment on Battle Harbour in a number of occupations, i.e., tour guide helpers, assistant maintenance helpers, assistant cooks, assistant house keepers, assistant office workers, and assistant store keepers and groundskeepers. The time is near when Battle Harbour's revenue will surpass the revenue of the fish plant in Mary's Harbour. Another factor which is often forgotten is the social impact the people working at Battle Harbour get including the students in their interaction with guests at Battle Harbour from all walks of life and all parts of the world. This interaction builds confidence for the workers. Battle Harbour can indeed be seen as a proof-of-concept. It has operated for 17 years without any operating revenue from governments and not being able as a registered charity of Canada to borrow from any financial institution (Slade, August 8, 2014).

For his extraordinary public and community service Gordon Slade has been recognized with such prestigious awards as the Order of Canada, the Gold Medal of the Canadian Geographical Society, and he will be awarded an honorary doctorate in the fall 2014 convocation by the Memorial University of Newfoundland.

Bringing such excellence and experience to the work of the Shorefast Foundation is invaluable. In various programmatic categories and in varying degrees, the other members of the Board of Directors play critical support roles in the planning and evaluation of Shorefast's development and performance.

Founding Brothers of the Foundation: Anthony Cobb and Alan Cobb

The membership of the Foundation's Board of Directors includes two other members of the Cobb family: in the roles of Treasurer and Chief Operating Officer is Anthony Cobb, and Alan Cobb, whose role is Secretary. Both of these board members bring a rich mix of talent and experience to the board. Anthony Cobb was a founding board member; from the beginning, he was an advocate for the Foundation's regional development model building. He has been the lead in the construction of the Fogo Island Inn. Alan Cobb too was a founding board member and supporter of the regional development goals of the Foundation. He keys on Board communications strategic level changes. Between the brothers, these economic sectors are represented in their past professional and organizational experience: private sector (both retail and wholesale; and in small and medium-sized businesses), public and policy sectors; technologies sector; and software. Both of these Board members have business process experience in strategy, operations, project management, regulations and team and consultative skills.

Other Members of the Shorefast Foundation Board of Directors

Other members of the Shorefast Foundation's Board of Directors round out the cast with diverse and extensive experience in the fishery, tourism, hospitality, social services and community service. Further, they bring their experience to the Board from local Fogo Island practice and from practice beyond the region. Thus, critical attributes for members of the board includes: a mix of locational backgrounds that are local and from away; strong entrepreneurial spirit; business acumen; and sharing a connection with a specific rural place (in their heart). For brief biographies of all members of the Board of Directors, refer to: Shorefast Foundation, n.d. Board of Directors.

Other Key Team Shorefast Members

The professional staff of the Shorefast Foundation perform as principal supporting cast to the Board of Directors. To understand the full range of expertise, experience and the Foundation's organizational capacity readers should refer to the section of the Foundation's Web site entitled "Our Team." It lists the various actors of the board and staff, i.e., "Other Key Team Members" and explicates their backgrounds and roles for the Shorefast Foundation (Shorefast Foundation, n.d. Board of Directors).

Founder and President Zita Cobb

Leader of the Team

Foundation President Zita Cobb's organization behavior style is to draw on the collective knowledge and experience of Shorefast's board members and the staff members (See Figure 44 for a photo of Zita Cobb). By means of this practice, she focuses on the Shorefast Foundation as a whole thereby seeking to develop widespread leadership capacity; this comports with the belief in shared leadership. Thus, Team Shorefast operates as a learning organization with an experimental mindset and behavior of organizational learning by means of systematic trial and error assessment followed by informed fine-tuning and perfecting; this is a tried and tested way to advance leadership capacity, grow champions and further develop board and staff. As we have conducted the research of the Fogo Island development experiment and model, two somewhat opposing issues have emerged.

On the one hand, we find people are quite taken by the life story of Zita Cobb, and they want to know more about her. On the other hand, Zita Cobb sees herself as a principal in this experiment and modeling, but she also knows that she has stood on the shoulders of many who have gone before and that the Fogo Island development strategy and its programs only can be advanced by means of a team effort. So even though she is most often the public face and spokesperson for the effort and the Foundation, she bridles from too much attention when her mindset tells her that recognition should be distributed across her many contributing neighbors, friends, relations and business colleagues – both from near and far. Having stated this, it is essential that we provide an informational outlet for those who desire to know a bit more about her. Such persons should seek out and read the chapter on, "Zita Cobb." It is the anchor chapter in an interesting slim volume entitled, *The Grit and the Courage: Stories of Success in an Unforgiving Land* by Steve Bartlett (2008).

Principal Public Face of the Foundation

In playing her role as the most visible and frequent public speaker for the Shorefast Foundation, she is quite active. A sampling of recent and forthcoming speaking engagements is revealing of the high interest and demand for learning about the Fogo Island Rural Development Model from the public and from professional specialist audiences:

Social Enterprise / Rural development:

- University of New Brunswick Pond Desphande Centre –East Coast Start-up Week (Fredericton, NB) – March 2013
- Georgetown Conference (Kings County, PEI) – October 2013
- Business Day 2014, Memorial University of Newfoundland, "Changing Tides" Panel Discussion (St. John's, NL) – March 2014
- C2MTL or "Commerce + Creativity Montreal" (Montreal QC) – May 2014
- Memorial University of Newfoundland , Affinity Dinner – Alumni (Calgary, AB) – June 2014
- Canadian Bar Association Annual Conference (St. John's, NL) – August 2014
- Philanthropic Foundation of Canada Annual Conference (Halifax, NS) – August 2014
- Address at the Award Presentation of the Dr. Gill-Chin Lim Global Award (Philadelphia, PA) October 2014

Geotourism:

- Adventure Travel Trade Association World Summit, "Anthem or Requiem?" 2013 (Namibia)

How Useful is the Fogo Island Model Elsewhere Without a Zita Cobb?

As greater awareness spreads of the Fogo Island Model, one may project the Shorefast rural development work being inspirational for customizing and shaping for place-specific fitting and use elsewhere. One should recognize that initial leadership in areas elsewhere can, and likely will come from sources other than from a local philanthropist such as Zita Cobb. Then the fundamental working details of a bold compelling vision, creative design and tenacious actualization of program goals and objectives being presented here can be revealed practically by analyzing, deconstructing and reflecting on the portability and localized matching of the operating principles underpinning the Fogo Island Rural Development Model. So, in the end, some of the highly unique circumstances of the Fogo Island region may be controlled intellectually for purposes of modeling while deriving inspirational and operational lessons about the intended role that culture, nature and place-specific imaginative functioning and synergies can play in creating and nurturing the exportation of local assets and thereby attracting needed inward revenue, income and investment to rural regions.

Simply, in today's globalized and networked environment, a locality must have sufficient leadership, championship and community ownership in the regional development process, whether well-funded or modestly resourced, in order to know the local assets and use or create and market them to attain intended development future end-states. Each place or region, by necessity must invent or reimagine its own development particulars – both in terms of the content and the process or development pathway to be followed to attain the alignment and collaboration needed for building a desired collective future. The Fogo Island case therefore, is an excellent one for the purpose of modeling rural development, because it is bold, visionary, nuanced, well supported strategically and still underway such that its on-going progress can and should be monitored and assessed so that further development lessons might continue to be derived for use by thoughtful learners elsewhere. Importantly, this narrative intentionally is offered in such specificity and operational detail that this rural development model can be empowering because of its transparency.

At the heart of the Shorefast Foundation's development strategy is the mobilization of the region's social capital and its other capital assets (Roseland, 2012) and the need to align them sufficiently so as to diversify the local economy by modernizing and intelligently enhancing the local core base industry of fishing and processing, and to that the Foundation's addition of art-based innovation, small business formation and the type of geotourism of the global well-to-do who seek both adventure and comfort. These initiatives require working from a new outward looking, global world view. The fishing industry and ocean literacy initiatives require both local as well as strategic and tactical planned attention to external regional and global practices and market forces. Working from her human capital development experience in business, including finance and technology, plus her international and global observations of social justice abuses and challenges has empowered Zita Cobb to be able to reflect, frame and will congruent and responsive strategic development actions back home in her native place of Fogo Island and the Change Islands region. These precedents and other factors have influenced and positioned her, her family, the Shorefast Foundation and its local and distant supporters to embark on this experimental pathway of social enterprise-based regional development, and in the implementation, demonstrate the working elements of and processes for a Model for Rural Development that others in rural places elsewhere may find useful as they too struggle with how to create better futures for their own regions in today's new globalized economic and socially interdependent and highly inter-connected environment.

Zita Cobb and Innkeeping

Lest one conclude that Zita Cobb is merely a creative and successful corporate strategist and inventive social entrepreneur (Business Education, May 6, 2013) practitioner, she is that and more. She brings other skill sets to the table as an inventor and champion of much of the content elements of the Fogo Island Model for Rural Development. She took off sometime early in her business career and served as an innkeeper in Costa Rica. One suspects that this hands-on experience had some role in informing such Fogo Island Inn guest-satisfying services and amenities as those introduced here, plus the many innovative physical and aesthetic capital investments that are listed above that enhance the guest's experience at the Inn both outside and in, for example:

- All full-board suites rates include a daybreak tray, breakfast, dinner (or lunch as it is called on the island), afternoon tea, snacks, supper and non-alcoholic beverages.

- Full use of all facilities within the Inn: cinema screenings, sauna, rooftop hot tubs, contemporary art gallery, gym and local heritage library.

- All gratuities are built into these room rates, including valet parking services for one's automobile, and more, such as personalized assistance in negotiating the ferry queues. Not having to bother with gratuities reinforces feelings by the guest that indeed they are being hosted warmly and sincerely by authentic long-time local "new friends."

In all seriousness, Cobb's innkeeper work may explain the micro attention that has gone into, for example, the strategy, design and execution of the Fogo Island Inn. Team Shorefast has integrated the following regional development ingredients to create this extraordinary facility. Indeed, combined with its highly inventive architecture, it forms a model for demonstrating ways of functioning as a place-based and cultural capital infused hospitality center. It not only houses well-heeled geotourist guests from around the world, but it also is on course to be a hub of community learning and employment for the current generation of local human capital (the Inn employed around 100 staff at the time of launch) and social capital. It also is planned to be an income generator for increasing the local community's economic capital and for the community stakeholders to decide how to invest that capital for its future intelligent development. At the time of this writing, the Inn as a recent start-up, is on a planned three-year trajectory to become profitable after expenses are paid. After this phase, community-based decision-making will determine how and to what target these resources will benefit and improve the Fogo Island and the Change Islands region.

Zita Cobb and the Unconscious Conspiracy

We must end this section on Zita Cobb and her role as leader of Team Shorefast with a kind of anticipatory warning. It is a warning for Team Shorefast and for those leaders elsewhere who become intrigued with the Fogo island Model and want to give direction and energy similarly, but in her or his own locality. The leadership guru Warren Bennis, who passed away recently, wrote a penetrating book entitled *The Unconscious Conspiracy*.

As Professor Bennis framed it, the unconscious conspiracy is: "routine work drives out nonroutine work, or how to smother to death all creative planning, all fundamental change in ... any institution" (Bennis, 1976: 20). This smothering includes routine work, but also the overall volume of work also is a factor. In the case of Team Shorefast and its leader Zita Cobb, we must make several points: (1) her creative work has not been smothered – yet; (2) simple delegation of the conventional variety may not be the only answer; and (3) one of the downsides that cannot be overlooked for an isolated rural location is that some of one's human capital or principal staff may have to be located distantly.

As the Fogo Island Inn now has come online, so to speak, it needs to be promoted and traveling appearances away from Fogo Island are necessary to ensure that the Inn gets off to a good start by attracting guests in sufficient numbers to create growth momentum and a widely distributed buzz about the Inn needs to be generated. Traditional delegation gets complicated when some of one's key support staff live distantly in Ottawa, Toronto and St. John's for example, and the likelihood of attracting human resources from far away to an isolated rural island can be quite a challenge. Volunteers, friends and neighbors are not likely to be satisfactory substitutes. Without being able to recruit the human resources needed to ensure that the leader of the team has the time to invest in reflection and necessary new ideas consideration, the leader has to scale back on the volume of incoming routine tasks or otherwise get them addressed through some additional level of delegation. Relatively isolated rural places need to give special additional thought to meeting the challenges of a possible unconscious conspiracy. The good news in the Shorefast case is that the routine workload has increased particularly because of the opening of the Fogo Island Inn; so, it is a good problem that is worth addressing.

Part VIII

The Model Interpreted and Imagined

☙

After our initial explorations and exposure in the field to the Fogo Island development approach in 2011-2012, we were sufficiently intrigued by what we understood of the early-stage development strategy that we knew we had to follow up and make a return in-depth working visit to the island. We determined that it was essential that we interview Shorefast Foundation President Zita Cobb and we had to stay at and experience directly the geotouristic product and services of the Fogo Island Inn. By way of a soft launch, the Inn opened in mid-May 2013 and we became early guests of the Inn's hospitality within a few days of that opening. Then and since, we were able to conduct face-to-face, e-mail and telephone interviews with a wide range of Foundation and Fogo Island Inn staff, workers and island residents and small-enterprise business people. With the context of having acquired a working knowledge of the early stages of Fogo Island's revitalized economic development programs by the time of our May 2013 return visit, the principal focus of the field interviews was to reveal the next steps of Fogo Island's planned development.

Our approach, as we initially conclude here, is to frame our Fogo Island development interpretations and findings and to translate our conclusions for regional development practitioners elsewhere so that they might learn of and from the accomplishments to date of the Fogo Island Model for Rural Development. Our motivation for sharing these detailed translations and our elaborated specific interpretations is to stimulate development professionals and development volunteers, at the sub-provincial and or sub-state scales, in North America for example, to engage in development strategy planning for their own rural regional home and work places – by using, in part, the Fogo Island Model – as a model, i.e. for motivation and mobilization, but not in mimicry or in a formulaic way. We adopt a life-cycle framework to next address this objective.

Imagining and Extending Our Interpretations

One of our primary purposes in preparing this monograph is to enable the reader to evolve a development planning mindset and behavior and to be positioned to practice informed decision-making and planning. This takes the form of making observations and of going beyond just reporting the findings of our research. So at times the narrative shifts from constructing current scenarios or reporting empirical results of our findings to stating imagined scenarios of what is likely to be or recommendation scenarios of what should be. This is our way of pointing out likely and normative future states as well as the current states that we have interpreted from our contemporary empirical analyses. The challenge for the planner on the ground of course, is to imagine and design the means and actions over time that are likely to realize the desired ends that respond to the demands and needs that were revealed from the actual empirical analyses and interpretations.

A Metaphor to Frame Our Conclusions

Newfoundland has a popular nickname of "The Rock." In framing our conclusions with this concept of nature's dynamics, we have been influenced partly by this nickname. As we got deeper into our research on the planned economic re-vitalization of the islands, we were reminded of the "cycle of erosion" concept that was conceived by William Morris Davis. He often has been called the "father of American Geography" (Rosenberg, n.d.). He formulated an easy-to-understand theory of landform erosion and creation. He conceived a simple life cycle of physical change driven largely by water working its power in concert with nature's tectonic forces on the earth's surface. For example, one may envisage a plain of land that simultaneously is uplifting while streams and rivers are carving v-shaped valleys into the plain; this stage may be called the river's youth. Over time, the uplifting and down-cutting forces widen the river valley; this stage may be called maturity. As these same erosive forces continuously work their joint influences, the river valley widens more extensively producing quite low relief and meanders in the river are a result; this stage is called old age. Lastly, as erosion and deposition proceed, a level, nearly flat plain at even lower elevation is produced; this plain is called base level. William Morris Davis termed this last phase a peneplain. If uplifting re-occurs then the erosion cycle can be rejuvenated when driven by similar physical processes.

When an analogous system of life-cycle stages is superimposed on the ecosystems of Newfoundland's culture, society, human capital, economy, physical capital and nature, then one might view the evolution of the Fogo Island development model in life-cycle terms. Therefore, inspired by the cyclical phases of landform evolution conceived by William Morris Davis, we have framed the region's Model for Rural Development in these analogue human and natural stages that are translated and interpreted below as: historical baseline; early stage resuscitation; next steps; and end states. Others also have used life-cycle models to frame and thereby understand better the changes over time to explain industry life-cycles and product life-cycles (Corey and Wilson, 2006: 203-204 and 213-214).

Historical Baseline

What are the pre-conditions that prompted the Shorefast Foundation to strategize and act? Simply, over the hundreds of years of human contact and settlement in the region of Fogo Island and the Change Islands, as well as the mainland of Newfoundland more broadly, people have relied on the cod fishery for their existence. Over this long time span there were economic cycles of ups and downs for ordinary people that ranged from modest prosperity to bare survival at the margin. This often vicious cycle rendered the fishers and their families across the outports of Newfoundland and its Fogo Island region dependent on the credit-based business practices of, what Zita Cobb has labeled, "distant capitalists." These were fish merchants based principally in Europe and St. John's, Newfoundland.

Over time, the fishery evolved from a local largely in-shore, small boat and hand line fishing practice to an internationally-scaled industry of large factory ships. These operations were based in a highly competitive global business environment that employed indiscriminant fishing methods that resulted in by-catch, i.e., also captured and destroyed many other species in addition to the targeted cod fish. So the evolution from pre-modern work to industrialized fishery precipitated the government-imposed moratorium of cod fishing in 1992. The result was a depression-like local economy that induced severe job loss and outmigration that halved the population of the Fogo Island and the Change Islands region. The remaining fishers and fish processors shifted from cod to other species thereby maintaining a greatly reduced job base. Thus, in the early 21st century, the economy of Fogo Island continued to be based predominantly on the single economic fishery sector, but now composed largely of snow crab and northern shrimp capture and processing rather than cod fishing.

Early Stage Resuscitation

Zita Cobb returned to Fogo Island in 2004 and re-set the Shorefast Foundation's philanthropy from granting scholarships to a social entrepreneurship-based effort to revive Fogo Island's economy. Based on feedback from the community about the early scholarship program, she re-focused the resources of the Shorefast Foundation on a new multi-programmatic agenda, the objectives of which are to create jobs and to diversify the local economy and sustain it -- including (1) maintaining and modernizing the island's long-standing economic-base of the fishery sector – and more; the new core strategy was to diversify the region's economy by means of (2) arts-based residencies that attract international artists to the islands; the artists' design and creative work is housed in contemporary-architecture studios and they live in near-by restored/preserved houses of traditional vernacular design that are distributed across and in multiple communities of the island; (3) a microfinance loan program that operates to form new and to upgrade existing local business enterprises; and (4) operate the new Fogo Island Inn with the intention of generating sufficient after-expenses revenues for the community to use in setting local development priorities for investment back into the development of the Fogo Island and Change Islands region. The latter-listed three programs are part of an underlying development strategy based on geotourism. The geotourism strategy especially is for tourists with means, and is supported in varying degrees by each of the Foundation's other programs. Geotourism by wealthy visitors and the permeation of a dynamic local enterprise culture are the glue that will hold together and catalyze the various new core strategic programs.

Critical to the function of this model of rural development is to connect the region to the global economy, and simultaneously seek to a balance between these external linkages while maintaining the most valued traditions of the local society and its unique culture. These new Shorefast Foundation programs were selected and resourced because the specific characteristics and heritage of the place informed them as priorities for investment to achieve each of the above-stated four programmatic objectives. In modeling elsewhere, other places would be expected to have a different set and mix of assets and traditions, and in many instances, significantly they would be functioning under different political economic systems, all of which would inform other types of programmatic initiatives.

In regional development life-cycle terms, these three programs still are early-stage economic activities. Realistically they will require much more time and experience to fully demonstrate their intended economic productivity, especially as measured by job creation and the generation of sustained inward revenue flows from the global marketplace based significantly on the strategy of attracting geotourists with their highly particular consumer demands and their ability to pay for them.

Geology at the Edge

While still in the early stages of the evolution of the Fogo Island Development Model and to continue the geological cycle of erosion metaphor, we introduce here some of the physical natural history that has produced today's Newfoundland; a place that merits the nickname "The Rock."

> Newfoundland has an interesting geological history since the western part of the island is an extension of North America and the eastern portion was once part of northern Africa. When the two parts collided, there was an upwelling of magma which gives us the mineral-rich deposits of central Newfoundland. The terrain of Newfoundland and Labrador is vast and diverse, ranging from boreal forest, to arctic landscapes, to bog and marsh lands to soaring granite cliffs and fiords. The province is affectionately known as "The Rock" as the last glaciation scoured the soil off most of the island. The soil was scraped off and deposited on the Grand Banks off the southeast coast of the island, leaving the terrain of the island with more rocks than soil (Loeffler, March 15, 2007).

Shorefast Foundation Business Assistance Fund consultant Jonathan Briggs supports the geological metaphor and references by adding:

> In addition to the Cycle of Erosion conceived by Davis, Newfoundland was the focus of two other prominent geologists in the mid-sixties who confirmed the action of plate tectonics using the rocks of Newfoundland (Harold Williams, 1964; J. T. Wilson, 1966) The rocks of Fogo Island are very interesting geologically, and are conveniently exposed

and scoured by ice, making observation and research practical. To further deepen the visitor's experience on Fogo Island Shorefast has initiated a Geology Residency program which blends local terrain and guides with professional geologists doing real research - and the Inn guests can participate and learn too (Briggs, December 16, 2013).

The geotourist visiting the Fogo Island and Change Islands region will discover an interesting and complex geologic history that is nearly 500 million years old.

> The islands we know today have changed from deep oceanic basins, to shallow and pleasant continental shelves, to river deltas, to violent volcanic landscapes, and then to a glacial desert. Fogo Island also preserves the turbulent buried reservoir of molten rocks ('magma chamber') that fuelled ancient eruptions – so that as a geologist walks from northwest to southeast across the island, he or she is actually walking down into the ancient Earth! The islands' modern landscapes were sculpted by ice sheets and glaciers, and by numerous changes in sea level. For the interested non-specialist, the islands provide an unparalleled opportunity to understand both the depths of geological time and the power of geological processes (Johnson GEO CENTRE, November 26, 2013).

This excerpt was taken from a lecture promotion entitled "Shorelines, Fire and Ice: Geological Stories in the Rocks of Fogo Islands and Change Islands" by Andrew Kerr, senior geologist with the Geological Survey of Newfoundland (Kerr, 2013). This was part of the Public Lecture Series offered by the world-class geological museum the Johnson GEO CENTRE, which is located in St. John's, Newfoundland. This is one of many educational geological touristic resources located around the province. It raises the issue of coordinating and networking affinity themes of interest for tourists – both local and from around the world.

In order to enable geotourists to take advantage of the islands' rich geologic history the Shorefast Foundation founded the Geology At The Edge initiative (Geology At The Edge Organization, n.d.). Similar to the Foundation's Fogo Islands Arts residency program. This is Canada's first community-based geology residency program (Geology At The Edge Organization, October 31, 2012). Kevin Sheppard is the geologist-in-residence. He was engaged to do "geotourism research and to provide education and outreach to residents and tourists alike" (Memorial University of Newfoundland, May 27, 2014).

While maybe not matching the level of Newfoundland's world-class geological history as noted above, what natural and or cultural assets does your place or region have that distinguishes your locality? What points of interest are of value to locals, say for education, as well as to persons from outside your region, say for touristic and exploratory purposes?

Next Steps

Once the Inn had opened in May 2013, it was essential for us to experience its physical presence and services directly. This also was the time that we needed to hear directly from Zita Cobb, with attention given to answering the question, what's next? The noteworthy take-aways from our return visit to Fogo Island included learning of future activities that are intended to move the entire regional economic change effort of Shorefast more fully toward complete implementation. Among other activities, these included: implementation of effective marketing, evaluation, business development processes and policy attention; the New Ocean Ethic; and the Fogo Island Dialogues. In varying degrees each of these already was underway to some extent.

Importance of Early Measurement and Monitoring

Prompted especially by the recent opening of the Fogo Island Inn for business, it will be important to set good and track their status in future. Measurement will enable the on-going monitoring and evaluation of business results and thereby provide the means for making mid-course corrections as needed. Such measurement and assessment needs to accommodate both the internal financial and business operations requirements of the Foundation and the Inn, and also the critical transparent accountability to and with local community stakeholders, thereby sustaining local ownership and sustained commitment to the whole regional economic renewal and diversification effort (Hodge, 1963).

How does the Shorefast Foundation plan to measure program performance? The mandate of the Foundation is to make a meaningful contribution to cultural and economic resiliency in Fogo Island and Change Islands. The leadership team of the Foundation has identified the following measurement milestones for use in monitoring and evaluating the status and results of its programming:

- Fogo Island and Change Islands are recognized as a sought-after geotourism destination, attracting affluent clientele from around the world.

- Fogo Islanders are employed in sustainable jobs through the Fogo Island Inn, Fogo Island Arts and tertiary activities; many of those who hold these jobs will be Fogo Islanders who have moved back home from away.

- There is an active and vibrant small business community and a spirit of entrepreneurial thinking in the community; new businesses emerge and existing businesses expand, attracting new people to the Islands.

- The percentage of the working age population receiving Employment Insurance is at historic lows.

- The Fogo Island Project is a model for rural economic sustainability.

- The contributions of rural communities are an integral part of Canada's economic strength, creating a direct connection to the international tourism market (Hodgins, May 16, 2013).

Some of these measures may be expected to be actualized earlier than others. On the whole however, and based on the deliberate pace of successful development experienced in most places elsewhere one should expect the full maturation and realization of these intended outcomes to be measured more in terms of generations than in decades.

Importance of Vertical Policy and Program Alignment

In addition to local community level development initiatives, strategically it is critical also to have government at the provincial or state level to cooperate and partner with local government and enterprises. The importance of improving the ferry service to and from Fogo Island and the Change Islands has been discussed in several contexts throughout this monograph. Mostly, this narrative has been focused on the reliability and capacity of the ferry service and the ferry vessel, but other ferry-related concerns also are at issue.

During the summer of 2013, the provincial government issued a request for proposals for the construction of a replacement ferry for the current aged ferry, i.e. the MV Earl W. Winsor, that normally makes the Farewell to Fogo Island run, However, in November 2013, the provincial government of Newfoundland and Labrador announced that the contract for the replacement ferry went to a European ship building company. The media reported relief that the new vessel was scheduled to go into service in September 2015. However, there was disappointment that the replacement ferry would not be built in Newfoundland or even in Canada (Robinson, November 19, 2013).

As announced, neither the vessel nor any components of the vessel will be fabricated in Newfoundland. The province thereby lost the opportunity for some local employment growth and the development of new skills capacities by the local workforce. The lesson for localities therefore is to do all in their power and influence to ensure that local citizen, government and business interests are heard and successfully aligned with the priorities and ultimate investment of public funds at the provincial (or state) level of government and political policies and decisions. The costs and benefits of investing only by means of lowest-bid decisions need to be re-assessed and weighed against the relative value to ordinary people of local job creation and human capital development capacities – with the local community having an effective voice and seat at the table.

For government actors at all levels that place ideology above basic substantive concerns such as local employment growth and talent development for the future, the electoral process is a ready means for insuring that the most fundamental community development requirements, in fact, get addressed. Such concerted and aligned action is dependent on civic vigilance, community organization, advocacy of collective civil priorities and inter-institutional collaborative behavior. Policy and programmatic congruence is an essential part of intelligent development (Wilson, Kellerman and Corey, 2013: 201-202).

Maturing

Explicit attention needs to be drawn here to a shift in perspective of this narrative. The nature of this discussion moves from the empirical and the actual to the possible, that is, speculative futures scenarios generating thinking based on the known realities that have preceded. The shift is from what is to conditions that have not yet happened (and might never happen in fact). However, these speculations are not mere wishful thinking or even boosterism driven by uncritical support for a promising new experiment. Rather, these desired scenarios are informed futures that are derived from the prior planned development stages that will have occurred already in the Fogo Island and Change Islands region. These scenarios are inspired by the stated inherent intentions and the embedded wills that are being driven and compelled by responding to the ultimate vision of the Shorefast Foundation and the local stakeholder development priorities.

Scenario construction is a highly recommended activity in strategic intelligent development planning. Such thought provocation can be an imaginative and creative way of building community-based ownership in and sustained commitment among diverse development stakeholders and thinkers. Comparison of alternative scenarios is an effective and relatively inexpensive way to tease out supportive nuances and subtle relationships among the variables being analyzed and strategized. Such systematic comparative analysis can greatly assist in setting development priorities for planned future private and public investments. Refer to: Corey and Wilson, 2006: 216 and Wilson, Kellerman and Corey, 2013: 213-250.

Even though it is too early to make a definitive judgment about the ultimate end-state development vision that is being intended and facilitated by the programs of the Shorefast Foundation, several extremely early public assessments have been made of the Foundation's work to date. These largely are qualitative measurements for now. Over time and with the added continuity of programmatic implementation, quantitative measurement will enable even more systematic comparison and analysis for monitoring and evaluative purposes (Hodge,

1963). In future, this further state of maturation will permit a more definitive conclusion about the status of influence and impact of the Fogo Island Model for Rural Development.

Initial Indications of Modeling Potential

Within days of the opening of the Fogo Island Inn, it was designated as a five-star accommodation. Further, four months from the Inn's launch, the *Travel + Leisure* 2013 Global Vision Award, was granted to the Fogo Island Inn. This recognition was made in the culture category, and embodies "responsible tourism and the remarkable ways in which travelers can give back to destinations visited." The award citation notes:

> Fogo Island Inn is recognized for its continued support of the local community through the embodiment of the island's indigenous culture, from locally sourced and foraged ingredients to hand-crafted quilts and furniture on the island (*The Compass*, October 15, 2013: 1).

In April 2013, the architecture magazine *Domus* featured the Fogo Island Inn; the article included stunning photography of the building and its dramatic site on the edge of the ocean. Since those early days, by the time of this writing, these are the awards and recognitions that have been conferred on the Shorefast Foundation initiatives:

- *Travel + Leisure*. It List, 2014
- CN Traveler Hot List 2014
- *Architectural Digest*. Ten Daring New Buildings Around the World, 2014
- Hospitality NL. Accommodator of the Year, 2014
- *AFAR*. The Experiential Travel Awards, 2014
- *Travel + Leisure*. Global Vision Award, Culture, 2013
- *enRoute magazine*. Canada's Best New Restaurants, 2013
- TIAC. National Cultural Tourism Award, 2013
- *Domus* architectural magazine feature, April 2013

These kinds of commendations are noteworthy. Such acknowledgements are suggestive of peer respect as well as popular admiration. This high profile attention can serve to bring the Shorefast Foundation efforts at rural revival to national and global awareness. With this kind of knowledge then the modeling qualities of this development work can be tested and in the testing can be refined and perfected.

Given that the role envisaged for the Inn to play in the implementation of the Model for Fogo Island's Rural Development is that of economic engine, it is noteworthy that by early August 2014 Zita Cobb was able to tell us that the market demand for rooms and suites at the Fogo

Island Inn was such that the minimum room rate – throughout the year – was then set at $1,600 per night. The summer of 2014 was experiencing nearly full occupancy each night.

During our field work on the island, as we interacted with local residents, fishers and other workers, we believe that it is noteworthy that we did not hear comments that suggested resentment or jealousy among these community members toward Shorefast or Zita Cobb. Indeed, several such informants indicated that they were a bit skeptical when the Foundation rolled out its vision and the initial, the early programs. However, after several years of operating Fogo Island Arts and Business Assistance programming, and now with the actual opening of the Inn, the inevitable nay-sayers seem to be keeping their own counsel or definitely were and are difficult to find today. What is needed are several more years of operations across the full range of Foundation and other spin-off programming to be able to even more firmly conclude that local positive perceptions are nearly ubiquitous.

Preliminary indications of some complementary development support have begun to be evidenced. The local government of the Town of Fogo Island established the staff position of Director of Tourism and Recreation to address the increased touristic demands and inquiries that it has experienced since the opening of the Fogo Island Inn. One of the early outcomes of this staff member is a new brochure for the growing numbers of general tourists who have been visiting the island. The label "brochure" does not do justice to the product. It is a most visually attractive map of Fogo Island with a highly detailed legend to guide new visitors to the sights, villages and other attractions of the island. Its informational detail and usefulness reminds one of the print editions of the yellow pages of the past. This new local information resource adds immeasurably to the quality of the exploratory experience of visiting Fogo Island. It is entitled "Fogo Island Tourism Guide" (Town of Fogo Island, 2013).

The September 2013 election platform statements of a number of the candidates for the council of the Town of Fogo Island ran on pledges to address several infrastructural issues that are chronic concerns to the island's citizenry and businesses. Clean running water and reliable ferry service that meet the needs of locals and visitors alike were among the highest priority issues raised in this context. If the initial Shorefast Foundation accomplishments stimulate the newly-formed local government to join with the Foundation in private-public partnership for the re-development of the island that is an early positive sign for the possibility of further cross-institutional cooperative ventures in future.

In the short-term, two critical transportation infrastructure needs are outstanding and will continue to require continuous joint attention by local government and the Shorefast Foundation. These are the ferry and the airport runway. Ferry service in Notre Dame Bay for Fogo Island and Change Islands: the good news is that the laying of the keel for the new $51 million ferry took place at Damen Shipyards in Romania on August 20, 2014 Delivery of the ferry is expected in September 2015. It is "an 80-metre ice-class vessel that has roll-on and roll-off capability and will accommodate up to 200 passengers and 60 vehicles" (CBC News, August

23, 2014). After years of recurring interruptions to ferry service due principally to aging ferry vessels and related issues of maintenance, ice, capacity and poor communication, the government of Newfoundland and Labrador expects the new ferry vessel to relieve these problems.

Both the local governments of the islands in coordination with the Fogo Island Inn and the Shorefast Foundation still will need to continuously review schedules and work with local authorities to manage the transportation network to ensure as smooth as possible the connections from airports to the front door of Inn – such fine-tuning is critical to enjoyable guest experience. Airport Runway on Fogo Island: currently the small airstrip on Fogo Island provides service to small aircraft. The Fogo Island Inn would like to expand the runway such that it accommodates small jets especially to be able to respond to the target market for Inn guests traveling from outside Newfoundland. Considerable investment will be required; Shorefast principals are working with the province to see how to move forward on the runway investment.

Infrastructure, Regulation and Learning/Training

Especially, in the context of the current work and the full entrepreneurial realization of the potential impacts of the Business Assistance Fund, some grassroots citizen-driven task forces should be considered to investigate the factors for and against such strategic development improvements in infrastructure as the following:

(1) management coordination for year-round ferry service that is reliable and with the vehicle capacity to better meet the changing needs of the residents and businesses of the islands and the seasonal demand of visitors from away;

(2) an extended and upgraded airstrip that can serve a growing high-end geotourist demand as well as the local business and resident air travel requirements, especially during icebound and other ferry service disruption times;

(3) internet ubiquity is needed across the entire populated areas of these islands and all of their settlements, that is the provision of affordable and accessible broadband infrastructure and services, plus offering the training and public education needed to enable the people, educational institutions and businesses of the islands region to participate digitally, especially with the new and upgraded enterprise-development opportunities available through competitive connectivity to the globalized economy. See Appendix 2 for the benchmark case of Connect Michigan and its approach for enabling rural and small town communities to assess their own local broadband services and requirements and then to formulate action plans to fill gaps (Frederick, September 24, 2013 and Connect Michigan, n.d.); and

(4) on-going research, including survey research, identifying the exact nature of the Unemployment Insurance eligibility issues and the related work-seasonality issues that currently make it risky for would-be business start-up persons if they have to give up off-season Unemployment Insurance benefits; such research findings should be used to seek appropriate regulatory change. Investigate further: if such recipients have to maintain several additional Unemployment Insurance-eligible jobs, then how can they invest sufficient time in their own new business venture also?

These impediments to new business formation were brought to our attention by Shorefast's Jonathan Briggs and would seem to merit further fact gathering, solid analysis and thoughtful follow-up advocacy (Briggs, June 21, 2013). This is the case particularly as the region's enterprise culture is expected to deepen and expand with maturation. (5) Explore better legal-organizational-regulatory structures that enable the operation and public accountability for the creation and implementation of social business enterprises. Social business is an emerging field in Canada. Social business is where for-profit economic activity contributes to positive social outcomes. Social businesses are appearing and having to invest in new types of business structures where rules are not clearly defined. There is no pre-determined box to fall into, no existing path to follow to success. Some economists recognize that there are issues with current capital markets and business structures; they are encouraging us to think of possible legal alternatives, including working from scratch and building from the ground up. Shorefast should continue to find insight from this work and seek to build a better legal-regulatory model and not just follow what we currently have. What is needed is "to develop something that is community centric with business as servant, not master." In her keynote speech to the Canadian Bar Association's August 2014 Legal Conference on "Converging Futures," she raised the issues of building for success by doing "old things a new way" (Cobb, August 17, 2014).

With the need for new ground rules to facilitate the innovations underway on Fogo Island, Team Shorefast should continue to press and put forward to government from these new issues that it is uncovering proposed experimental pilot opportunities to test the incentive power of modeling from Fogo Island for similar other selected places in the province to stimulate new-business formation and regional development innovation. It is important that provincial government continues to partner with the Shorefast Foundation, the Town of Fogo Island local government, and the individual businesses and individual citizens to ensure that these collective local voices and particular interests are heard and get response and priority in government resource allocations. The more that the collective Fogo Island development programs mature and attract additional tourist and other attention, the more that thoughtful, informed advocacy is likely to prompt higher and earlier priority for resource allocation setting from provincial government. Refer to Appendix 7 on Some More Principal Components of the Fogo Island Model for Rural Development and an elaboration on special roles that islands can play in catalyzing innovation in development, thereby meriting investment priority consideration from government and business.

Institutions, Information Infrastructure, Information Accumulation, Affinity Networking and Training

Once the early-stage programs of the Foundation have sufficiently matured and demonstrated their sustained economic productivity, then it is time to have addressed these systematic business and process improvement issues. By this stage, it may be possible for some of these above physical and other infrastructure quality improvement factors to be convincing that the Fogo Island case warrants additional investment to demonstrate some of its innovative experiments with the goal of generating proof-of-concept empirical evidence that could be used selectively elsewhere in the province and beyond the province to provide a spur for initiating innovation in regional development that is intended to result in more diverse and economically viable regions across targeted demonstration areas.

Why are such institution-development initiatives, including information infrastructure and information accumulation so critical? Our research into the role of islands and small countries in development has found that institutional quality "can explain the relatively strong economic performance of islands and small countries" (Congdon Fors, 2014: 34). The trust that accrues from the information about a local functioning, productive and beneficial organization or institution creates social value; when the flow of this kind of information creates social networks of people who know each other on the island, then the "accumulation of social capital" may explain stronger development performance from institutional quality on small islands (Congdon Fors, 2014: 52). Additional research suggests that improving information infrastructure that generates decentralized information improves management incentives and increases productivity. Better accumulated information has the value of sending clearer signals to the market thereby "enabling reliable relative performance evaluation" (Acemoglu and Zilibotti, 1999: 30-31). These authors remind us that transformation to a modern and global economy necessitates accumulating data "to improve our understanding of the development process (Acemoglu and Zilibotti, 1999: 31). With intelligent information accumulation and improved understanding, better informed decisions about the range of products, services, productivity, the organization of the enterprise and better selection and task assignments can be realized (Acemoglu and Zilibotti, 1999: 31).

Analogously, some fishery sector regulation experiments might prove productive. Over a several-year time span a student-led faculty guided coordinated business research effort might be conducted on these issue areas (University Center for Regional Economic Innovation, n.d.). This is a best-practice or good-practice (Vettoretto, 2009) way to harness the contemporary learning of young minds and their recently-learned formative analytic and business strategy methods. It might build on and extend the memorandum of understanding between the Shorefast Foundation and the Memorial University of Newfoundland (MUN) (Cohoe, May 16, 2013). Students from MUN's Faculty of Business Administration and their professorial supervisor Natalie Slawinski already have a working relationship with Zita Cobb. Particularly, on research into innovation-based development work, our experience with such student-learning projects often serves to generate fresh perspectives and demonstrates creative solutions (University Center for Regional Economic Innovation, n.d.,). By laying this kind of new multi-generational assessment and reflective groundwork during this maturation stage, the whole Fogo Island rural development effort may be prepared in its most fully realized end-state phase to fill in and refine the inevitable gaps and evaluation-informed improvements that every innovation-based planned change regional development effort requires.

As the New Ocean Ethic initiative continues to evolve and as the Fogo Island Dialogues regularly generate fresh inputs for and approaches to rural development, such programmatic activities will influence local and external perceptions of Fogo Island and Change Islands regional development possibilities. Based on improving production, indications of increasing community cohesion and collaborative effort among the region's various institutional and individual actors, the Fogo Islands likely will be more attractive to investors, donors and other external well-wishers interested in supporting the growing momentum of Fogo Island toward development success. This future state suggests that an active and effective fund-raising and investment partnering effort will have been realized and is sending the message that this case is establishing itself as an increasingly promising Model for Rural Development – especially one that can serve as a best practice of rural social entrepreneurship and social business development (Vettoretto, 2009).

As noted earlier, a selection of Newfoundland's leading innovative eco-dining chefs convened for the October 2013 Canadian Thanksgiving weekend. They used this meeting to confer and collaborate in preparing a creative multi-course holiday menu and meal that drew on traditional Newfoundland foods and practices and contemporary foods and practices from their experience and exposure both in the province and from away. This peer-invitational event at the Fogo Island Inn has set an example and laid the groundwork for a possible collaborative of eco-dining creative producers for geotouristic consumers. Such peer gatherings might be expanded to the end-state stage of realizing the evolution of an affinity network of additional like-minded and so-inclined food production innovators across the province. As such communication and networking might deepen and develop, the thorny issues noted earlier relating to food sourcing, logistics, supply chains and organizing supplier systems with similar values can be tackled.

The cumulative and synergistic relationships of this maturation stage in the life cycle of Shorefast Foundation rural development investments might also be expected to catalyze some additional small business formation, both as part of the Business Assistance Fund program, but also as a result of island residents and island alumni observing new firms being created, and in the process, gaining increased confidence in the region's emergent enterprise culture.

The example of the initial gathering of Newfoundland chefs is a hopeful indicator of possible further collaborative business relationships in other economic production and consumption sectors at the provincial level. At the Fogo Island level there needs to be comparable movement toward collaboration among the internal business players and would-be business players. Such collaboration within the islands region could take advantage of scale economies and capitalize on linkages that result in related businesses working together to offer, provide and deliver a coordinated and holistic system of touristic services to visiting consumers across functionally affiliated enterprises in lodgings and accommodations, tours and guides, crafts, food, events and transportation. Such close cooperation and cross-functional alignments among the islands' firms would enable the marketing of higher-quality and more reliable tourist products as a coherent and integrated services sector.

Shorefast's Jonathan Briggs introduced us to the parable about "Newfoundland lobsters stuck in a trap. Only one lobster can find a way out, but the others pull it back into the trap. What's the learning? Extreme unity? No success for just one? No reward for being smarter? Don't stand out? Selfishness?" (Briggs, June 21, 2013). As the benefits of collaboration and strategic cooperation, both internally and with external-to-the-island partners like the chefs, are evidenced and celebrated, then the evolving local enterprise culture may accelerate and put down deeper sustainable roots for the next generation of the young, for the older islanders, and for the women, as well for men. Such acceleration and wider diffusion of an enterprise culture may be stimulated by programming in business training and education. If more widespread business options are developed then seasonal income insecurities might be reduced while self-reliance and independence might be increased and imprinted on entrepreneurial civic behavior. This could be an enhancement in the local quality of life if space also can be created to enjoy the family and to re-group after the hectic multiple demands of the warmer seasons. It is important to preserve some of the good of past cultural values while also enjoying some of the benefits that can come from engaging in new enterprises. Internal balance and options will need to be managed in order to continue to take advantage of the region's unique social and natural assets in the context of the networked and highly connected global economy and society (inspired by Briggs, June 21, 2013).

The most critical and strategic factor underpinning the possible positive acceleration of the already-upward trajectory of this particular stage of maturity assumes that the Fogo Island Inn is attracting affluent geotourists at surplus-generating levels of guest occupancy. Thus, effective targeted marketing is the critical independent variable in the success of this planned business model. Refer to the discussion on Surplus Allocation in the Concluding Remarks below.

End States

Based on likely and feasible evolutionary trajectories, these are some of the rural revival outcomes that might be expected in future. These may be stimulated in part from Shorefast leadership, investments and leveraging of additional resources for critical asset development, and from the engagement of new entrepreneurial behavior, partnering and ownership more widely by the people and communities of Fogo Island and Change Islands – and from the external influences of the geotourist visitors and artists-in-residence from across the globe.

If demonstrated to be economically and socially promising and profitable then these new economic base modes of doing new business development may spill over and spread to other locations in the province. With these emergent networks of producers and consumer-serving alignments beginning to form, in time, one realistically can envisage not only locality-based collaboratives and networks beyond chefs engaged in eco-dining innovation, but the incorporation of other economic sectors and industry sub-sectors in both goods and services and for affluent geotourists and the more numerous and seasonal generic tourists.

The tourism sector as a whole can be an even more important means of bringing income and revenue into the province and its localities. For example, during the 2013 May through October season, the province experienced 64 cruise ship port calls "to 23 Newfoundland and Labrador ports by 16 cruise operators with 20 ships." These calls generated 61,820 visitors; 41,376 passengers and 20,444 crew (The Pilot, November 4, 2013). The environmental and infrastructural impacts of the generic more mass tourist market will require close monitoring and attention by the appropriate local and regional planners and regulators of the province. From the results revealed by this monitoring the responsible elected officials and actors will need to be held accountable by informed civic and institutional players across the province. Tracking the key tourism measures and indicators by citizen and business stakeholders will be required to provide feedback for the goal of ensuring responsiveness to the demands and needs of Newfoundland's regions and localities (Newfoundland and Labrador Tourism Board, February 2013).

However, in the case of the Fogo Island and Change Islands region, continuing leadership from Shorefast by means of refining and perfecting its social entrepreneurship developmental approaches and its strong community-based empowerment philosophy certainly will be critical as scaling up and spreading out of new development benefits and the inevitable unplanned costs manifest themselves. By the time of this end-state future rural development, the Shorefast Foundation will not be the only geotouristically experienced institution in the province. It likely will have attracted multiple partners of influence and donors of wealth with shared progressive regional development aspirations. So, in the full flowering of a revitalized Fogo Island and rural Newfoundland and beyond, the Shorefast Foundation may well have gone a long way toward realizing its vision for an economically diverse home place that has been able to retain its core culture and traditions while at the same time learning how to responsibly engage the global economy with all of its promise and unintended consequences. In the process of striving to have attained these accomplishments, it seems reasonable to conclude that some modest number of new jobs on the islands will have been created and some alumni from the region and beyond will have returned; some to start up or expand their own businesses and some to maintain second homes for regular return stays with relations and friends. How might some developments by selected programmatic sectors support such speculative musings and scenarios?

The Fishery

A viable and sustainable fishery will have been attained that has found its place in the regional and global market, while simultaneously practicing responsible utilization of the fishery's assets. These practices will be informed and sustained because the fishers, processors and managers of the fishing enterprises and the Fogo Island Co-operative Society now will be aware of and sensitive to the science and modern business requirements needed to achieve and maintain a healthy local marine environment. Such a knowledge-based fishery culture will have strengthened and imprinted over time, such that the Fogo Island and Change Islands region will have been recognized as a leading producer of some of the cleanest, most flavorful seafood products available. These branded products will attract top prices because the Fogo Island product name will have become known for highest quality based on solid science and values of the best stewardship practices. Indeed, because of its special contributions to and membership in worldwide networks of marine and ocean knowledge and education centers, the New Ocean Ethic of Fogo Island will be recognized as a leader in responsible business behavior that functions in ways that both conserves the natural resource of the fishery and provides a reliable livelihood for its participants. Being strategic in the matters of markets and financial investment, the Fogo Island Cooperative Society will be operating according to best business practices that are generating profits and along with resulting local control and ownership of the sector's means of production. Further, given such success, one may expect that some sons and daughters of today's fishers will participate in and contribute to the rejuvenation and continuous improvement of the local fishery.

Fogo Island Arts

The diverse activities of the Shorefast arts programming will have been established both globally and locally. It functions as an open system (Corey and Wilson, 2006: 212-213) of continuous innovation in relationship and synergy with the other principal programs of the Foundation. The annual cycle of Fogo Island Artists-in-Residence will provide on-going infusions of fresh and creative external intellectual and business stimuli to the local community culture of the islands. In turn, the cultural assets of the local people, their society, and their physical and natural environments will inspire the international and national arts visitors to experiment and advance their own writing, filmmaking, new media, the visual arts, design, music, dance, thinking and curation. These interactions are encouraged via collaborations between visitors and locals.

By means of on-going publishing, both distant and local exhibitions and digital communication and networking, Fogo Island artistic production from international visitors and local residents alike will have become known, appreciated and respected by art consumers around the world for its unique brands of ingenuity, imagination and improvisation that take forms that are contemporary, traditional, global, local and fusion, and that are identifiable as Fogo Island in origin or influence. At this more mature and advanced stage in the development life cycle of Fogo Island Arts, the routine operation and commercialization of the program's production is advancing and contributing to the economic sustainability of the social enterprise-based business model that includes the Fogo Island Inn and Shorefast's overarching geotourism-centric strategy. The after-expenses assets of this business can be routinely invested back into the community for the benefit of its collectively determined local development priorities.

The freshness and innovativeness of Fogo Island Arts in particular and the other Shorefast programs more generally are maintained in part because of the dynamics of the Fogo Island Dialogues. These interactions bring strategic value-added enrichment to the local region because they tap into emergent issues and forward-leaning trends that are shaping diverse tastes and fashion around the world in culture, economics, and ecology that may offer opportunities to and present challenges for rural communities and regions. In turn, specific issues resulting from development changes taking place in the Fogo Island and Change Islands region are able to be regularly addressed as part of these external and internal exchanges.

By having the Fogo Island Dialogues held in strategically important artistic and intellectual centers of innovation, opinion setting and education, the message of the Fogo Island Rural Development Model will have generated growing and more widespread interest and attention. Subject to demand for Fogo Island arts production, gallery and exhibition locations will have been established in selective global hubs of artistic debate and leadership. These dialogues and conferences will have stimulated the formation of partnerships with key institutions; these relationships will have served to deepen the presence and influence of Fogo Island Arts on the global arts stage. Nicolaus Schafhausen, Strategic Director, Fogo Island Arts, with his cosmopolitan skills in curation, artistic leadership and management will have been effective in facilitating the connection of Shorefast programs to the relevant artistic networks in Europe and cosmopolitan areas in other regions of the global marketplace, e.g. the Asia-Pacific region.

Business Assistance Fund

As one peers into an end-state future, informed by the prior groundwork of research, realistic scenarios for development, debate and strategy determination, it is feasible to envisage the emergence of an increasingly lively and spreading enterprise culture across the Fogo Island and Change Islands region. Tapping into the possibly under-utilized entrepreneurial assets represented among some of the women, men, youngsters and seniors of the islands who might be less economically engaged during the November through the end of March seasons also might be possible. Refer to Appendix 5.

For example, once the Fogo Island Inn has demonstrated that it is able to generate profits and a sustained net surplus, then it may be possible through training and targeted marketing to alumni from the islands who had moved away to have some of them return home and become owners of new businesses. Such returning, especially of younger-generation Fogo Islanders, might have a contagion effect among some older current residents, such that some multi-generational enterprises might be started up.

Finally, as one envisions an end-state future for the island's arts production, the demand for the program's creative products might suggest some additional capacity and modest locational expansion in Shorefast's arts and other programming. The early vision for the artist studios was for six facilities. In time one may want to make a case for a multi-programmatic facility on the Change Islands both to serve needs of the people there and to tap into the unique assets of that place – which is yet another location even more "away" and isolated than Fogo Island. If the original six studio vision were to be realized that also might mean expanding the artist studio spatial distribution to the Seldom-Little Seldom area and the village of Fogo area, among other Fogo Island locational possibilities.

Fogo Island Inn and Spin-Off Scenarios

The on-going activities of the Fogo Island Inn may well operate to have attained the vision of a world-class destination and business function. Plus, its special and innovative use of social entrepreneurship and community development methods may be functioning effectively by being in the forefront of global high-end geotourism through its priority on providing continuous highest-quality hospitality services and business process improvement. Balancing the particular global and local reasons d'être will be important during the on-going fully evolved phase of the Inn's business development. Even though the Inn will have reached the stage of "routine" business operations performance, it still needs to be in the mode of continuous innovation, invention and process improvement. Its operating staff needs to remember that it has established and now is implementing a new business and new social-enterprise that is a "not-just-for-profit" hybrid organizational entity. This demands on-going forward-leaning and active attention to ensuring that both the surplus-generating requirements and the well-to-do geotourist customer satisfaction and high-quality service standards are being met and exceeded – especially since the Inn is a global pioneer in its particular brand of remote rural-place affluent geotouristic hospitality creation. During this end-state phase, such a groundbreaking niche position will be explored regularly for additional business and regional development spin-offs and spillovers – both in the region and beyond.

Even before and during Shorefast's early-stage strategic shift from a scholarship-based philanthropy to a multi-programmatic social enterprise philanthropy of arts, architecture, heritage-preservation, small-business expansion, high-end geotourism and modern responsibly-practiced fishery, other related geotouristic and global/international business start-ups will have emerged and are evolving in other Newfoundland location. A highly-selective sampling of illustrative contemporary examples of food, art, architecture and lodgings attractions include: St. John's based The Rooms museum and the Bacalao (cod-fish, especially dried and salted cod) restaurant, known for its Nouvelle Newfoundland Cuisine along with other restaurants, such as: Raymonds, Chinched, Blue on Water, and Mallard Cottage and the Oppidian at the Sheraton, all in the St. John's region. The Goose Cove Retreat (n.d.) designed by architect Robert Mellin is a private getaway for families or management teams, it is located in the Trinity area; and nearby is the eco-dining innovative Two Whales Coffee Shop and the top-ranked rural inn of Fishers' Loft in Port Rexton. In the Corner Brook area of Newfoundland, the tourist has available Gitanos' Supper Club and Tapas Bar and the Humber Valley resorts nearby; and the high-end boutique hotel; and finally, a geotourism project conceived by Canadian television personality Shaun Majumder in his home town of Burlington, Newfoundland (Bozikovic, July18, 2013).

It can be noted that these are examples of enterprises that might be patronized nowadays by geotourists from outside Newfoundland and Labrador in particular. To list such businesses here, it is not necessarily an endorsement or a judgment statement on the success of these firms. Some of these companies have been profitable for their investors and others less so, or not profitable. Of course profitability partly is a creature of business cycle, so variability in return on investment should not be unexpected. These business initiatives illustrate more contemporary and up to date development activities, many of which are more aligned with a clientele from the global marketplace that may be interested in geotouristic products, where previously in Newfoundland, Labrador and indeed in the Fogo Island and Change Islands region, such new demands were non-existent in these places.

From the perspective of Shorefast and the Fogo Island's Inn's strategy of attracting wealthy geotourists from the global marketplace it makes sense to consider the broader context for Fogo Island. Some of these wealthy geotourists heading to the Fogo Island and Change Islands region will want to do some exploration traveling to and from the Inn. As a consequence, the principal points in noting geotourist-serving enterprises beyond the islands region is twofold: (1) in recent years, outside of the St. John's city-region, the touristic support infrastructure is better and deeper for wealthy geotourists from outside the province; and (2) there may be some benefit for these businesses to engage in some forms of collaboration and networking.

For the geotourist and the general tourist alike these are some of the many attractions available for such travelers, and again ranging across highly selective cultural, physical and nature heritage attractions, include: the Beothuk Interpretation Center Provincial Historic Site in Boyd's Cove in proximity to the highway route from Twillingate to the ferry terminus at

Farewell for sailings to the Change Islands and Fogo Island; the Beothuk Center is an important public education and awareness institution focused on explaining the life and 1829 extinction of these aboriginal people (Such, 1978); the Twillingate area's Amber Retreat saltbox house, Above the Tickle restored merchant house and commercial fisher David Boyd's Prime Berth Twillingate Fishery & Heritage Centre; root cellars there and the nearby popular and well-reputed Doyle W. Sansome and Sons Ltd. Super Lobster Pool; the Eastport area's highly localized homey and unadorned countryside assets of the Little Denier restaurant, known widely for its fish and chips, and other traditional and home-cooked dishes of Newfoundland; the comfortable family-run Inn By The Sea B&B, and the Inn at Happy Adventure and its restaurant in Happy Adventure, Newfoundland; New Bonaventure's Random Passage settlement re-creation and film site; Trinity's Rising Tide Theatre Playhouse; Port Union's new entrance and community gathering place arch built by students from Toronto (Bozikovic, July18, 2013); the historic trans-Atlantic seaplane terminus in Botwood, Newfoundland; the Barbour Living Heritage Village in Newtown, a sealing industry and fishery outport in the Wesleyville region; L'Anse aux Meadows National Historic Site, Viking Settlement circa 1000 AD; Labrador's Red Bay National Historic Site and the Battle Harbor National Historic District (Battle Harbour, n.d.),; and the extraordinary geological and natural-science assets of Gros Morne National Park; Terra Nova National Park; and the Cape St. Mary's Ecological Reserve, an important visually accessible bird sanctuary. With many more nature, contemporary and heritage sites that one could nominate, a wealth of geotouristic attractions are distributed throughout the province and nearby, such as the French Island of Saint-Pierre et Miquelon.

As a cultural and natural enhancement, a kind of provincial scale geotourism trail of digitally-supported virtually linked via social media and actual sites might be constructed for the benefit of the well-to-do geotourist, as well as the generic tourist from within and beyond the province who is engaging in more thematic, recreational and educational tourist demand and satisfaction. For the international and affluent geotourist whose primary destination is the Fogo Island Inn and its integrated offering of rich local cultural and natural exploratory activities, such a holistic province-wide tourist information networked resource might stimulate and enable longer stays in Newfoundland and Labrador and or return trips. Given the large scale of the province and the length, cost and effort of the long inward and outward journeys to Fogo Island, such visitors might well benefit from having additional touristic options that are organized, marketed in bundles of integrated explorations and made easily facilitated logistically by means of multi-media enhanced and enriched with mobile and social media applications. Such an electronically enabled "geotourism trail" would provide synergistic value-added benefit both for visitors and local businesses alike. Putting together such a trail initially for example, by student-led and faculty supervised projects over several years' time would be a highly feasible task that would bring many benefits for all (University Center for Regional Economic Innovation, n.d.).

An additional component that we would have welcomed as we journeyed to and from Fogo Island for our research and field work would have been a geotourism system of feeder accommodations. This might consist of comfortable, well-designed and visually attractive lodgings and with light meals available to the geotourist who has had to take an entire day with possibly several stops for air connections to get to especially the airport town of Gander for example. It could consist of a re-purposed structure or a house worthy of preservation, i.e. a special bed and breakfast type of facility that would serve as a complementary transitional quality accommodation intended for visitors to the Fogo Island Inn. Initially, it might be established and run directly by the Shorefast Foundation/Fogo Island Inn and then later franchised out to other quality-appropriate local operators, or it might be commissioned from the beginning of such a feeder accommodation project. This would depend on sufficient volume of demand of geotourists traveling to and from the Fogo Island Inn throughout the year. Depending on demand, such feeder accommodations further might be considered for Deer Lake and St. John's airport proximity locations. These geotourist feeder locations would be served by totally coordinated ground and or air transportation service providers.

We are reminded that the people of Newfoundland and Fogo Island are some of the most welcoming and hospitable people that one is likely to encounter when traveling. By the very nature of this quite place-unique asset, the province and the Fogo Island and Change Islands region would seem to be ideal environments for supporting a vibrant center for hospitality-industry education and research. Such a start-up service sector initiative might be initiated by existing local educational institutions and or in partnership with established and highly-reputed organizations and institutions outside the province, e.g., hospitality-industry schools.

Given the hospitality sector nature of the above discussion, the Fogo Island Inn itself ultimately might well build on the case of the initial peer and affinity gathering of the Newfoundland chefs noted above. One's futuring imagination can envisage the possibility of forming cooking classes cum chef's school devoted to educating local and external students in the arts of eco-dining and high-end tourism especially tuned to the particular issues encountered in remote rural locations. Such a business start-up might be Fogo Island Inn championed initially and moved later into a multi-actor provider network that more fully taps into the widening range of creative food talents in the province that already are functioning and able to be expanded in response to a larger, more vibrant and more diverse tourist and hospitality industry in Newfoundland and Labrador. As this Fogo Island Inn-inspired and locationally distributed and networked venture in hospitality entrepreneurship might gain traction, then additional analogous affinity networks in local vernacular arts, for example, might be conceived. Quebec's Economuseum Network, could serve as a stimulant for a hospitality-sector movement worth piloting for the whole of Newfoundland and Labrador.

Extending the hospitality network throughout the region is a logical expansion of a provincial level hospitality network strategy. Even in the current early phases of the Fogo Island rural revival effort, opinion-setters in other provinces are noticing and being stimulated to emulate the Fogo Island model of identifying their own local area and specific assets for development attention and priority. For example, rural community stakeholders in Cape Breton, Nova Scotia are assessing that locality's "great musical culture, a fraternity of writers, theatre experiences and event promoters" as possible means of building on and the learnings from its annual nine day Celtic Colours International Festival (Bates, October 21, 2013). These Fogo Island, Newfoundland and other provincial hospitality industry network-supportive and place-based initiatives, in time, might be planned and implemented in partnership with selected educational hospitality and tourism programs of universities, resorts and world-class hotels from around North America and the global economy.

New Ocean Ethic, Literacy and Responsible Practice

Central to the full realization of this multi-faceted programmatic priority of the Shorefast Foundation is successful fund raising. Such financial development and significant donation attraction needs to be preceded and complemented by the cultivation and mobilization of individuals and institutional partners. Such collaboration and alliances need to come from partners who are: persons and families of wealth and influence; other non-profit institutions such as other foundations, but also from research and educational institutions that have related, interdependent objectives; and with for-profit corporations with value systems and business practices that are progressive and developmental with respect to sustaining the natural environment, source locally, practice of fair and equitable labor relations, and the empowerment of communities and individuals whose health and quality of life enable them to retain and accumulate some of the resources that their labor and ingenuity have produced, and thereby contribute substantively to the advancement of local civil society.

Governments at various levels, national, sub-national and local, also need to partner, especially by co-investing in fundamental infrastructural modern living and working requirements that address both basic needs such as clean running water, contemporary communications and digital technologies and transportation facilities that support business and job and income generation, these include such facilities as ferry and air services that are in demand and deemed by local island society to be essential. Simply, Shorefast can catalyze and inspire with innovative vision and some investment, but to be truly "owned" by local and regional society and sustained well into the future, there must be significant shared commitment and investment across a range of economic sectors and administrative jurisdictions (Lachapelle, 2008). To be a fully-elaborated model of rural development and having generated widespread impact it should demonstrate a high level of ultimate buy-in and shared mission from such representative actors of regional and local society. Such localized self-determination, initiative and self-reliance are essential in an era when government investment too often is uncertain and meager.

The New Ocean Ethic, Literacy and Responsible Practice initiative of the Foundation merits this kind of systemic attention, support and priority because this effort fills a critical and strategic niche on behalf of the global stewardship of natural environmental assets and responsible natural resource utilization interests. The Fogo Island and Change Islands region is an historically significant fishery hot spot for the northwestern higher-latitude Atlantic Ocean (Bolster, 2012). Its empirical reality and multi-national heritage make it an ideal place for having a science-based ethic-inspired center for ocean awareness, education and informed utilization of ocean resources.

At least two ocean thrusts might serve to advance the Shorefast Foundation's ocean vision and interests: (1) a physical facility that houses and hosts ocean awareness and education programming that is informed and supported by world-class cutting edge science; and (2) in concert with other institutions, the formation of a global ocean science and education network that is complementary and technologically connected. In the global knowledge economy and the global information society electronic networking and connectivities continue to create development opportunities and new complementarities.

The Fogo Island Ocean Ethic and Literacy Center concept may be well positioned to attract the funding and to instigate the planning required for playing a needed strategic ocean ethic niche role globally and certainly at the North American level to network, collaborate and thereby complement other ocean knowledge, ocean education and ocean advocacy organizations and centers. By framing and stitching together a coherent holistic network of the currently diverse centers of ocean and marine knowledge generation and dissemination, the Fogo Island Ocean Center should be able to benefit from the earlier science and education development work of ocean knowledge pioneers from around the world, e.g., Jacques Cousteau. By means of a division of labor and purpose, the Fogo Island Ocean Center thereby can focus its effort and knowledge production and ocean resources practices improvements on its unique self-declared niche of ocean ethic research and knowledge transmission leading to responsible use and sustainability of marine resources.

By having an explicit exploratory effort to take maximum advantage of contemporary information and communications technologies (ICTs) and networking opportunities, ways should be sought to collaborate and conduct two-way (outward and inward) electronic communications (including on-going oceans educational exhibits from network partners) with some of the various kinds of ocean research and public educational functions that were referenced in the previous paragraph. As a consequence, the Shorefast Foundation may assume a global regional leadership role especially focused on literacy-based ocean ethic development and practice by means of citizen science. By being able to use, and having the capacity for year-round and remote ICT access to and transmission of ocean education and ocean knowledge dissemination, the Fogo Island center (and the Inn's e-Cinema facility) would not have to replicate all of the needed oceans literacy content on its own. Such an ocean network and collaborative partnering would be cost-effective and more powerful in penetrating global and regional consciousness and markets of the oceans component of the global-environmental science and policy research communities.

Massive open online courses (MOOCs), in particular, should be explored and piloted for the development of ocean-knowledge consumption both within the Fogo Island and Change Islands region and from sources external to the local region. Once the proof-of-concept has been established and developed for delivery, of both non-credit and credit knowledge and practice content in ocean science, ocean research and ocean ethic utilization should be analyzed and benchmarked for additional customization, tailoring and application for particular empirical contexts globally. The costs and likely revenue-generating benefits of ocean ethic MOOCs programming should receive early evaluation.

Merely for the purposes of illustration, some initial would-be members of an ocean network and collaborative partnership, for example, might include the Sylvia Earle Alliance (Saeks, August 10/August 11, 2013), the Monterey Bay Aquarium, the Memorial University of Newfoundland, Simon Fraser University, the Seacoast Science Center in New Hampshire and other selected universities and ocean research-production centers such as the Smithsonian Environmental Research Center (SERC). For example, an ocean-related niche of SERC is its focus on "ecosystems on edge."

> Seventy percent of the world's population lives in the coastal zone. Biologically, coasts are the most fruitful ecosystems on Earth. They are also some of the most fragile. Discover the challenges of life on the coasts and what scientists and people can do to save them in these videos created by the Smithsonian Environmental Research Center (Smithsonian Environmental Research Center, n.d.).

So place-specific eco-systems, regional customization and maximum localization of the ocean programming should be advocated and implemented also by local citizen scientists and local industry practitioners. As the global ocean network gets beyond its formative stages additional complementary ocean centers to the network should be welcomed so that diverse eco-systems are represented including all continents and latitudes from polar to tropical. The few example ocean institutions noted here are merely illustrative of representative network partners.

Importantly, the ocean initiative of the Shorefast Foundation will have targeted the region's youth. It is critical strategically that some students from the Fogo Island and Change Islands region be exposed to career and advanced ocean science educational options. Some portion of the local youth should have white collar occupational opportunities facilitated via local education and distance learning programming. The scale of such a local education priority would seem feasible from a numbers perspective. For example, the Fogo Island Central Academy in September 2011 had a K-12 student population of only 282 (Nova Central School District, November 20, 2013). A strong and continuous emphasis on ocean science education in particular and science research and practice education in general from the earliest grades through to graduation, might go a long way to address the Foundation's earliest objective of job creation and student retention. For example, by having local schooling made available as a high priority in ocean science and other related science studies, there is likely to be a higher proportion of students from the local region either practice more responsible local fishing or leave the region for more advanced science education and earn white-collar salaries but with the likely wherewithal ultimately to be able return, invest locally, vacation and retire back home. This is the pathway followed by Zita Cobb.

Given the deep roots of the local culture, and family ties and place ties that are so characteristic of the people of the Fogo Island and Change Islands region, it seems realistic; that some later-generation well-educated islanders would follow in the footsteps of Zita Cobb and maintain regular connections with home. Scholarship support from the Foundation for the best of local science students would certainly address the early Shorefast concern of the need for job creation to benefit the local community. The ocean science and science education priority would likely result in both blue collar and white collar job creation for an important proportion of the region's graduates, some of whom might remain as working residents and some might have the ties and income to maintain varying degrees of alumni linkages with home.

Fogo Island Dialogues

These regular periodic soundings are important for bringing into the on-going Fogo Island rural development experiment fresh ideas from outside the islands region. This will ensure that continuous feedback stimulates a stream of innovation and to provide opportunities to re-consider and possibly update earlier decisions. Such dialogues should continue to be held at international and Canadian venues and in Newfoundland, including in the Fogo Island and Change Islands region. The Shorefast leadership has expressed interest in expanding the Dialogues to include economists into the mix of participants in the future along with various other fields of expertise.

Further, the global arts scene needs to be heard, not only in Western Europe and North America, but also from the worlds other principal culture regions. So that affluent geotourists and art consumers from the most likely high-demand market regions of the global economy become aware of Fogo Island's unique assets, key locations in the Asia-Pacific region should be cycled occasionally into the Dialogues scheduling. This is important not only for marketing and spreading the word about the unique cultural and natural assets of the Fogo Island region, but also for calling attention to the global need for responsible and intelligent use of ocean resources, and to cultivate investment partnerships among individuals, institutions and corporations from such major seafood consuming populations, maritime economies, and environmental and ocean science leaders as Japan, South Korea, China, Taiwan, Singapore, Australia, New Zealand and Russia.

Economic Development

Even though the actual accomplishments of the Shorefast Foundation-led economic resuscitation of the Fogo Island region currently is in what one might label "an early adult life-cycle stage," it may be concluded that various business development indicators already are promising. The Arts programming and the Business Assistance Fund have been established and underway several years before the more recent opening of the anchor program of the Fogo Island Inn. With the Inn having completed only its first year of operation, at some point, it needs to demonstrate the ability to generate sustainable surpluses for re-investment. Such revenue generation capacity needs to be demonstrated not only annually, but also during each year's seven seasons (See Appendix 5), which of course, includes the highly challenging winter months.

The major next-stage programming is the New Ocean Ethic, ocean awareness and ocean literacy center initiatives. These then are the four principal development programs or the substantive drivers of the goal to revive and diversify the island region's economy; i.e. (1) Fogo Island Arts Program, (2) Business Assistance Program, (3) Fogo Island Inn and (4) the New Ocean Ethic programming. These recent Shorefast Foundation and community development efforts are intended to build on top of the historic economic base of the fishery. In future, as the ocean initiatives are more underway and produce their planned results, then there should continue to be on-going enhancements and modernization of the fishery's business processes, practices, marketing and profitability.

Critical to meeting the goals of the principal development programs should be several operational and program-support activities by the Shorefast Foundation. The marketing and business development activities in support of filling the guest rooms of the Fogo Island Inn are essential. The success of the overall development strategy is dependent on the Inn being able to produce surpluses for the community to invest. The challenge of marketing to well-to-do geotourists globally and attracting them to the remote Fogo Island Inn in sufficient numbers is the primary means for driving the multiple programs of the Fogo Island development strategy. It is imperative that this challenge be met.

An additional crucial program-support function is the realization of productive investment partnerships with donors; these include persons and institutions of wealth, corporations and the further leveraging of governmental expenditures. During the early stage development period, the Shorefast Foundation already has produced significant private investment partnering – especially in support of the Business Assistance Fund and its initial infrastructure. This strong performance to date is buttressed further by generating impressive return-on-investment numbers for the government investments. Through various levels of taxation $12 million has been recovered. "It is estimated that the total return to governments (on their $16 million contribution) will grow to $27 million over the next five years" (Hodgins, August 8, 2013).

An effective investment partnership and fund raising program is needed to fully develop the Foundation's ocean programming. Among the various ocean activities noted above, a center for ocean awareness and ocean literacy will require sufficient funding to construct an ocean education and research facility. It should serve the public both local adults and youth, and it also should serve visitors to the island from away. Such infrastructure is needed in order to establish and develop its globally strategic niche function of establishing and advocating a New Ocean Ethic for responsible use of the ocean's resources. So that such a Fogo Island Ocean Ethic Center can take advantage of, and complement the world's other ocean and maritime science and education centers, a digital network connecting to those other global centers would seem to be an essential fund-raising target so as to be a contemporary transmitter and receiver of new ocean knowledge.

Both the Fogo Island Inn marketing challenge and the fund-raising investment partnership development needs are most likely to be successful if these two strategic tasks are supported by a systematic and regular sensing of the global environment and marketplace. As a consequence, the Fogo Island Dialogues should be maintained and the feedback that is collected from them should have particular attention paid to the changing demand factors of affluent geotourists, to the contemporary global art market and to shifting forces in ocean science-based utilization of ocean resources and assets. Recently, Zita Cobb reiterated her core business strategy: "If Fogo Island is going to survive, we have to remain relevant. We have to be woven into the fabric of the world, but on our own terms" (Donaldson, n.d.).

It is critical therefore to ensure that the on-going production and on-going profitability improvement of the base economy of the fishery and the more recent thrusts for the diversification of the local economy be fresh and continuously brought to bear on the ways and means of the region. It is critical that the principal internal traditional economic driver of the fishery and the new Shorefast Foundation stimulated economic drivers are responding profitably to the external global consumer demands for the Fogo Island and Change Islands region's commodities, goods and services. This exporting strategy is at the heart of the success of the islands' Model for Rural Development. For those interested in learning from by the Fogo Island Model, they also should practice these principles of effective open systems planning and implementation (Wilson, Kellerman and Corey, 2013: 224-225; 247-249).

Another cluster of challenges that needs to be faced and met is to continue to ensure that local demands and interests also are routinely built into the on-going practice of the local development model. Maintaining a healthy balance between the external environment and the internal local environment raises yet another set of challenges that require attention and sensing for the Fogo Island Rural Development Model to be successful and thereby serve as a useful guide for development elsewhere. Opportunities for feedback from local stakeholders need to be routinized and the resulting feedback factored into the refinement and perfection of existing programming such as the Artists-in-Residence program and related activities and the Business Assistance Fund's operations and process improvements. The Foundation's Jonathan

Briggs has observed, "areas of business training and market development are where Shorefast could add much value to accelerate the process" locally (Briggs, June 25, 2013). He has stated further:

> Due to the (present) strong seasonality of visitors, new businesses (with a physical product) on Fogo Island & Change Islands have the most chance of success if they also develop, in parallel, off-Island markets. However reliable and fast access to the Internet has only come to Fogo Island & Change Islands recently (some communities still do not have it) and is still a relatively new and hence unfamiliar business tool. This lack of market knowledge and access is a 400 year old problem.

> Future economic development themes and actions include: (1) directing energy at empowering youth and businesses with knowledge is essential; (2) finding new ways to translate that knowledge into meaningful jobs in the Fishery or geotourism, or new sectors, on Fogo Island and Change Islands is essential; (3) the Fogo Island Arts Dialogues which are stimulating conversations in many areas (Shorefast Foundation (2013 and 2014); and (4) with the New Ocean Ethic the Shorefast Foundation is providing a platform for conversation about oceans and the fishery.

Over time, and especially as particular economic sectors and localities prosper the Fogo Islands region may begin to realize a more diverse and sustainable economy, then the internal requirements for doing business and for living will need to be considered for additional development attention. For example, the infrastructural needs of clean water, seasonally responsive and reliable ferry service, upgrading of the airstrip and high-speed broadband access for every enterprise and household should be prioritized for local investment. By working on both internal and external development priorities that address the strategic economic production fundamentals, and the local consumption and quality of life issues should be coordinated so that a working balance is achieved that is informed, responsible, equitable and sustainable. Such ultimate end-states will make the Fogo Island Model for Rural Development one that is compelling for developers elsewhere to consider for their own place-specific customization and emulation.

Social Entrepreneurship

INSEAD is one of the world's most highly reputed and largest graduate business schools. It is headquartered in Fontainebleau, France. INSEAD scholar Filipe Santos has defined social entrepreneurship as:

> The process of pursuing sustainable and innovative solutions to neglected problems in society. Social entrepreneurs can adopt for-profit models and create new ventures or work within existing organizations. What distinguishes social entrepreneurship from

commercial entrepreneurship is that the goal of value creation is more important than the goal of value capture. This allows social entrepreneurs to tackle difficult issues, where markets have failed, and adopt open business models based on empowerment (Business Education, May 6, 2013: 9).

As a consequence of such a goal, the programs and projects supported by the Shorefast Foundation may be seen as intending to challenge notions of value; what has value in this context – in particular, it is to highlight the intrinsic value of place and the development potential that is created when community-owned value-added assets empower the local economy.

A significant outcome of the Shorefast work and the emerging model is the concept of the social business. This is an emerging field:

> Where for-profit economic activity directly contributes to positive social outcomes typically served by the non-profit community. [The] Shorefast Foundation is a leader in this emerging space, creating not-just-for-profit businesses that maximize return on sacred capital (natural, social, cultural) alongside economic capital. The goal is to create a next generation economy of strong resilient communities – a global network of deeply local places (Shorefast Foundation, Shorefast Controller Position, July 31, 2014).

Shorefast is using business minded ways to serve social ends. (Refer to Figure 37 Social Enterprise). The Foundation's modeling aspirations and practices seek therefore to showcase the power of the specific to inform the universal. At its deepest level, the often publically stated ambition of the Shorefast activities in the Fogo Island and Change Islands region is to become a model for other rural places; that is, for how they too might reflect, plan, act and flourish.

The thoughtful and creative rural development strategizing and leadership by Zita Cobb and the Shorefast Foundation is a work in progress. This work will not be completed any time soon. The timeframe and life-cycle for realizing the vision elaborated above must be measured in decades and generations. Indeed, if the seeding of transformative change that currently is underway in the Fogo Island and Change Islands region continues its promising trajectory and flowers further, there never will be a "completion" to the work that the Shorefast Foundation's leadership and inspiration have set in motion.

Back in the spring of 2012, when we first saw several of the visually iconic artist studios and the then partially completed structure of the Fogo Island Inn all perched dramatically over the gale-force wind-roiled waters of the North Atlantic Ocean we asked ourselves "what does this effort mean?" We now have a much better handle on some of the many answers to that question. The effort to date already has meant that for the nearly 2,800 or so residents of the Fogo Island and Change Islands region, there now is hope for the future, where just a few years ago there was little or none. The effort indeed also has meant that a glimmer of the possible is on the horizon for students and practitioners of rural development elsewhere. Even in these early-stages of the creation of the Fogo Island Model for Rural Development, it has been demonstrated that thoughtful, experimental innovative strategizing and partnering among various stakeholders can generate priorities sufficient to attract multiple and significant financial investments – even in a remote and isolated small place "on the edge of the earth."

Given the initial accomplishments of the Fogo Island experiment, there is such high potential and promise embedded in the imaginative, holistic and ecosystems regional development work being done there, that we conclude that the provincial and federal governments and other societal and philanthropic investors would do well to consider using the Fogo Island and Change Islands region as a test-bed for further experiments in private and public collaboration and partnering for development. The work there to date has served as a creative and fresh early-stage pilot effort.

This start-up momentum might well be used to demonstrate more systematically that social entrepreneurship can be a basis for having a tested proof-of-concept case for pulling together and aligning the best functions and purposes: (1) of a value-creating enterprise that empowers local society; (2) of the relevant governments to align and target their development priorities and investment allocations in ways that exemplify responsiveness to new needs and demands of local society; and (3) of the regional citizenry living up to its responsibilities to govern and be governed in an informed proactive manner that is intended to be self-deterministic, equitable and in the best interests of future generations. Such an extension of experimental practice should lead, among other experiments, to fundamental assessments of regulatory and licensing affairs in fisheries, food sales, processing and inspection, transportation infrastructure, logistics and supply chains, and natural resources utilization and environmental protection sectors, among other societal assessments that are needed to be more responsive to the new dynamics and differentials brought about by technological and globalization relationships with local places. We believe that the initial case has been made in Fogo Island for modeling much of this intelligent development behavior. It would be a pity not to reinforce and more fully capture and invest in the modeling advantage that has been initially established in the Fogo Island and Change Islands region.

The individual leadership and resource mobilization talents of Zita Cobb and her Shorefast Team have been instrumental in enabling the Shorefast Foundation's take-off actions that have set this cycle of erosion (Rosenberg, n.d.) or regional development life-cycle evolution in motion. She has accomplished this by marshalling her business experience and lessons from a world view that that has been formed from a pragmatic blending of local life struggles and global-scaled observations of corporate behaviors that took from the vulnerable and greedily extracted the natural and intellectual resources of those susceptible and powerless and returned little. This coming together of realizations forged a philosophy of commitment and determination to test the belief that "we the people," even rural people, might in turn resurrect a fresh approach for the future of a special place and culture deemed to be worth the effort.

Such a belief was possible because it seemed feasible that the forces and potentials of the new global economy and new globalized informational capabilities offered new options for local development, while at the same time preserving some of the best of a rich culture and heritage that might bring benefit and satisfaction to locals and visitors alike. This effort also has demonstrated the criticality of leadership, learning from doing, maintaining focus and tenacity in quest of a resilient, but coherent core vision and having the organizational and management ability to strategize and operationalize for success.

Now It Is Up To You

Can these elements and processes be modeled elsewhere by others? That is the challenge that has been laid down by the Shorefast Foundation's example, along with complementary exemplars of selected individuals and the people and supporters of the Fogo Island development vision. If the reader has been inspired from the still-evolving development model of Fogo Island to join with their near neighbors to mobilize the energies and efforts of their own rural region elsewhere so as to be able to make a good run at revitalizing another place, then the hope of Zita Cobb and her Foundation team for producing a model for rural development in today's new world will have been realized. Are you interested in helping meet that challenge?

In seeking to practice intelligent development – that is the utilization of theory and concept to inform and stimulate solutions to local empirical needs and aspirations – it greatly aids the strategy and planning process to have both actual examples and conceptual frameworks feeding off and reinforcing each other. This monograph has sought to provide the reader with both the empirical and the conceptual.

Throughout the preceding narrative on the development of Fogo Island's model, there have been explicit reference to and implicit use of concepts, theories, methods and techniques as they were being used in the regional development work being executed in the Fogo Island and Change Islands region. Some of these have included: economic base theory; relational theory; the use of tradition as a development pathway; community capital as a framework for sustainable development; learning organizations and systems management; benchmarking; best practice and good practice; open systems planning; force-field analysis; the program planning model; economies of scale; economic spill-overs and spin-offs; and among other notions, life-cycle or cycle of erosion concepts.

To answer the question posed above, if you are interested in taking up the challenge of using the Fogo Island Model for Rural Development in your own region, then we have offered here a pathway toward addressing the opportunity inherent in the Fogo Island example. Since your region is different in its specifics, you now may model and customize your development approach and processes in part to the thinking and logic that was explicated here for Fogo Island. Conceptually you may consult other more generic sources that complement and support specific empirical analyses and action planning by reviewing and practicing the recommended actions that are outlined in chapters 11 through 13 of *The Global Information Society: Technology, Knowledge and Mobility* (Wilson, Kellerman, and Corey, 2013). This two-fold blended empirical and conceptual follow-on pathway in intelligent development is intended to aid in your modeling process, or in the translation of more universal ideas to the enhancement of the particularities of a concrete place in time. By mobilizing the awareness and imaginations of neighbors and other local stakeholders where you live and work, you too may be able to emulate for your own place a development effort that puts your rural and small town community on a path toward renewal by means of improved prosperity and quality of life. Also, refer to Corey, Wilson and Fan (2015) for using a self-designed pedagogic approach to local regional development.

Remember that the development model that is being constructed by the Shorefast Foundation, with the leadership of the Shorefast Foundation, and the participation and support of Fogo Island's residents and business persons has been grounded in the aspirations of self-determination and community control of its assets, thereby earning some command over its future. Consequently, be guided not only by the effectiveness of the model's attention to the specificity of local asset valuation, but importantly also by the progressive values that are embedded in the execution of social entrepreneurship (Business Education, May 6, 2013).

Shorefast Foundation President Zita Cobb has drawn on and recommends the advice of distinguished systems theorist, designer, inventor and futurist Buckminster Fuller when he stated: "You never change things by fighting the existing reality. To change something, build a new model that makes the existing model obsolete." Finally, to actualize the Fogo Island Model for Rural Development in your region, Zita Cobb has advised:

> As we rise to the urgency of building new operating models that bring a better balance between money and wellbeing, we need to be respectful of and give a strong voice to all of our human ways of knowing. We know things from our schooling of course but we mustn't lose sight of what we know culturally, what we know through artistic processes and of course through our ecological intelligence. Even though most of us are urban people now, there are still those remaining rural people who live deeply entangled with the natural world, who know things the rest of us don't know ... we must seek them out, listen to them and help them hold on to their ways of knowing ... for all of our sakes (Cobb, November 9, 2013).

Part IX

Concluding Comments:
A Model of Informed Actionable Rural Intelligent Development

☙

The preceding narrative has been guided by Shorefast Foundation's Zita Cobb's admonition that a place has inherent value and revealing its development assets is at the heart of rural revival. To be informed by the Fogo Island Model of Rural Development therefore others need to reveal the core assets of their locality and its region; further, the additional new assets and/or new impetus that represent what is needed to rejuvenate the local economy also must be identified. In the Fogo Island case, to date, that has meant principally the layering of four programmatic new initiatives on the fishery, i.e., the base economy of the Fogo Island region, plus the diversifying programs of: (1) the Fogo Island Arts; (2) the Business Assistance Fund; (3) the Fogo Island Inn; and the New Ocean Ethic.

We have derived two major findings from our own prior development work. First, stakeholders in development learn best how to plan and implement development when that have before them examples of what others elsewhere have done in similar development situations. Second, from our experience in working with rural region stakeholders imported ideas and models from elsewhere only seem to have the power of informing and stimulating effective action and imagination when the outside models are presented in sufficient specificity to enable the stakeholder learner to get inside the "black box" of the model's regional development work that has been done by others. Then, with sufficient commitment, tenacious dedication to the development task locally and emboldened by imagination and strategic courage is there a likelihood of a development model from outside becoming, with localized shaping, imprinted in a different place. That said, such an overall adoption process begins at the origin location of the modeling effort; in this case that is in the Fogo Island and the Change Islands region. Consequently, in crafting this monograph, we have been guided by the self-imposed mandate that detail is needed. So, in order here to operationalize a potentially useful model of rural regional development we have sought to take the reader deep into the strategic and tactical planning processes, the planning organization's culture, the execution of the planned programs and the reasons that particular approaches were selected to produce specific intended results.

By walking a mile in the shoes of the Shorefast Foundation team and the Fogo Island residents and business persons our aim has been to enable regional development practitioners elsewhere, both professionals and volunteers, to be stimulated and inspired to experiment with their own innovative locally tailored approaches in effective planned development for their home place. Would-be local professional and volunteer development planners and practitioners are advised to attend to essential elements of modeling.

Armed with the Fogo Island region's development details and with the motivation of having learned that other rural and small town stakeholders are working with some hope and reinforcement to turn around their local economy, we remind ourselves that effective modeling requires simplicity and this framing of model development that aids in keeping the task simple requires: (1) transparency; (2) the model must be understandable; and (3) it must inform action (Lee, Jr., 1973). With these traits in place, broad-based ownership among a region's principal development stakeholders in the evolving model is likely to be realized (Lachapell, 2008). Such ownership, of course, is imperative if an adopted model is to be effective elsewhere. How have these elements of modeling played out on the Fogo Island stage?

Transparency

Looking beyond the current action programs, an important coming activity for the Shorefast Foundation and the Fogo Island and Change Islands communities should be to design and implement a transparent monitoring and evaluation system. This is critical on several levels. For example, revenue surpluses after expenses are paid by the Fogo Island Inn go to the community for its use. Community ownership is likely to strengthen further as the financial performance is regularly shared. Such openness, combined with awareness of the profit and loss particulars may have the effect of generating suggestions for improvements and even deeper engagement in the entire islands' revitalization enterprise. Community accounting should occur in particular once sufficient maturation of the various programs has been attained. But preparing during the run up to that point is essential. Having a hand in early discussion of some of the metrics to be used in the assessment system design is an additional impetus for even greater community ownership. The Shorefast Foundation and the Community has begun these preparations for having transparency.

Surplus Allocation

It is anticipated that the Fogo Island Inn will begin to turn a net surplus from operations during calendar 2016 (in its third fiscal year of operation). Surpluses will be allocated to the Shorefast Foundation, sole beneficiary of the Business Trust which holds operations of the Inn. Presently two means for this allocation are under development taking into account the Shorefast Foundation's Board mandate of stewardship over these surplus funds. At the time of this writing these are the proposed means; they include:

- Direct Contribution to Economic Development fund with the Town of Fogo Island (For background refer to Town of Fogo Island, Home Page, n.d.).

- Interest in developing a cooperative relationship with the Town in pursuing economic development activities. Discussions are continuing towards an agreement with the Town

- Shorefast initiatives are only part of the overall island momentum – Town is central in managing many others

- Discussion in works on how economic engines of Shorefast can make direct contribution to Town led initiatives

- Plan is to create a Business Development Fund, led by community oversight committee created to give direction and oversee spending

- Will have at least one Shorefast Board representation on oversight committee

- Percentage of Inn surpluses would be allocated to this Fund directly (via Shorefast)

- Execution of the activities of the fund would be managed by the Town, likely through business development officer (Town employee)

- Community Advisory Committee (reporting to the Business Trust)

- Plan to establish Business Advisory Committee to provide insight into opportunity for business cooperation and provide comment on surplus contributions

- Committee will be made up of a variety of community members with representation from each Island community

- Hoping to generate participation from each of Town, Fisherman's Co-op, community hospital, community school, youth representative, etc. so as to obtain broad scope for input and consideration

- Committee would report to the Trust board quarterly on potential projects

- Depending on nature of project, would bring in other partners that are a good match to provide additional funding / operational support for initiatives (Other business owners, Town, province, Federal funding partners).

For many generations, Fogo Island working fishers and the working members of fishers' families experienced having their own surpluses flow out of the locality and the region. Too often these resources flowed to distant fish merchants as was discussed earlier in this monograph. Simply, they had little effective autonomy or control over their earnings. If nowadays the Fogo Island Inn is able to generate income for the community, one can expect the descendants of the earlier-fisher ancestors to make collective investment decisions for the community's benefit that keeps the value-added in the region. At long last they will be able to have the autonomy to control the locally generated resources for the locality. This and the early-stage accomplishments of the Shorefast Foundation-led development programs should be imbuing the ordinary people of the Fogo Island and Change Islands region with added confidence and increased hope for the future.

Preliminary Metrics for the Fogo Island Model for Rural Development

It is premature, at this early stage in the life cycle of the model building process, to judge the "success" of the entire range of programs being executed by the Shorefast Foundation and its various community stakeholders. To reiterate, some of these local stakeholders include: the Town of Fogo Island; the Fogo Island Co-operative Society Ltd; recipients of loans from the Shorefast Business Assistance Fund, the provincial government, the federal government and so on. Still, we asked the Foundation's leadership to share with us, for the readers of this monograph: (1) the kinds of metrics or indicators that are being considered initially for measuring and monitoring the status of on-going programs implementation, and (2) the respective results and outcomes even at this youthful stage in the life-cycle of the experimental and modeling process. These are some of the preliminary metrics being considered:

- Number of jobs created in Shorefast projects
- Island population growth
- School enrolment (young families in the community)
- Number of residents returning for employment
- Sales of cod pot cod
- Business Assistance Fund: New applicants, successful repayments and new business startups on Fogo Island
- Quality of International partnerships developed with other organizations (art, community development, geotourism)
- Shorefast donations & program support plus residency sponsorship (Fogo Island Arts, Geology at the Edge)
- Number of tourists visiting Fogo Island

A perennial problem in less developed economies is lack of information (Acemoglu and Zilibotti, 1999). We see that situation here. The information that can be reported, by necessity, is generally nominally scaled, rather than quantitative in nature (Hodge, 1963). These are the simplest forms of measurement; nominal measurement permits classification and conceptualizing one topic from another; thus, it nominally is a measurement. Therefore, most of our comments on these metrics and their respective outcomes must be limited to qualitative descriptions. Over time, with maturation in the work that makes up the current Fogo Island development experiment, it will be important to generate quantitative numerical information that enables arithmetic operations and statistical analysis – in addition to qualitative analysis. Now, we turn to the results information that we have for the metrics list above.

Jobs: there are about 85-100 employees on the payrolls, i.e., principally those who work at the Inn and for the Foundation. There are other modest numbers of irregular workers who are part time or on-call, for example to do housekeeping or tour guests around the island as part of the Community Host program and so on.

Island Population Growth: the intended objective here is, over time, to record some increase, particularly of former residents returning in recognition that the local economy is perceived to be on the up-tick. A long-term target of 5,000 people as been mentioned from time to time.

School enrollment: in parallel and interdependence with the population growth metric, the objective here is an increase; especially of young families with school-age children.

Number of Residents Returning for Employment: basically, this is the same overall measurement intention as the population and school enrollment metrics.

Sales of Cod Pot Cod: This metric of cod pot sales suggests that more of the islands' clean tasting cod is being caught in the cod traps that are indicative of wider use of these more natural resources conserving technologies, the cod-catch of which commands higher price points than conventional net-caught cod. Last year about 8,800 pounds of cod pot cod went into the market to selected and targeted business consumers (Hodgins, August 21, 2014), including the Fogo Island Inn's fine-dining restaurant, Nicole's Café also located in Joe Batt's Arm and Bacalao Restaurant, among several other restaurants in the St. John's area (CBC News, August 14, 2014). The Shorefast Foundation saw the potential for the experimental method for catching cod with new cod pots that were developed by the Marine Institute in 2007 (See Figures 45 and 46 of the new green netted cod pots). The design does not damage the floor of the ocean; and currently fishermen using the cod pot "were receiving two-and-a-half times as much for their cod as the regular fisheries." At a cost of about $1,000 each, the Foundation purchased 75 to ensure over time that they would get "in the water" (McClelland, June 2014: 2). We asked Shorefast Foundation Chair and Ocean Adviser for an update on this metric; he reported:

> Five fishers [are] using Cod Pots. We have a total of 65 cod pots, 10 were loaned to the Marine Institute two years ago to test their use in other parts of the province and they still have them. The 65 pots we now have [are] sufficient to supply cod to the restaurants we are selling to. Our plan is to build another 100 pots when we find the financial resources and have another 10 fishers involved. Ten pots per fisherman is fine for the three week cod fishery on Fogo Island. When the Government of Canada lifts the moratorium on Northern cod then more pots will be required per fisher (Slade, August 27, 2014).

Business Assistance Fund -- New applicants, successful repayments and new business startups on Fogo Island: All the metrics and their results are combined in the narrative here and excerpted from the Foundation's Chief Financial Officer Gary Duffy in an e-mail to us.

> To date, the Fund has advanced a total of $340,592 in startup support for small businesses on Fogo and Change Islands. The average size of loan disbursed is $26,199. A total of two businesses receiving funding have not succeeded, and ceased operations. All of the remaining businesses continue to operate as of March 31, 2014. Three of the new enterprises have fully repaid their loans. Excluding the two failed entities, four are meeting their repayment terms and the remaining four continue to operate, but are in arrears on their loan repayments (Duffy, August 27, 2014).

Whether a business has been assisted by the Business Assistance Fund program or not, some of the firms in general that serve visitors seem to be doing well. The increase in tourist visits seems to be uplifting a number of businesses on the island. One hears good things about the boat excursions offered aboard the motor vessel Ketanja which, for example, was part of the "Fishing for Cod" package that was marketed through the Fogo Island Inn during two periods in July-August and September of 2014 (Refer to Figures 47 and 48 and view two photos of the Ketanja motor vessel with icebergs nearby). We visited the Hart House Museum last year and were charmed by the experience. Other good stories are heard about the nature hikes taken by guests of the Inn, and the addition of an outside seating area/deck seems to have benefitted the bakery/café. But, word of mouth buzz is nice; for the near-term future, measureable information needs to be collected routinely, thereby enabling business process improvement and more effective management. This should be an action item for the discussions upcoming between the Town of Fogo Island, the Shorefast Foundation and with representation from the business community included.

Quality of International partnerships developed with other organizations (art, community development, geotourism): this is a metric that is being worked on as opportunities arise during the implementation of the core programs of the Shorefast Foundation. The objective here is to develop affinity relationships that build on common worldviews and thematic interests. The relationship between the Shorefast Foundation and Simon Fraser University is an example of an early partnership in the presentation of the ocean lecture series. The Fogo Island Dialogues and various fund-raising efforts are ideal opportunities for such networking and partnering initiatives. The many speeches by Zita Cobb also enable the initiation of future partnership development.

Shorefast Donations and program support plus residency sponsorship (Fogo Island Arts, Geology At The Edge): several proposals to foundations have been submitted by Shorefast and are pending. An example of a successful proposal is one that is intended to contribute to building a network of deeply local places.

Number of tourists visiting Fogo Island: in future, these data still need to be collected, compiled and made readily accessible publically. It is principally a task for the Town of Fogo Island and would be a natural topic as the Foundation and the Town continue to engage the issue of how best to decide on the use and allocation of the surplus revenues that are expected from the after-expenses income from the Fogo Island Inn and other enterprises such as the Fogo Island Shop for the sale of furniture and furnishings from the Inn (See Figure 49 for a view of the punt chair). Also, see Kellner (2014) for the latest listing of furniture and other products that are made on the island. In the meantime, we can draw on the latest perceptions of an informed local stakeholder, Alan Cobb, the Secretary and Member of the Board of Directors of the Shorefast Foundation:

> As for the information on the overall tourism picture on Fogo Island, there is a paucity of data. Our anecdotal evidence is that the number of tourists coming to Fogo Island continues to increase quite substantially. We have been told by provincial government officials that the Farewell/Fogo Island ferry service carries the second highest traffic volumes (people and vehicles) of any of its 17-vessel fleet in province (second only to the Bell Island service which provides transport for Bell Islanders commuting daily to/from work in the capital, St. John's). The provincial government added a second ferry to the Farewell/Change Islands/Fogo Island route in order to handle the increased volume of visitors over this summer. The provincial government has launched a ferry improvement initiative with the first new ferry from that procurement program scheduled to enter the Farewell/Fogo Island service in September 2015. The provincial government has already commenced work at the ferry docks to prepare for the arrival of the new vessel next year.
>
> We understand from our municipal officials that there has been a marked increase in the number of visitors to the Island's various museums and that donations at these locations have increased substantially this year. A further piece of anecdotal evidence is that the Artisan Guild retail store is reporting historic high sales to the extent that their inventories are at record lows. And, of course, the Fogo Island Inn is operating at occupancy rates that are exceeding our expectations throughout the June/September [2014] period (Cobb, August 26, 2014).

In the years ahead, as the Fogo Island rural development modeling experiment continues, we expect that these and other measurements will be fine-tuned to take into account the inevitable needed calibrations that get revealed from daily operations. Such metrics and their respective outcomes are important so as to be able to perform mid-course corrections and other essential management functions of the islands' various new development enterprises (Acemoglu and Ziloiboti, 1999).

At the heart of a responsible civic and social business enterprise transparent modeling effort is accountability. A development effort that is seen as inclusive, open and understandable is more likely to engender some needed degree of local trust, and thereby can add to the social capital that is so critical to produce confidence in the priorities and the responsiveness of resource allocations to the community's principal economic demands and social needs. These dynamics also may be seen to have drawn some inspiration from the autonomy and independence of the collective decision making and behavior that formed and were practiced during The Fogo Process of the 1960s. In those days it was reaction to the threat of resettlement that catalyzed Fogo Islanders to organize, to adopt independence of thought and to take collective thoughtful action.

Today and tomorrow, the catalyst is more a function of having both the legacy connection of The Fogo Process to draw on and the added spur of the Shorefast Foundation's community mobilization built around the suite of new programs that arise from, and add value to the islands' specific intrinsic assets. These then are some of the benefits that can be realized from investing in a transparent development model. In the years ahead, it will be important to invest in building a better more measureable information infrastructure. Among other benefits, this will enable more "reliable performance evaluation." Therefore, as a society accumulates more capital, it also accumulates more information, and achieves higher managerial effort and productivity (Acemoglu and Zilibotti, 1999: 34)

Understanding

The mindset to accomplish a working knowledge of the model is to rely on what we have labeled Intelligent Development. By that we mean that along with appropriate empirical analyses, applicable planning theory should be used routinely "in the formulation of policies and the planning of communities for exploiting the potential of a place [within] the context of the global knowledge economy and network society" (Corey and Wilson, 2006: 205-206). It is this "local meets global strategy" that Fogo Island development practitioners have adopted in order to revitalize the islands-region economy. Specific programs have been designed and are being implemented; additionally, they are intended to be complementary and as a result of their interaction and synergy these interventions are expected to be transformative. That is the local economy should be congruent with the external, i.e., the global economy, and thereby seek to be sustainable by means of diversity and resilience.

To review the programs; first, Fogo Island regional stakeholders are seeking to build on and continuously modernize the fishery, i.e., the base economy of the local region, while simultaneously having invested in the Fogo Island Arts Program, the Business Assistance Fund and the opening and operation of the Fogo Island Inn; the Inn is green, small-scale with limited capacity in the number of guests, it is luxurious and it is architecturally bold and attention-grabbing so as to be attractive to wealthy geotourists from the global marketplace. These programmatic initiatives have formed the principal cluster of actions for the early stage of the intended transformative development strategy's life-cycle. The next stage of the development strategy includes expanding the New Ocean Ethic programming, continuing the Fogo Island Dialogues and engaging in on-going process and business improvements, including global marketing and scanning the external environment and among other process improvement initiatives to explore appropriate legal and financial business organizational structures that are enabling and accommodating to the multidimensional ways that the Shorefast Foundation has used to date to get the whole experiment off the ground.

But is it sustainable? Across the above programs and activities, the Shorefast Foundation has organized around a core geotourism-based concept that targets wealthy geotourists in particular. The selection of this cohort of the global marketplace has the benefit of maximizing revenue generation while keeping numbers of such tourists low, thereby minimizing impact on the local environment. This combined with using the principles of green building construction and localization strategy of natural resource use will go a long way toward rendering the Fogo Island Experimental Model for Rural Development to be a sustainable effort.

Inform Action

To be effective, the model should move both local and external stakeholders collectively to invest and direct effort and resources to the accomplishment of the model's goals and objectives. Understanding the reasons and dynamics involved in executing the model is the means; attainment of the goals and objectives are the intended ends of the modeling activity.

Translating the development approaches of others elsewhere so as to inform action on development in one's own region and locality requires a systematic, thoughtful process that is customized sensitively to the particulars of the receiving place. Actionable knowledge is what is needed to fuel and impact decision making and action taking in planful and strategic ways. It helps to initiate, maintain and draw on tested frameworks to organize the empirical complexities of the local and global society and economy.

The authors of this monograph have developed frameworks that were designed and intended to guide and mobilize development stakeholders in places around the world to engage in Intelligent Development or integrated empirical and theory-based planning and decision making. Our 2013 book, *Global Information Society: Technology, Knowledge and Mobility* concludes with an "Intelligent Development Charrette" (a time-intensive workshop event or series of events) that seeks to empower local community stakeholders to initiate and "practice the process of establishing an intelligent development strategy for a local community" (Wilson, Kellerman and Corey, 2013: 235). The predecessor volume, *Urban and Regional Planning: Planning Practice in the Global Knowledge Economy* lays the methodological groundwork for practicing Intelligent Development, especially by means of developing and applying the ALERT Model (Corey and Wilson, 2006). This organizational learning-action construct moves the stakeholders through the planning stages of: Awareness (evidence); Layers (context); E-

Business Spectrum (content and linkages); Responsiveness (to economic demand and social need); and Talk (continuous engagement) (Wilson and Corey, 2008).

Framing these complex dynamics helps to clarify and manage the relationships and diverse connectivities of the local and the global. The key here, that Zita Cobb suggests "is linking to markets directly, so people don't have to go through a merchant or broker and can control their destiny" (Bartlett, 2008: 115). In the Fogo Island context, this is the long-delayed vision that Fogo Islanders can attain the autonomy in their daily living and working that was denied their ancestors from the earliest days of colonial Newfoundland and through to the resettlement period of provincial Newfoundland.

First Principle: Plan for Who and What You Are

In the end, there is one nearly universal principle that should be put into operation when seeking to invent one's own local model for development. Every place and region has its own unique and particular history, mix of individual people, its selective patch of nature and a diverse use and particularized utilization of technology; so, when using these elements together to construct one's own local regional model of development one might well benefit by imitating a first principle of the Shorefast Foundation's model for rural development from Fogo Island. It is:

> the intent is to find ways to take things the people of the islands have always done well and connect the products of those activities with outside markets. ... Imagine then, that you have an economy that is based on who you are. That is absolutely how you preserve culture (Bartlett, 2008: 114-115).

Today, in talking to Fogo Islanders, one senses a spirit of hopefulness there. Seemingly, it derives from the opportunity to join with friends and neighbors to chart a course for tomorrow's development; the spirit draws on the possibilities that are embedded in this principle. Its liberating qualities can confer a high degree of personal satisfaction as well as enabling the community's collective stakeholders to operate with a real sense of self-generated freedom in shaping some part of their collective future. This is what civil society can and should be. It is a healthy reminder for others beyond the Fogo Island and Change Islands region, and Newfoundland that places elsewhere also might pursue intelligent development and derive their own personal and societal satisfactions thereby producing needed community transformations and vitality.

Ordinary Folks: Another First Principle

We end the monograph with the observation that the Shorefast Foundation has practiced – and continued a noteworthy Newfoundland tradition – of what amounts to another first principle. This principle should be explicit and standard operating procedure for development stakeholders of any other region or place that is considering using the Fogo Island Rural Development Model to inspire and guide their own planned development. John Friedmann, distinguished planner and professor of community and regional planning at the University of British Columbia has stated this principle simply, "place-making is everyone's job, local residents as well as official planners" (Friedmann, 2010: 149). The planned development underway in the Fogo Island and Change Islands indeed has followed this principle. "Ordinary folks," as Professor Friedmann calls them, need to be at the regional development planning and decision making table. Ordinary folks include the most vulnerable in any society. Ordinary folks represent the lion's share of economic producers and consumers in every place. Consequently, their social needs and economic demands should to be driving a significant component of new strategic development direction in any place whether rural, small town or urban region.

Particularly today and in tomorrow's complex global information society and global knowledge economy; balanced credible information and knowledge are essential ingredients in serious place-making. Informed decisions need to have public and civic support, especially from research, learning and higher education institutions. In the Fogo Island case such support long has been provided for the region by Memorial University of Newfoundland (MUN and the National Film Board of Canada (NFB). The pioneering Fogo Process of the late 1960s with its participatory media impacts comes to mind (Crocker, 2008). In varying degrees such support has influenced Fogo Island culture for over a two generation period of time. Since early in the turn of the new 21st century, the Shorefast Foundation, along with MUN and NFB again, Fogo Islanders and Change Islanders have benefitted from the information and knowledge services that these institutions have facilitated. Information and knowledge have come from other sources too, but the point here is that effective development requires widespread stakeholder involvement, and participation that has the capacity to sift through complex information and to come out of that process with the ability to make informed decisions and set development priorities that drive resource allocations for the benefit of the whole of the region – as well as for some special interests, such as the most vulnerable in society and for social businesses. These businesses that generate revenues and serve social ends are particularly valuable to rural places and regions.

Role Models: From the Ordinary to the Extraordinary

Given the enduring and inventive nature of the nearly 500 years of human behavior and settlement in Newfoundland and the Fogo Island region, today one may identify a certain local spirit of independence, interdependence and courage that has produced a resilient and tenacious people and individuals some of whom are positioned to engage contemporary rural development opportunities and challenges. Some of the named individuals mentioned here in this monograph are exemplars and models in their own right with the kinds of mindset, behavior and commitments that are required to demonstrate for others how rural revival may be achieved. Such Newfoundland-grown indigenous values and mindsets have been passed down the generations to produce ordinary folks who have transformed themselves into extraordinary folks. These include, for example this sampling: Harold Williams, Leslie Harris, Gordon Slade, and Zita Cobb, among many other residents of the Fogo Island and Change Islands region and Newfoundland.

Rural and small town Newfoundland has produced native sons and daughters who have succeeded in professional careers and were people-centric throughout their lives. To illustrate a few select exemplars, geologist Harold Williams, was instrumental in advancing the modern science of plate tectonics. He reinterpreted the Appalachian mountain chain using modern plate tectonic theory; this was a significant advancement in geoscience. He has been quoted as saying that in 'making a complex hypothesis accessible to ordinary people,' "He wanted people to understand his work because, he said, 'the truth lies in the rocks.' (Sullivan, October 11, 2010).

Similar to Zita Cobb, Leslie Harris was the child of a fisher. He has been described as "outwardly common and elemental," yet his inward talents and perspectives enabled him to become a "powerhouse" in the development of the province (Slade, September 17, 2008: 2). He was an outport school teacher; a student of history, both of Newfoundland and as a London-educated scholar on South Asia; he served thereafter as a professor and university leader who ultimately became President of the Memorial University of Newfoundland. His work and dedication to scholarship and public service, e.g., he served as Head, Review Panel on the Northern Cod Stocks, empowered him to advance the various communities of which he was a member; these roles and service earned him much recognition and many awards (Refer to Northern Cod Review Panel, and Leslie Harris, 1990). After his death in 2008, the University's regional policy center was named The Leslie Harris Centre of Regional Policy and Development. Because he articulated "how the 500 years of living by and from the sea had created a unique cultural identity for the province, Dr. Harris' essay on "The Outport Phenomenon" "is something every Newfoundlander and Labradorean should read" (Slade, September 17, 2008: 2).

Readers elsewhere interested in deriving development lessons from the Shorefast Foundation Rural Development Model also will want to consult this essay on outports by Leslie Harris. Gordon Slade is the Chair and Ocean Advisor of the Shorefast Foundation. For a biographical sketch, refer to Shorefast Foundation, Board of Directors, n.d. Earlier in the monograph his seminal work in the resurrection and preservation of the historical settlement of Battle Harbour, Labrador was outlined. He is noted here again as we conclude this monograph because, for us, he exemplifies the profile of today's "ordinary person" whose civic and environmental passions have compelled him to become an extraordinary person too. In particular, he has worked at the seam of the local and the extra-local, including at the global. As a Newfoundlander, he has invested his energies over the decades to community development enhancements through the province and Atlantic Canada. And today somehow he further has made time and effort for contributing to an additional concern at the international level, the Arctic. He is active in the development of a new Canada-Norway dialogue, the Arctic Forum. Thus, this ordinary and extraordinary person brings a lifetime and career of wisdom to the Shorefast Foundation's debates; his participation there not only advances the Foundation's ocean programming, critically also his presence ensures that the local and the global are front and center on Shorefast's continuous rural development agenda.

Lastly, Zita Cobb. Since her vision, experience and loyalty to place have permeated the entire monograph we will give her only brief note here. But she must be included now to remind the reader, that while she too is an ordinary person cum extraordinary person, especially in her exemplary leadership role of team actualizer, indeed as Foundation President she also must perform the lead actor role in Shorefast's drama of reviving the rural Fogo Island region. She has a profound commitment to the centrality of the team and the collective effort of the full cast of characters in place building; so, in respect of her preferred member-of-the-team role, we will here conclude further reference to her individual talents and accomplishments.

A Reminder for Would-Be Users of the Fogo Island Model: Place-Making is Everyone's Job

John Friedmann, is one the most distinguished, respected and thoughtful scholars and commentators in the field of regional development planning. He draws on a lifetime of development experience throughout the world. His wisdom, especially for us here, comes from having honed an insightful and equitable global perspective. His attention to the position and role played in societies around the globe by ordinary people compels him to call for people-centered planning (Friedmann, June 2010). His advocacy makes a strong case for having local "ordinary folks" at the globalized policy-making and priority-setting table – along with official planners, elected officials of all levels of government, business persons and investors and other establishment stakeholders. Otherwise, local residents, would-be small business people and other vulnerable members of societies, such as children and elders run the risk of being resettled, displaced and or have their fragile social infrastructure marginalized. We believe that his concerns are valid not only for cities; but they are also legitimate concerns for small town and rural places.

Finally, for us, this narrative has come full circle. We began this monograph by acknowledging the support and facilitation of Michigan State University, especially MSU Libraries; the MSU School of Planning, Design and Construction; the MSU Department of Geography and the MSU Center for Community and Economic Development. Without the commitment of MSU and these MSU units to execute the Land-Grant mission of knowledge generation and knowledge utilization for ordinary people we would not have been encouraged and supported in the research, production, distribution and accessibility of this monograph. In turn, this research has informed, been derived from and has enriched our teaching and public service work. Without providing such scholarly services to ordinary folks, as we have seen in this case from Newfoundland and Labrador, and Michigan, the democratic processes of Canada and the United States would be poorer. Such services merit on-going community and public support today and for future generations so as to have and ensure an active and intelligent civil society that is prosperous, healthy, just, happy and sustainable.

Our Final Comments on the Model's Roots and a Vision for Its Future

A Model for Rural Development: An Experiment from Fogo Island, Newfoundland

Several generations from now, it will be known whether or not the Fogo Island rural development experiment has served its ultimate goal of being a good practice or best practice benchmark or model for rural development around the world (Vettoretto, 2009). In the meantime a useful start will have been made toward that goal. The overall preliminary analysis here suggests that it is a case with promise that merits on-going monitoring into the future for those with practical and intellectual stakes in innovation and thoughtful experiments in rural region revival. This detailed early-stage assessment has documented planned strategic processes and detailed operational development content that are sufficiently lesson rich even at today's early phase to be able to influence and stimulate analogous innovative development thinking and doing elsewhere.

As we near the end of the monograph, it is useful to provide a *working definition of the Fogo Island Model for Rural Development.* Particularly, what is its composition and what are its distinctive characteristics? This is our distillation:

> Unlike many other rural and small community development strategies, the Fogo Island Model explicitly embraces the development possibilities of the external world, i.e., beyond the islands region. In order to revive, diversify and have a sustainable local economy, the globalized economy and society are being engaged by means of attracting high-end geotourists to the Fogo Island Inn and its world-class level of dining and hospitality. The Inn's role is to be an additional economic engine for Fogo Island and the

Change Islands region. The presence of these geotourists are expected to stimulate spillover effects into the local legacy fisheries-based economy; to nurture business start-ups, expansions, profitability, job formation and the production of quality services and products for visitors, especially as these economic outcomes complement and advance ecotourism, local culture preservation-celebration and the responsible utilization of natural resources resulting in sustainable environments. These business development intentions are supported by the micro-financing and assistance provided by the Business Assistance Fund.

In order to instill into the local mindset and behavior a contemporary culture of continuous innovation, both from scratch and from old ways to inventing new things, art, architecture, design and artists from away play an overt role by doing and demonstrating original creativity production. Thereby, innovation and imaginative thinking are at the tables of the island's everyday living and working and are being infused into the routine behavior of the region's ordinary people. These initiatives, when fully producing, represent a kind of hinge between the external global economy and the internal local economic base of the fishery complemented by the early, largely commercial small business revival that is underway.

The approach of the Model's leadership is open, participatory and based on teamwork and partnering with the communities of the islands and beyond. The organizational culture underpinning the Model's respective enterprises may be framed as social entrepreneurship, distinguished by value creation and stakeholder empowerment that results in the promotion of social business wherein for-profit economic activity directly contributes to positive social outcomes. The Model is initiated and executed by the region's neighbors, relations and friends and institutions, both local and from away. The new key stimulant and organizational frame for this development work is the Shorefast Foundation, a federally registered Canadian charity. The team-driven leadership of the Foundation intends to share this experimental Model with others elsewhere.

This then is a condensation of the many details that have been explicated throughout the monograph. In framing this distilled statement of the Model, we have sought to capture the essentials of the still youthful Fogo Island Model for Rural Development. Even as the experiment continues to evolve through its life cycle, we believe that it is not too early to envision how the Model should be shared.

We did derive additional learnings. We have compiled them in an appendix for your consideration. These various and diverse components include: more discussion of islands; the interface of the local and the global; use your own pre-conditions; organize your own human capital; and rural and urban – each can teach the other. See Appendix 7, Some More Principal Components of the Fogo Island Model for Rural Development.

Activating the Model Elsewhere: From Pilot to Demonstration to Worldwide Implementation

A distinguishing characteristic that we propose is that the Shorefast Foundation strategize and plan for taking the action needed to get the Model into the hands of ordinary people elsewhere. The usefulness of the Fogo Island Model can be accelerated by taking a leaf from the original Fogo Process and fund-raise/partner to be positioned to actively extend the Model to rural people and places around the world (Williamson, 1989). How so?

In 1967, there was a convergence of actors who, given their respective roles, came together to create The Fogo Process and later it was actively extended to other parts of the world. Many people deserve acknowledgement for bringing the process to fruition; the lead actors included: National Film Board (NFB) of Canada filmmaker Colin Low; NFB founder John Grierson; Memorial University of Newfoundland (MUN) field officer Fred Earle; and Donald Snowden, then Director of MUN's Extension Department (Newhook, 2009).

> He [Donald Snowden] led a process whereby community members were able to articulate their problems, ideas and vision on films that were later screened to community members at facilitated community discussion forums. Through the films, the people of Fogo Island began to see that each village on the island was experiencing similar problems and became aware of the need for community organization. The films were also used to bring distant politicians face-to-face (or face to screen) with the voices and visions of people they seldom heard. Government policies and actions were changed, the people of Fogo began to organize, and the history of the island changed forever (Editors' Note to Snowden, 1998: 1).

What were the essential factors for the diffusion of the original Fogo Process to influence other places around the world (Williamson, 1989)? And how would these kinds of factors inform adoption elsewhere of today's Fogo Island Model for Rural Development? The answer below is filtered through the lenses of the contemporary world. To illustrate, in a particular rural place and region that would be selected for demonstrating the Fogo Island Model, representative members of the community would be asked to verbalize their "problems, ideas and vision;" these are recorded in audio and modern video by means of inexpensive portable equipment that can be operated by ordinary people. After appropriate editing and post-recording preparation, these recordings would be viewed across the communities of the demonstration place and region, such that ordinary people get to see and to hear each other's issues and comments on what is needed for a better community in today's highly networked and globalized new economy and information society. Common ground and perspectives would be identified; these function as possible community organizing points for collective strategizing and action taking. The recordings then would be shown to and heard by external, often distant, individuals and institutional representatives who make or may make decisions that affect the people and places that are included in the demonstration of the Model.

Today, we would not limit this decision-maker audience to politicians; they would be included, but also included would be various levels of all the pertinent governments and their officials, private sector for-profit representatives, non-profit non-governmental organizational officials, foundations and individuals of wealth and influence and others whose roles in society position them to influence the development of the targeted demonstration region. But what might tip the balance toward adoption of the Fogo Island Model would be active facilitation by trainers, mentors and consultants, initially partly weighted from outside and increasingly over time more from home-grown training, some graduates would be on the ground in the demonstration region. With support from distant trainers the needed learnings would be transmitted via electronic information and communications technologies. Local trainers and facilitators would perform the lion's share of translating lessons into program and project.

As to the on-going evolution and deepening of the Fogo Island Model's life cycle that will continue to be underway, it is reasonable to expect that within the next few years, the current pilot of the Model will have evolved into a more fully illuminated and more routinized operational proof-of-concept that it may be able to be demonstrated and diffused to a limited number of diverse locations globally so as to gain additional new experience and feedback on how the Model plays out in varying situations, including at different levels of development, in different political-economies and within diverse and heterogeneous cultures. Institutional capacity and level of initial local buy-in and receptivity would be critical criteria to be assessed in a careful location selection process. A handful of such thoughtfully selected demonstration and networked test bed locations would be sufficient to be able to calibrate and update the Fogo Island Model based on these respective demonstrations and the comparative and evaluative re-designs that will be necessary to achieve greater generalizability as to the application of the Model. After this demonstration phase, then decisions can be made on the readiness and feasibility of moving toward broader diffusion of the then more thoroughly tested, updated and proactively delivered Model to a wide range of rural areas around the world. Given other development innovations that have diffused globally, e.g., the Grameen Bank (Grameen Bank, n.d.), we envisage time lines of decades for pilot, to demonstration to full implementation of a sharing process for the Model globally.

These generalized diffusion processes noted here are simple illustrations of the kind of scenarios that might be used to effectively and widely activate the Model. But while variations on the best ways to share the Model would have to be fully debated, the critical point here is that a strategy must be developed that proactively and supportively gets the Model diffused and adopted beyond the Fogo Island region with the necessary localized shaping and tailoring to be feasibly implemented elsewhere.

It is one thing to have constructed and piloted a model toward the goal of having realized a proof-of-concept that the model, in its original home test bed "works" in the sense that it addresses and largely meets the local needs and demands of that home place and its region; it is quite another matter to have the model adopted and ultimately be similarly successful elsewhere under different and varying conditions. At minimum, what is required is a robust carefully designed and well-resourced strategy for diffusing the model, i.e., the model adoption innovation, and have it get underway and eventually become imprinted in the demonstration locations.

Even as the early-stage of the Fogo Island Model continues to evolve and develop, some serious consideration should be given to the pre-conditions necessary to be in place for the time, in the not too distant future, when the Model is to actively be diffused elsewhere for demonstration purposes, continuing perfection and locality-specific tailoring. There are plenty of theoretical-methodological and empirical precedents and a vast literature from which to draw lessons and guidance for the next stage of moving from pilot to demonstration. For example, we can provide some initial direction.

Theory and Method

The applied behavior science literature should be consulted. The early program planning and evaluation work of Andre L. Delbecq, Andrew H. Van de Ven and Richard Koenig, Jr. is particularly informative on diffusing and operationalizing a pilot-to-demonstration model innovation (Van de Ven and Koenig, Jr., 1976: 167; Delbecq and Van de Ven, 1976). The classic *Diffusion of Innovations* by Everett M. Rogers provides an early framing of and conceptual/graphic background for the adoption of innovations by relative time and categories of adopters, their personal characteristics and communication behavior (Rogers, 1962: 162 and 185).

To illustrate just a few of the detailed levels of preparation and behaviors that will need to be designed into the transition activities for implementation at demonstration sites for successful diffusion of an innovation such as the Fogo Island Model; just seven factors are outlined here; a thorough search of today's research literature is necessary, and that search would reveal more relevant findings:

(1) the design integrity of the original model needs to be maintained; thus some demonstration locations need "nearness" along with the education and training of the receiving personnel who will be leading the demonstration effort elsewhere.

(2) The greater the diffusion of information about the innovation, i.e., the model, to potential adopters through personal contact between the models' planners and the demonstration location's personnel, the more likely there will be successful transfer of the model elsewhere. Question: nowadays, after some level of face-to-face familiarity has been achieved, can electronic nearness substitute or only complement physical distance?

(3) The pilot Model planners need to supervise and be involved in its diffusion as a demonstration.

(4) The more that there is participation by some actors from the demonstration in the execution of the pilot development, the more likely there will be a successful pilot-to-demonstration transfer.

(5) Similarly, the greater the number of "boundary-spanning roles" between model planners and potential adopters for demonstration, the greater the likelihood of adoption elsewhere;

(6) The closer that the model's inherent core values and norms are to those of the demonstration actors, the better are the chances of adoption.

(7) The greater the perceived prestige of participating in adopting the model, the better the case can be made for the demonstration place and region to activate the model.

There are other such factors that are known to influence the diffusion and adoption of innovations, and they need to be thoroughly researched. Hopefully, these selections are sufficient to convey the point that theory and method involved in activating a model beyond its place of origin needs to involve much more than unveiling it and inviting rural revival stakeholders nationally and globally to run with a model on their own.

Empirical

On the empirical side, there is a rich past experience of the original Fogo Process such that it is widely known and respected. In recent years the Shorefast Foundation has maintained contact with the National Film Board of Canada in establishment on the island of the e-Cinema project and re-housing the cinema within the Fogo Island Inn. Further, the Foundation and the Memorial University of Newfoundland have signed a formal cooperative agreement. So the original partners of the Fogo Process are in recent relationship. This might suggest discussion among these three actors for looking to their possible joint interests in collaborating to prepare for the activation period of the Fogo Island Model. Here, again there is some additional history to draw on. The University of Guelph in Guelph, Ontario hosted a two-day conference in 1998 entitled, "Partnerships and Participation in Telecommunications for Rural Development: Exploring What Works and Why" (University of Guelph, October 26-27, 1998). Interestingly, it was preceded by a three-week pre-conference. These activities drew directly on the early Fogo Process work of the late Donald Snowden. His work in diffusing the Fogo Process from Fogo Island, Newfoundland to the Arctic, India and Africa headlined the conference call. Of course there is empirical guidance in the literature to draw on as well. For example, one can consult Donald Snowden's own writings and other early discourses of those days (Editors' Note to Snowden, 1998; Nemtin and Low, May 1968; Williamson, 1989). More recent narratives also might be informative on the ways and means that were employed in the diffusion of the original Fogo Process (Ferreira, September 2006; Crocker, 2008; Newhook, 2009).

Fund-Raising, Resources Generation and Investment Partnering for Model Activation

An additional and strategically critical task is to raise the support necessary to demonstrate the Fogo Island Rural Development Model. Exploring the history of the original Fogo Process and the supporters who aided its dissemination will reveal contemporary investment leads. These, for example, were the sponsors of the 1998 University of Guelph conference noted in the previous paragraph: the International Development Research Centre (IRDC, n.d.); Industry Canada; Telecommons Development Group; and Foundation for International training. Further, current activities of the Shorefast Foundation might be stimulative to preparing for Model activation.

The first task, for example: seek funding to initiate a small pilot program that parallels and takes inspiration from the Foundation's current programming in Artists-in-Residence and the Geologist-in-Residence programs (Memorial University of Newfoundland, May 27, 2014). This pilot would be a "Model Extension Agents-in-Residence" program that would issue a call globally for applications and proposals to take up a role on Fogo Island, with similar visiting time frames as the Artists-in-Residence program. They would be development practitioners learning by doing support service through the Shorefast Foundation for the institutions, businesses, local government and on the behalf of ordinary people in the Fogo Island and the Change Islands region. One might envisage a half-dozen or so participants from around the world; they would need to have some form of support (to be determined later) from their home government or a home-country institution or business). By having to apply, and propose reasons for their respective applications combined with local support, there would be at least and implicit show of interest from these places beyond Fogo Island in possibly hosting the diffusion of the Fogo Island Model in their home region. The presence of the Model Extension Agents-in-Residence in the Foundation for a working period would provide the initial hands-on knowledge of the Model and later by returning home would serve to seed in the knowledge and experience of the Fogo Island Model, thereby facilitating the transfer from pilot-to-demonstration. We should not take up the space here on the possible operational details, but one can envisage drawing on selected features from programs like the Fulbright and Humphrey Fellows programs in the U.S. for constructing some of the operating and procedural practicalities. Early-career and mid-career applicants should compose the likely pool from which such applicants would be selected for the Model Extension Agents-in-Residence program.

The second task is the current project, "Rural Community Toolkit for Entrepreneurial Action," is being implemented by the Shorefast Foundation as a result of funding from The Dobson Foundation, to the extent possible, this project might be shaped to address some of the needed preparatory tasks in anticipation of planning for the activation and demonstration of the Fogo

Island Model. The building of a global network of "deeply local places" would seem to be a relevant support system from which to build the necessary two-way awareness for places elsewhere to learn of the Fogo Island Rural Development Model, and in turn, for the Shorefast Foundation to get to know of potential candidate regions and places to participate in the demonstration and diffusion phase of the Model's evolution.

The third task uses a cooperative agreement between the Memorial University of Newfoundland and the Shorefast Foundation, these partners should explore the feasibility of developing a student-led and faculty guided project focused on planning for the activation of the Fogo Island Model. This might be run for a number of semesters with a stream of student groups. Ideally, multiple fields, professions and disciplines would be involved from policy studies, to business, to communications, to geography, international relations, extension and outreach, and so on. For more on how these service-learning and action-research projects have been operated from another university, refer to: University Center for Regional Economic Innovation, n.d.

The final task is preparing for the pilot-to-demonstration activation of the Fogo Island Model while the pilot phase of the Model's development continues to evolve is possibly to prepare for two phases; one within Canada and the next phase for demonstration outside Canada. The original Fogo Process was exported to Newfoundland's Northern Peninsula, Labrador and then to the Keewatin district of the central Arctic of Canada. Poor regions of the U.S. and other international locations, including India, were involved from the inception of the Fogo Process. Canadian foundations, corporations and governments whose primary interests are for community building investments in Canada may enable the Shorefast Foundation to leverage international sources of support more readily after further testing and fine-tuning of the Model inside Canada.

These four above examples, should be sufficient to suggest that the need and the opportunities may well exist for setting in motion soon, preparations for demonstrating the Model beyond the Fogo Island and the Change Islands region – even while the current Model continues to be dynamic and to mature and be perfected.

Deep Explication Combined with Our Intended Value Added

Finally, we end the narrative of the monograph here with the observation that we have sought to immerse you deeply into the content and processes of the experiment that is underway in the construction of the Fogo Island Model for Rural Development. True to Zita Cobb's philosophy we have intentionally taken you through the operational details and specificities of the Model as we have perceived it. We hope that our interpretations and translations have been true and will prove helpful to you as you experiment with the Fogo Island Model in your locality. Lastly, rather than just report our findings we have injected our own views and used our imaginations to make suggestions for improvement and to go beyond the stated parameters of a particular program or initiative. This is our value-added. With the members of Team Shorefast and the residents of Fogo Island and the Change Islands region doing the development of their home place, we reckoned that our contribution in pulling together so many of their development efforts and actions that we should bring to bear our third-party perspectives including our best informed positions and recommendations.

Why Are Some of Us Doing This Work?

It is good to be reminded periodically that the past should inform the future. We are completing this monograph as the 100th anniversary of the death of Martha, the last passenger pigeon, is being observed. She died in the Cincinnati Zoo & Botanical Garden on the afternoon of September 1, 1914 (Engel, August 23/August 24, 2014). This case is relevant to a discussion of the future development of the Fogo Island and the Change Islands region. The extinctions of the local Beothuk peoples, the Great Auk and the catastrophic over fishing of the cod fish all were local events that certainly are reminders for us today of what we humans should and should not do. In the discourse earlier in this monograph were discussed the circumstances that necessitated the 1992 moratorium on the commercial harvesting of the cod. The Great Auk used nearby Funk Island as an important nesting ground. The birds were massacred every spring inexorably such that by 1810, every bird was gone from Funk Island forever. After 1844, no other Great Auks were seen anywhere on earth.

Today, a sculpture of the Great Auk may be viewed on Fogo Island near the Long Studio. One may hike to the sculpture and view it from the sea; Ketanja Boat Tours advertises this opportunity. The sculptor Todd McGrain is the artist in residence at the Cornell Lab of Ornithology. He has dedicated the last decade to The Lost Bird Project. The Project "is an ode to vanished times and vanished species." In addition to the Great Auk and the Passenger Pigeon, the Project also helps us remember the extinct Labrador Duck, the Carolina Parakeet and the Heath Hen by means of sculptures of each bird. McGrain worked untiringly to locate each sculpture in the place where each bird was last seen in the wild (McGrain, 2014). We thank The Lost Bird project for granting us the use of the image of the Great Auk sculpture on Fogo Island for the cover of this monograph.

As part of the remembrances of Martha, the last passenger pigeon, John W. Fitzpatrick, Executive Director of the Cornell Lab of Ornithology, provides us with an apt finale.

> It seems that whenever humans discover bounty, it is doomed to become a fleeting resource. The fate of cod fisheries in the late 1990s mirrors that of the passenger pigeon a century before. Pacific Bluefin tuna, down 96 percent from their unfished numbers, may be next in line. Countless such examples exist around the world, but the

good news is that we still have time to reflect on them before their populations dwindle down to their last respective Marthas (Fitzpatrick, August 31, 2014: 6).

The Shorefast Foundation and the people of the Fogo Island region are in the midst of reflecting -- and acting on these concerns with its New Ocean Ethic and its other ocean programing. We hope you too will reflect, act and follow into the future the status of the support that the Foundation attracts for engaging the global issue of natural resources utilization while being both responsible and sustainable. We hope also, that for your own home place and region you work with your neighbors, relations, friends and the relevant local institutions to do your own reflection and action – especially in using the Fogo Island Model for Rural Development to practice intelligent development and planning.

Appendices

Appendix 1

Geotourism Elaborated

Definitions of geotourism are not so cut and dried. In fact, defining geotourism is a complex and debatable business. The origins of the concept go back to the seventeenth century. Academics and practitioners from the United Kingdom and Europe more generally have defined and re-defined geotourism.

This European form appears to have risen from the need to conserve local geological and geomorphological sites, especially ones like mines and quarries, the post exploitation stage of which demands rehabilitation and environmentally sensitive reclamation. Using tourism to advocate and fund the remediation of such damage to nature was seen as a means to finance restoration and protection of the natural environment. Such 'alternative' tourism relied on "educational, environmental, nature-based and heritage travel" (Hose, Markovic, Komac and Zorn, 2011: 339). Geological interpretation and the promotion of geoconservation for tourists has been a primary purpose of early geotourism. Thus, the geological basis is the foundation for geotourism; certainly in Europe and globally most of the publications on it were premised on this basis (Hose, Markovic, Komac and Zorn, 2011: 339).

More recently, North American thinkers and doers have adopted and experimented with a more inclusive, interdependent and holistic extension of the geotourism concept. The Shorefast Foundation has referenced the more thematically comprehensive definition of Jonathan Tourtellot of the National Geographic Society (Center for Sustainable Destinations, n.d.). This definition in effect puts people and economic development explicitly in the travel picture – along with the environment, including understanding and actionable concern for the geology and geomorphology of localities and regions. The Tourtellot definition of geotourism can encompass human culture, heritage, art, architecture, design, technology, food, music and among other human constructions, the sustainable utilization of nature including science-based stewardship of land, the oceans, fresh water and the planet's atmosphere and earth-space. Already such educational travel and tourism, facilitated by the pervasive networking of information and communications technologies globally, has begun to gain traction in a number of places. By means of geotourism, the promise of new employment and economic development especially in rural and small town regions is in the air.

Beyond North America there has been some notable experimentation and innovation especially in the European interpretation of geotourism. A new model, the geopark has emerged. It is defined as "a nationally protected area containing a number of geological heritage sites of particular importance, rarity or aesthetic appeal; ... a geopark should aim for the development of the local territory and support local communities and products" (Farsani, Coelho and Costa, 2011: 72).

There are at least 64 geoparks located around the globe. Twenty-two of these are in China. The remainder principally are in Europe, the Asia-Pacific, including Japan and Australia, and Brazil in South America. Japan and China have developed domestic geoparks. They have been organized into a Domestic Geopark Network. Such proximal organization aids and supports "close collaboration" among the local-area stakeholders among all tourism-relevant sectors and institutions from business to education, among other actors.

Geoparks, a form of sustainable tourism, are seen as a solution for rural-area economic development. The vision for geoparks is that they can generate new spillovers such as jobs, new products and services, and new recreational and public education functions for local rural economies (Farsani, Coelho and Costa, 2011: 79-80).

Source: The Authors

Appendix 2

Connected Community Engagement Program of Connect Michigan

Eric Frederick, Executive Director, Connect Michigan

Rural regions throughout North America have many places and areas that are under served or not serviced at all for broadband connectivity and access.

In today's global information society and global knowledge economy such rural regions are at a significant disadvantage and are limited in their capacity to do business, to access distant educational programs and opportunities, and to communicate and search for information, social interaction and entertainment among other needed functions that require digital networking such as using government services and programs.

What support does Connect Michigan provide to empower Michigan's small town and rural regions to help their citizens and business persons take a lead in conceptualizing, planning and implementing a local broadband strategy that might be used to leverage accessible and affordable internet services from for-profit corporate providers and to bring such needs to the attention of government?

Part of Connect Michigan's programming is to help communities assess their local broadband landscape (by benchmarking themselves against standards from the U.S. National Broadband Plan), and then formulating an action plan to fill gaps in that assessment (called the Connected Community Engagement Program). Connect Michigan has been working on the ground with 28 communities in Michigan to help them through this process. Technology Action Plans have been completed in more than half of these communities so far, while others are working to complete their plans. Below are links to a sample of representative 2013 plans. All of these plans are for small town and rural area counties. Three of these counties are located in the Lower Peninsula of Michigan and one county is located in the Upper Peninsula of Michigan. Parts of the plan contents are similar, and even some of the suggested projects are similar, but local context and the grassroots teams established in each of these rural and small town regional communities dictate how the Technology Action Plans are implemented (Connect Michigan and Ogemaw County (2013); and Delta County (2013); and St Clair County (2013):

    Antrim County
    St. Clair County
    Ogemaw County
    Delta County.

While the Connected Community Engagement Program results in a local Technology Action Plan for the community, the process of benchmarking and plan development is, arguably, more important. The Connected program seeks to bring together local stakeholders from across sectors to facilitate a broadband and technology conversation. Connected teams are often comprised of representatives from the following; chambers of commerce, local government, schools, libraries, economic development entities (both local and regional), workforce development offices, emergency management, county and regional planning, broadband providers, healthcare establishments, institutions of higher education, non-profit organizations, and others. Teams comprised of these entities oftentimes have never met with each other around the topic of broadband or technology. The Connected program works to bring all parties together to collectively discuss technology as a driver of improved community and economic development. Connect Michigan offers Connected teams a facilitated process, education, and connections to resources to empower local stakeholders to take charge of their broadband future. More information on Connected and its progress to-date across eight U.S. states can be found online (Connected Nation, Fall 2013).

Contact information for Connect Michigan:
    6546 Mercantile Way, Suite 5
    Lansing, Michigan 48909 USA
    info@connectmi.org

Source: Frederick, September 24, 2013

Appendix 3

Product Business Outline: A Project to Kickstart the Cottage Industry for Handmade Goods

(Excerpt From Proposal)

Rural Newfoundland has a rich and long tradition of making things by hand. Besides boats, fishing gear, houses, flakes (a platform built on poles for drying cod-fish) and barrels that were needed for fishing the North Atlantic, objects for the home were made at home. Hooked rugs, furniture and quilts were always produced locally and not only provided necessary household goods but created a social network for the women (mostly) who made them. Thankfully, today on Fogo Island those skills survive intact.

In designing the Fogo Island Inn, priority was given to locally sourced crafts such as quilts and rugs and all the wooden furniture was designed and crafted by local carpenters to reflect traditional Newfoundland Outport Furniture. The results are nothing short of awesome. Before the doors of the Inn were even open, we identified significant commercial demand for these products.

While the skills used in making these products are ancient, the marketing of them to the broader public is a newer concept.

Traditionally, handmade objects were made with recycled materials and put to immediate use by the maker. Today, professional design is the language of modern commerce. Fogo Island artisans can anticipate a strong market demand for their products if they are provided with contemporary, professional advice on design and marketing, and seed funding to acquire materials that appeal to today's discerning buyers.

An investment in "Kick-starting the Cottage Industry for Handmade Goods" will allow us to create an industry for beautifully crafted Fogo Island products and market on a global scale – online, through catalogues and in retail spaces on Fogo Island and beyond.

Consider this a unique IPO - an Innovative Private Offering. Contributions serve as expansion capital, monetizing the initial investments already made on Fogo Island. It is a growth model where social and economic returns are achieved in tandem.

A contribution to this project is a perfect example of private investment for public good. As with all Shorefast Initiatives, investments made go back to the community providing employment and sustainability far into the future.

We are rebuilding an economy of care, craft and culture that has existed on Fogo Island for hundreds of years.

Source: Hodgins, January 28, 2014?

Appendix 4

Economic Cost-Benefit Assessment:
2012 Fogo Island Partridgeberry Harvest Festival

The weekend event costs about $10,000 annually to organize – for example to rent the Iceberg Arena costs $1500, there are radio and other advertising costs, and performers to be paid – and it takes many hours of planning throughout the year, including two days to set it up, and one day afterwards to take it all down.

However the positive social and economic impact is far greater than the cost:

Vendor sales in 2012 were estimated to be well over $23,000.
(11 of 24 food & craft booths reported sales totaling over $17,000)

Many B & B's were sold out all weekend. This represents over $2000 added to the Islands economy.

Restaurants and grocery stores benefitted from the increased weekend population over the Thanksgiving weekend by at least $1000

The Ferry had a very active weekend – we estimate 70%+ of attendance was by non-residents. That represents 800 passengers and about 400 visitor vehicles using the Ferry, bringing a further $8000 to the Island's economy.

The monetary impact is ongoing – many visitors intend to return, and crafts vendors are still receiving orders for their work.

Source: Fogo Island Partridgeberry Harvest Festival, n.d..

Appendix 5

The Seven Seasons of Fogo Island and the Change Islands Region

Spring – April, May
Easterlies and Northeasterlies; icebergs; some rain and fog; occasional frosts.

Trap Berth Season -- June
The season during which a location or place on the fishing ground where a cod trap is placed; the position is assigned by lot.
Can act like spring or summer; boats are back in the water; Southwesterlies; fishing season.

Summer – July, August
Southwesterlies; gentle cleansing winds; blueberry time.
Fresh and clear air; temperature +20C; fishing time; long days, 16 hours of light.

Early Fall – September, October
September, partridgeberry time; October, lovely drying Westerlies; lots of sun.
Fish-making time; lovely Westerlies and Northwesterlies; temp 12-15C.

Late Fall – November
Northwesterlies; powerful storms; gathering firewood.
Boats are out of the water; rough seas; birding season; Northerlies and Northwesterlies;

Winter – December, January, February
Snow; wind; glitter; temperatures -10 to 0C; short days, 16 hours of darkness; snow shoeing; cabin retreats.
Make and mend gear; skating on ponds; snowshoeing; crafts season.

Ice Season -- March
Ice Season; pack ice comes; icy winds; icebound; clear; sunny; sealing season.

Source: Coates, n.d.

Appendix 6

A Shorefast Foundation Reading List

Diane Hodgins, Director, Investment Partnerships
Shorefast Foundation

The references listed below are read and serve to inspire and influence Shorefast Foundation team of staff, board members, friends and neighbors. These are examples from the literature that have been shaped inspiring ideas and approaches for intelligent development strategies and tactics in the formulation and implementation of the Foundation's programs and projects. The principals of the Foundation place "great value" especially on the "next generation" of such creative global-issue economists and development thinkers as: Mark Roseland, Peter Senge, Charles Eisenstein and Tim Jackson, among others. These selections provide some insight into the substantive and philosophical threads that have been used in constructing the Fogo Island Model for Rural Development. In particular, these influences from the development-related literature have informed a core value of Shorefast's rural development work that business should serve social ends. A driving intention in the creation of a Model for Rural Development is to experiment and test how to put a social business model into each place where rural stakeholders seek to position the local to engage the global.

A key guiding phrase which business models follows has been derived from this literature; it is from Tim Jackson's (2009) book, *Prosperity Without Growth*: "Avoiding the scourge of unemployment may have less to do with chasing after growth and more to do with building an economy of care, craft and culture." Writings by some of the other economists represented in this reading list have provoked operating tenets for ensuring that business serves social ends in local and regional development:

- The economists listed below have aided Shorefast Foundation actors to recognize that there are issues with current capital markets and business structures, encouraging us to think of possible alternatives, i.e., building from the ground up.

- Social business means investing in new types of business structures where rules are not clearly defined ... there is no pre-determined box to fall into, no existing path to follow to success. Continue to find insight from their work to build a better model, not just follow what we currently have – develop something better that is community centric with business as servant, not master.

- In the Dialogues that have been initiated by Fogo Island Arts, we are looking to expand the Dialogues to include economists into the mix in the future along with various other fields of expertise being represented.

Note: for the use of the readers of this monograph, a number of these readings below are accessible as free downloads via the links provided with each entry. The other references are available from local lending libraries or by purchase.

Gaston Bachelard, *The Poetics of Space.* Boston: Beacon Press, 1994.

Julian Barnes, *Nothing to be Frightened Of.* New York: Vintage, 2009.

Various books by Zygmunt Bauman; for example: *The Art of Life.* Hoboken, NJ: Wiley, 2008.

Wade Davis, *The Wayfinders.* Toronto: House of Anansi Press, 2009.

Charles Eisenstein, *Sacred Economics.* Berkeley, CA: Evolver Editions, 2011. Twelve-minute film summary available online: <http://sacred-economics.com/film/>

Tim Jackson, *Prosperity without Growth.* London and New York: Earthscan, 2009.

Mark Kurlansky, *Cod.* New York: Penguin Books, 1997.

Mark Kurlansky, *Salt.* New York: Penguin Books, 2003.

Mark Kurlansky, *The Big Oyster.* New York: Random House Trade Paperbacks, 2007.

Barry Lopez, *Arctic Dreams.* New York: Vintage, 2001.

Sara Maitland, *The Art of Silence.* Berkeley, CA: Counterpoint Press, 2010.

Various books by Tim Robinson, for example: *Setting Foot on the Shores of Connemara.* Dublin: Lilliput Press Ltd, 1997.

Mark Roseland, *Toward Sustainable Communities: Solutions for Citizens and their Governments,* 4th Edition. Gabriola Island, BC: New Society Publishers, 2012.

Tomas Sedlacek, *The Economics of Good and Evil.* New York: Oxford University Press, 2011. Transcript of an interview with the author: <http://www.carnegiecouncil.org/studio/multimedia/20111005/0434.html/_res/id=sa_File1/>

Peter Senge. *A Necessary Revolution.* New York: Doubleday, 2008. An 8-page summary is available online from the Society for Organizational Learning; you must provide your name and contact information to download the summary. <http://www.solonline.org/?page=Download_TNR2>

Note: The links to the websites were added by the authors.

Source: Hodgins, January 28, 2014

Appendix 7

Some More Principal Components of the Fogo Island Model for Rural Development

As noted relatively early in the main narrative above, we have drawn on past experience in the building and the utilization of models in planning and development. We have learned that an effective model should meet these three criteria: (1) have transparency; (2) be widely understandable; and (3) clearly be able to inform action. With these attributes having been realized, a model is more likely to gain community ownership, and therefore be used locally as well as elsewhere (Lee, Jr., 1973). Past experience also teaches us to keep large-scale models simple; complicated models do not work well or at all. Being guided by these lessons and these three criteria that are known to be critical in the development of ownership by the principal local development stakeholders, we have identified below some of those principal components that make up and drive the Model for Rural Development in the region of Fogo Island and the Change Islands of Newfoundland. In deriving these factors, we have been mindful that our core goal here is to provide readers elsewhere beyond the Fogo Island region with a set of operating principles that might serve to inform planned actions, especially in those other rural regions.

Note, with the exception of the component, the focus of which is on the comparative advantage of islands, there is no particular order to the components that follow. The island discussion begins the components narrative because a case can be made for the Fogo Island and Change Islands region to be considered for additional investment and partnering based on its potential for being a useful proof-of-concept case for innovative regional development initiatives that need piloting and demonstration before fully implementing a formative idea.

The Fogo Island Model for Rural Development Merits Further Investment and Attention: In General and Because It's an Island

What Should be Targeted for Additional Investment in Fogo Island?

It is early days for the development work that is currently underway in the Fogo Island region. In this monograph, we have raised the notion that, even in its initial phases, this work has demonstrated a high degree of freshness, i.e., an unusual level of creativity and initiative that is compelling. The Shorefast Foundation and the people and businesses of the region have demonstrated to us that the Model merits continued investment and attention. The investments to date have been substantial and noteworthy. The Shorefast Foundation, the government of the province and the federal government, as well as some philanthropy from individuals has been forthcoming and has served to move the development work well into its start-up stage, our preliminary assessment here concludes that to be a more fully fleshed out operational model for other rural places much more program implementation work should be done, especially in critical infrastructure systems such as:

(1) marketing and relationship building within the global tourism industry;

(2) completing the needed airport runway;

(3) ensuring that all ferry access and ferry capacity requirements are met throughout the seasonal variation of annual demand;

(4) ensure that dependable electricity power provision, and high-speed, high-volume broadband and networking services are accessible, affordable and spatially distributed to all settlement clusters throughout the low population region of Fogo Island and the Change Islands; and

(5) expand the ocean programming toward the establishment of the working culture of the New Ocean Ethic for a commercially profitable local and regional fishery that practices the responsible utilization of the ocean's natural resources in a fully sustainable manner. Suggested early in this monograph, the island character of the Fogo Island and the Change Islands region confers a comparative advantage on the place. This advantage should be capitalized by means of the discipline to build a broader stakeholder base. A tenacious and continuous campaign for this purpose is strongly recommended.

Parallel with the five infrastructural investments noted immediately above, also needed is (6) value-added investment in on-going research and monitoring of the business processes that are underway by the Shorefast Foundation, including the Fogo Island Inn; the Fogo Island Arts programming; and expanding the proof-of-concept and demonstration capacity of the Business Assistance Fund work by not only continuing the needed work of seeding new business, but also transforming existing businesses, enabling the growing of businesses and innovating through partnerships.

For an illustration of starting up a cottage industry for handmade goods from the islands (See Appendix 4). Explicit cross generational and in-region and away-region partnerships would be particularly valuable. With the tiny current island population of younger residents plus former Fogo Island "alumni" who have engaged business careers elsewhere, such partnerships, coupled with the additional support systems investment advocated here, might be rendered feasible. Impediments to taking up new business initiatives by island residents, such as the seasonal regulations for unemployment benefits may be particularly strategic targets for piloting reforms. The already demonstrated excellence of the work of the Business Assistance Fund's lead, Jonathan Briggs, combined for example with the business expertise and potential business student practical learning interest from the Memorial University of Newfoundland (MUN) might be explored for mobilization of additional innovation through partnerships. Dr. Natalie Slawinski of MUN's Faculty of Business Administration would be an additional resource in developing this proposed programming.

The Island as a Promising Investment Target: Two Cases

Over the generations of our own travel and scholarly observations of islands such as strategy, Singapore and Hawai'i we have learned that islands and the people who occupy them have evolved their own adaptations and approaches to living and working in response to the concrete specificities of their "islandness." Distinct cultural responses get constructed. For example, in Sri Lanka, policies of counterurbanization were effective and maintained, even as they spanned cycles of electoral partisan party political changes and differing philosophies. While the neighbor mainland countries in the region were experiencing significant population movement from the countryside to the big city-regions, off-shore island Sri Lanka stayed the policy course for encouraging rural residence and employment. The neighbor countries might well have benefitted from considering the adoption with tailoring of the unique tried and tested Sri Lankan Model of Counterurbanization (Corey, 1987).

Another island case to note is Singapore's economic development and societal transformation. In August 1965, the Federal Government of Malaysia expelled the Government of Singapore from the union that the two governments had formed two years earlier (Sopiee, 2005). At the time of this unexpected event, the newly independent island city-state of Singapore was a tiny, poor developing country. Singapore was a colony of the United Kingdom until 1963. Its seaport and airport and other transportation infrastructures and housing stock were terribly dilapidated. Little modernization and investment had occurred since the end of World War II. By the 1990s however, Singapore's highly effective strategic planning and program implementation over the previous generation had positioned its economy to the level where its (1) internal economic development was productive and successful, based principally on its planning, promotion and development of a dynamic industrial sector; (2) "Singapore started to share its town-planning and industry development expertise with other cities" (JTC Corporation, n.d.; Singbridge Corporation Pte Ltd, n.d.). The selling of these services was a means to build a strong export leg to its base economy. Refer to the "Sharing Singapore's Experience" section of the Singbridge Corporation's home page. It has conducted major urban development projects in: Indonesia, India, and Vietnam. Many of its projects have been in the People's Republic of China. These have included projects in Chongqing, Jilin, Tianjin (the pioneering Eco-City project) and two projects in Guangzhou (including two Knowledge City projects). To gain an impression of the innovative nature and large scale of these projects, refer to the "Our Portfolio" section of the Singbridge Corporation's home page.

To signify the strategic centrality of information technology in its urban development strategies, Singapore branded itself as the "Intelligent Island (Menkhoff, Chay and Loh, 2004). So, the point of the Sri Lanka and the Singapore island cases here is to know that both performed creatively and well above expectations in their respective regional development programs. In the Singapore case, the strategy of exporting urban development services from a strong well-performing internal economic base that has been successful. Further, it has leveraged significant investments for its overseas partners and income for its participating businesses at home. The Fogo Island Inn's furniture is in line to be marketed for sale as a means of producing income for the island. Might the Shorefast Foundation, like Singapore also be positioned in future to sell it services beyond Fogo Island by means of a spin-off not-just-for-profit enterprise? We fully recognize that the population size difference between Singapore island at 5.4 million population and Fogo Island at about 2,800 persons is beyond comparison. However, the Shorefast Foundation is committed to sharing its rural development practice and experience with others. In time, given the full maturation of its modeling effort, the feasibility of the Shorefast Foundation exporting its Rural Development Model expertise as an income and revenue generation strategy for Fogo Island's economy should be anticipated and considered. It took Singapore a generation from the time of its independence from Malaysia to export its urban development practice and experience.

Preparing for such a day in the Fogo Island case might be a goal for the Shorefast Foundation to put forward for targeted prospective investment partners to review. The Fogo Island Dialogues already are in place to support such preparation. For example, from the Dialogues purpose statement:

> While the topics addressed by invited speakers are international, the discussion will take as its focus Fogo Island, the current site of an ambitious rural project. The Fogo Island Dialogues will refer to the example of Fogo Island as inspiration and catalyst for the exploration and understanding of other locations. Using the idea of island as a metaphor for any rural locale, the concept of the island-as-laboratory is tested through dialogue (Fogo Island Dialogues, n.d.).

The literature on the unique attributes of islands and certainly from our experience of island cases suggests that investment in a worthy, especially island-based, not-just-for-profit rural development proof-of-concept pilot enterprise might be tested as a social entrepreneurship demonstration for starting up a social business. Preceding such an initiative should be some comprehensive and in-depth research that explicates further the comparative advantage of islands and investigates good practices of island-centric rural development. Such research should begin with the imaginative 2012 book by Steven Roger Fischer entitled *Islands: From Atlantis to Zanzibar*; Fischer is drawn on in the next part of this section. Networking and collaborative organizational structures should be part of such preparatory investigation; for example, Singapore island development leadership explored and later developed with overseas partners, some of the earliest growth triangle efforts. These "triangles" are cross-border collaboratives with at least a total of two partners that complement the development strengths of the respective partner country regions. For example, Singapore provided finance and strategy, while Malaysia and Indonesia provided land and labor for joint development projects. Such cooperative arrangements have been developed or conceptualized throughout East Asia (Thant, Tang and Kakazu, 1998).

Islands of the Mind

If only at the intuitive level, islands are special places, especially for doing exploratory proof-of-concept and early-stage life cycle regional development work and investment. Islands are bounded, that is they are separated; they have a certain degree of isolation from the "mainland." As a result, spatially and physically, external influences may be perceived as more clearly identified, measured and thereby controlled in a development experiment. The relative isolation may aid the implementation and measurement of an experiment in unpacking and thereby improve our understanding of development processes. Also, and critically significant for our purposes here, islands have an advantage for using the lessons derived from the knowledge acquired from such analysis and understanding; they seem to stimulate the imagination. Islands, unlike many other kinds of places generate meanings and images that are powerful constructs. As such, the island of the mind can help facilitate imagining and creating approaches and solutions that can move us from what is to what should be. The power of islands stimulates images and wish-for futures confer on them advantages for planning strategies policies that inform action. Steven Roger Fischer, for example, states that over the past 200 years some Pacific Ocean islands have comprised an "ideological testing ground" for Western nations. The evidence he offers in support of this include perceptual changes have occurred over this period from an earlier formation of mental meanings in the case of many Pacific islands being perceived as dangerous, cruel and savage shift to being imagined as places of paradise, sensuality and supporting freedom of behavior not found in the "civilized societies" of the West. In turn, the indigenous Pacific islanders have been "intellectually occupied and conceptually shaped by the West." These natives also manifested shifts in culture and behaviors and "have sometimes influenced Western understandings of itself" (Fischer, 2012: 256).

Thus, this and other researches into these "islands of the mind" have revealed that non-islanders and islanders construct differing psychological spaces and interpretations; and these distinctions affect various meanings such as "the creation of a landscape, the psychological process of identification and can include a transference of self-image to location" (Fischer, 2012: 262 and 263). These abstract and nuanced island-based mindset formation dynamics demand deeper examination and reflection in order to better understand and translate this emerging body of island knowledge into effective regional development practice. Attracting the investment needed to support such knowledge acquisition holds promise and would seem to merit the effort.

Capitalize on the Intersection of Local and Global

From the perspective of today's and tomorrow's development realities and opportunities, the most strategically significant decision taken has been the selection of the engine intended to drive and transform the Fogo Island regional economy into a more prosperous future. The decision was to design programs and actions for "the local to meet the global and vice versa." Embracing the development potentials of the economic, social and technological world beyond the Fogo Island region will have a high impact on the local people, their local economy and their natural environment and natural resources. Managing these changes and influences will be a major challenge. To accomplish this, the ordinary people of the islands need to be involved in this management process. Indeed, with its neighbors and friends, this is the course that the Shorefast Foundation has embarked upon. The explicit intention is to strive for the Fogo Island Inn in particular to produce after-expenses surplus profit that the community will decide how to invest these resources. Given the time, additional revenue-generating instruments will be conceived. Most recently the Fogo Island Shop has been launched as the retail mechanism for the sale of the unique locally designed and fabricated furniture and other furnishings of the Fogo Island Inn. Handmade quilts and the wallpaper patterns of the guest rooms of the Inn may be purchased. Eventually textiles may be available through the Fogo Island Shop. The creative outcomes of the Fogo Island Arts program represent possible income sources also (Refer to Kellner, 2014).

Draw Vision and Action from Your Pre-Conditions

A key factor in the formulation of the Fogo Island Model for Rural Development is pre-conditions. For example, the Fogo Process and the life and particular mix of complementary working experiences of both Zita Cobb and Gordon Slade are just some of the significant pre-conditions that have been instrumental in setting the table, so to speak, for Fogo Islanders to grasp the need for and nature of the Shorefast Foundation's development strategy and initiatives. Historically, other Newfoundland outports functioned under similar cod and fish merchant economic domination and exploitation conditions, but the separate island-based community identity and community organizational stimulus of The Fogo Process was instrumental in resisting re-settlement. Thereby, Fogo Island became fertile ground for a fresh approach for the future of the place.

The work and career experiences of Zita Cobb and Gordon Slade, for example, enabled them to determine that indeed by embracing the development opportunities from the increasingly connected and networked outside world, in the form of the globalized new economy, it might be feasible to design and actualize a vision of local economic development that would breathe new and additional economic life into Fogo Island. Exposure to doing successful business globally and gaining experience and confidence by doing successful local innovations such as the Battle Harbour preservation project and staying abreast of advances in science and sustainable practices in the responsible utilization of the ocean's resources were combined to frame realistic strategies that could engage and mobilize ordinary people, the region's neighbors, relatives and friends in collective decision making and action taking to experiment and "road test" the Fogo Island Model for Rural development. So, not only is the identification of intrinsic place assets important for utilizing the Model, but also assessing a region's and locality's human capital assets may be invaluable. Look for possible competitive advantage in local people's work experience, education, travels, origins, social capital networks, special skill sets, and so on.

Organize and Develop Your Local and Regional Human Capital to Do the Job

As it was demonstrated in the discussion of the Shorefast Foundation's functions, organizational structure and ethos, effective leadership and development is not the work of one person. Rather, this work is a shared and collective undertaking. So, shared leadership, teaming and interlocking divisions of labor are central to development work, as are other explicit process tactics of experimenting and learning by doing. This work is most effective when the actors, i.e., the key stakeholders are engaged participants in some aspects of the collective community undertaking. This might mean involvement in leadership, governance, visioning, program design, prioritizing and investing resources, program implementation and assessing program status, and suggesting mid-course corrections. What is essential are people who possess and or are willing to develop and perfect these qualities, knowledge and skills. Individuals and ideal candidates to be involved in the regional development effort need:

- Energy and passion to support development in long-term
- To be embedded in the place; acquire a deep understanding of its history and social dynamics – be in the "thick of it"
- Be impacted themselves by the changes they are undertaking; that is, be a community member

- To have experience both in the place as well as other world experience; be able to compare and contrast
- To build working relationships with and recognize the many community individuals and community groups so that strong bonds are maintained with the development initiative throughout the community and its region

In the end, we have explicitly sought to drill down into the specificities of the Fogo Island and Change Islands communities and region. By getting deep into the assets and processes of the place, its people and its institutions, we have sought to offer would-be rural development actors and stakeholders elsewhere the inspiration and means for achieving better and happier places.

Might the Fogo Island Model for Rural Development have Anything to Say to Urban Development?

We believe that the answer to this question is an unequivocal, yes. Zita Cobb has made this point in some of her speeches. Since so much of what is needed to practice intelligent development is process in nature, rural versus urban. Whether rural or urban, the planned development of a place or region requires such essentials as leadership, championing the strategy, research into the internal dynamics and external connectivities of the area its people and institutions, a measured understanding of the functional themes of the region – especially its economic production and consumption functions and quality of life factors, investments that are prioritized and responsive to economic demand and social need, monitoring and evaluation of the programs and projects being implemented, and among many other factors, the active participation of the region's stakeholders who are being impacted by the programs being implemented and so on.

Professor John Friedmann's incisive journal article on "Place and Place-Making in Cities," he:

> introduced a number of criteria by which we can determine the degree to which neighborhoods are places: being small, inhabited, cherished by most of those who live there, and centered as revealed in its sacred places, reiterative social practices and rituals. Above all, it is a space where the daily drama of small events is enacted for the benefit of everyone who cares to watch (Friedmann, 2010: 159).

Except for the word "neighborhoods," one can apply Professor Friedmann's city criteria for what makes up a place comfortably to the rural region of Fogo Island and the Change Islands. Each criterion is as integral and important to the Fogo Islander and Change Islander rural area stakeholder representatives as they sit at the strategic planning tables over Shorefast Foundation programs or the respective local government initiatives as their counterpart urban stakeholders in Beijing or any other big city place. Nowadays, with the ubiquitous communications technologies, the overwhelming sources of content and programming emanates from city-regions and penetrate throughout most small town and rural areas. So, the rural isolation of yesteryear has been greatly diminished. Simply, the urban influence is widespread in today's global knowledge economy and global information society. Consequently, readers from city-regions also may be able to derive benefit from the development innovations currently underway in the rural Fogo Island and Change Islands region.

To demonstrate the kinds of urban-to-rural (and vice versa) parallels that were noted above, earlier this year we briefed one of our Michigan State University faculty colleagues, Professor John Beck on the efforts underway to revive the Fogo Island economy. He had recently co-edited a book that discussed the development efforts in the city of Detroit, Michigan to tap into the city's rich culture and vibrancy in order "to create a new community out of the old." The 2014 book is entitled *Detroit Resurgent: A Counternarrative of Hope and Vision*. Professor Beck immediately recognized some of the comparabilities between rural Fogo Island and urban Detroit. To his mind, these included: the initial stirrings of local social and economic forces; the role of art in catalyzing these new dynamics; the key roles being played out by particular individuals; the notion of creating value and re-investing it locally; the centrality of proactively engaging freshly the new opportunities provided by the pervasive globalized information and communications technologies; while simultaneously preserving some of the best of local culture, among other analogies. Refer to Bossen and Beck, 2014: 10-11.

The notion of modeling development that has many commonalities across both urban and rural environments is noteworthy, even across these two quite different places. There is a core message in this case that regional re-birth is possible among the places where ordinary working people with the will and imagination to capitalize boldly on local assets and can benefit from their contributions to the globalizing world. Analyzing such efforts across the miles and borders can be a useful way for identifying commonalities and in the process inform modeling from which others might learn and be inspired. In the end, readers, even those with principally rural development stakes can learn from and derive possibly useful approaches from urban places, and vice versa.

Source: the Authors

Figures

Image Credits and First-Reference Page Location in the Text

Front and back cover illustrations

These images capture some of the idiosyncratic characteristics of Fogo Island's heritage, culture and use of natural resources.

The **village sign for Joe Batt's Arm** represents the kind of quirkiness that one finds throughout Newfoundland in general and Fogo Island in particular. This unique place name comes from the first Europeans to settle there in the 1700s. The "arm" label comes from the shape of the inlet to the sea on which the village is situated. The new Fogo Island Inn is located in the settlement of Joe Batt's Arm.

Photo: Paddy Barry.

The person-sized statue of the **Great Auk** is an icon that symbolizes the extinction or near extinction of people, birds and fish in the Fogo Island and the Change Islands region, Newfoundland area. The Beothuk were hunter-gatherer aboriginal people who had sparsely occupied much of Newfoundland before Europeans began to settle permanently on the island. With the death of Shanawdithit in 1829, the Beothuk people were believed to have become extinct. The person-sized statue of the Great Auk was erected by the Lost Bird Project on the edge of the sea near Joe Batt's Arm. Globally, this large flightless sea bird became extinct in 1844; it became extinct around 1810 from the nearby Funk Island located east of Fogo Island. Lastly, in commercial terms, cod fish had been so over-harvested by industrial-scaled fishers from around the world that the Canadian government declared a moratorium on commercial cod fishing in 1992. This resulted in massive job loss, economic depression and out-migration for Fogo Island and Newfoundland.

Photo courtesy of the Lost Bird Project.

Figure 1. Map of the Fogo Island and the Change Islands Region (Photo courtesy of the Shorefast Foundation) First mention in text: page 9.

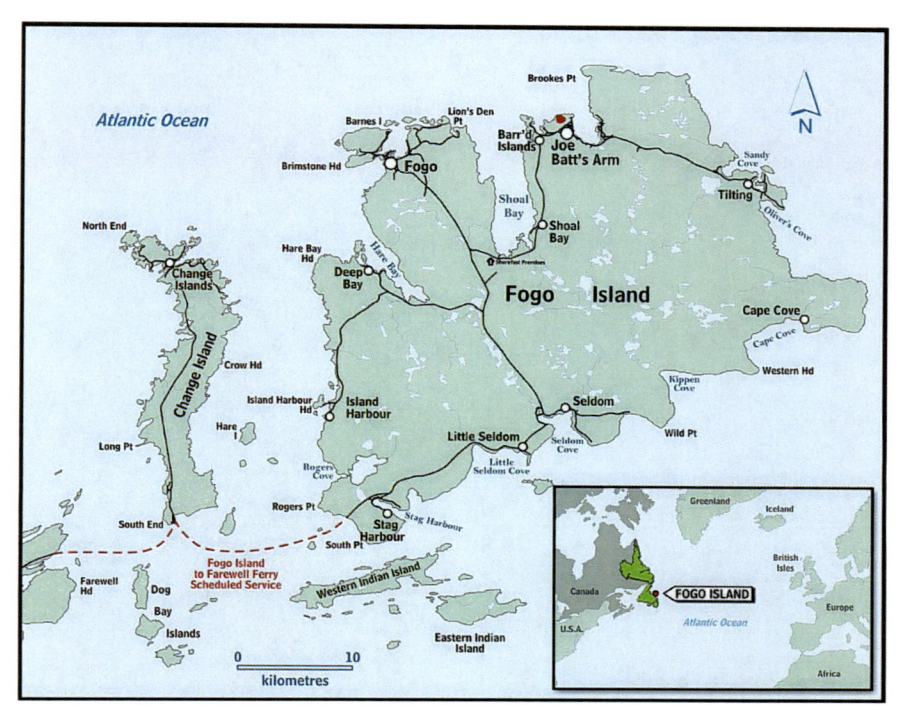

Figure 2. Landscape of Fogo Island Region Countryside (Photo: Paddy Barry) First mention in text: page 9.

Figure 3. Seascape of Fogo Island Region Countryside (Photo: Alex Fradkin) First mention in text: page 9.

Figure 4. Iceberg Near the Fogo Island Shore (Photo: Paddy Barry) First mention in text: page 9.

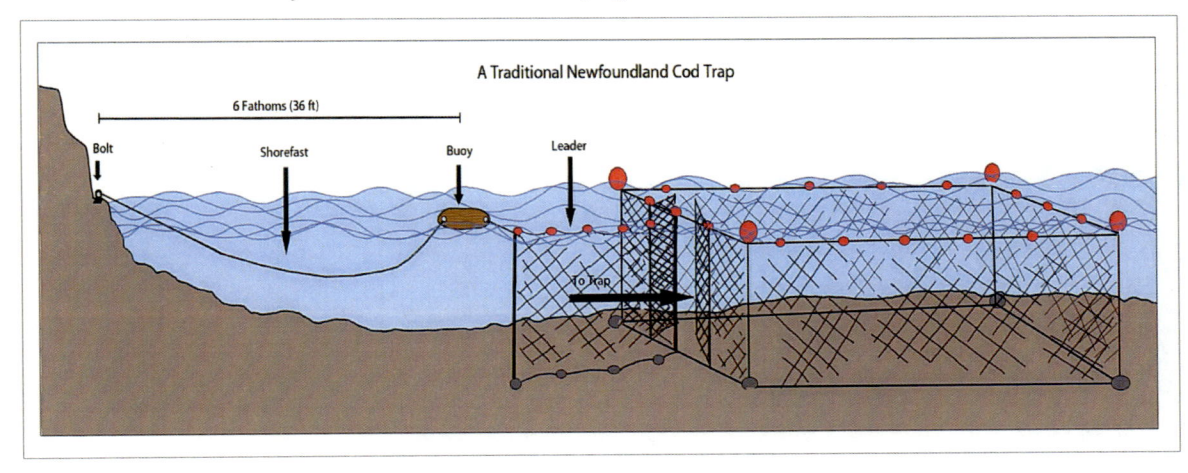

Figure 5. Diving Whale off Fogo Island (Photo: Paddy Barry) First mention in text: page 9.

Figure 6. A Traditional Newfoundland Cod Trap with Shorefast Cable (Photo courtesy of the Shorefast Foundation) First mention in text: page 11.

Figure 7. View of Cod Face (Photo: Paddy Barry) First mention in text: page 20.

Figure 8. Full View of Cod Fish (Photo: Paddy Barry) First mention in text: page 20.

Figure 9. Cinema Located in the Fogo Island Inn (Photo: Alex Fradkin) First mention in text: page 25.

Figure 10. Carpenter Working on a Fogo Island Punt Boat (Photo: Jamie Lewis) First mention in text: page 44.

Figure 11. Close-Up View of Mural in the Guest Elevator of the Fogo Island Inn (Photo: Eric Ratkowski) First mention in text: page 49.

Figure 12. Fogo Island Inn Guest Room: View and Sound of Sea from Open Window (Photo: Alex Fradkin) First mention in text: page 49.

Figure 13. Fogo Island Inn Guest Room: Note Bath Tub and Hand-Made Furnishings (Photo: Alex Fradkin) First mention in text: page 49.

Figure 14. Fogo Island Inn Suite with Wood-Burning Stove and Punt Boat Rocker (Photo: Alex Fradkin) First mention in text: page 49.

Figure 15. Dining Room of the Fogo Island Inn (Photo: Alex Fradkin) First mention in text: page 49.

Figure 16. Food Presentation # 1 (Photo: Alex Fradkin) First mention in text: page 49.

Figure 17. Food Presentation #2 (Photo: Alex Fradkin) First mention in text: page 49.

Figure 18. Murray McDonald, Executive Chef of the Fogo Island Inn with a Mummer (Photo: Paddy Barry) First mention in text: page 50.

Figure 19. Nicole's Café for Modern Interpretations of Newfoundland Regional Cuisine (Photo: Paddy Barry) First mention in text: page 50.

Figure 20. A Garden-to-Table Source for Some of the Produce for the Fogo Island Inn (Photo: Joe Ip) First mention in text: page 50.

Figure 21. One of a Number of Gardens that Source the Fogo Island Inn Kitchens (Photo: Paddy Barry) First mention in text: page 50.

Figure 22. Local Garden Carrots on Their Way to the Fogo Island Inn's Dining Tables (Photo: Jamie Lewis) First mention in text: page 50.

Figure 23. The Bar of the Fogo Island Inn: Its Signature Cocktail is the "Rockin Fogo" (Photo: Paddy Barry) First mention in text: page 51.

Figure 24. Profile of the Long Studio (Photo: Paddy Barry) First mention in text: page 54.

Figure 25. End View of the Long Studio (Photo: Bent René Synnevåg) First mention in text: page 54.

Figure 26. Tower Studio with Colored Rock in Foreground (Photo: Bent René Synnevåg) First mention in text: page 54.

Figure 27. Tower Studio: View of the Dark Side (Photo: Bent René Synnevåg) First mention in text: page 54.

Figure 28. Bridge Studio (Photo: Bent René Synnevåg) First mention in text: page 54.

Figure 29. Squish Studio: With Blue Sea and Blue Sky (Photo: Bent René Synnevåg) First mention in text: page 54.

Figure 30. Squish Studio: With Iceberg, Growlers (pieces of floating ice) and Waves (Photo: Paddy Barry) First mention in text: page 54.

Figure 31. Squish Studio: At Sunset (Photo: Bent René Synnevåg) First mention in text: page 54.

Figure 32. Wells House: Refurbished and Modernized Residence for Artists-in-Residence (Photo: Joe Ip) First mention in text: page 54.

Figure 33. View of the Fogo Island Inn from the Sea (Photo: Alex Fradkin) First mention in text: page 54.

Figure 34. Fogo Island Inn: A View on the Diagonal (Photo: Alex Fradkin) First mention in text: page 54.

Figure 35. An End View of the Fogo Island Inn (Photo: Alex Fradkin) First mention in text: page 54.

Figure 36. A Night View on the Angle of the Fogo Island Inn (Photo: Alex Fradkin) First mention in text: page 54.

Figure 37. Social Enterprise: Business Minded Ways that Serve Social Ends (Image courtesy of the Shorefast Foundation) First mention in text: page 56.

Figure 38. Barr'd Islands Church has Been Re-Purposed as a Space for Performance (Photo: Paddy Barry) First mention in text: page 59.

Figure 39. The Dr. Leslie A. Harris Heritage Library is Located in the Fogo Island Inn (Photo: Alex Fradkin) First mention in text: page 70.

Figure 40. A Cozy Spot to Read in the Harris Library of the Fogo Island inn (Photo: Alex Fradkin) First mention in text: page 70.

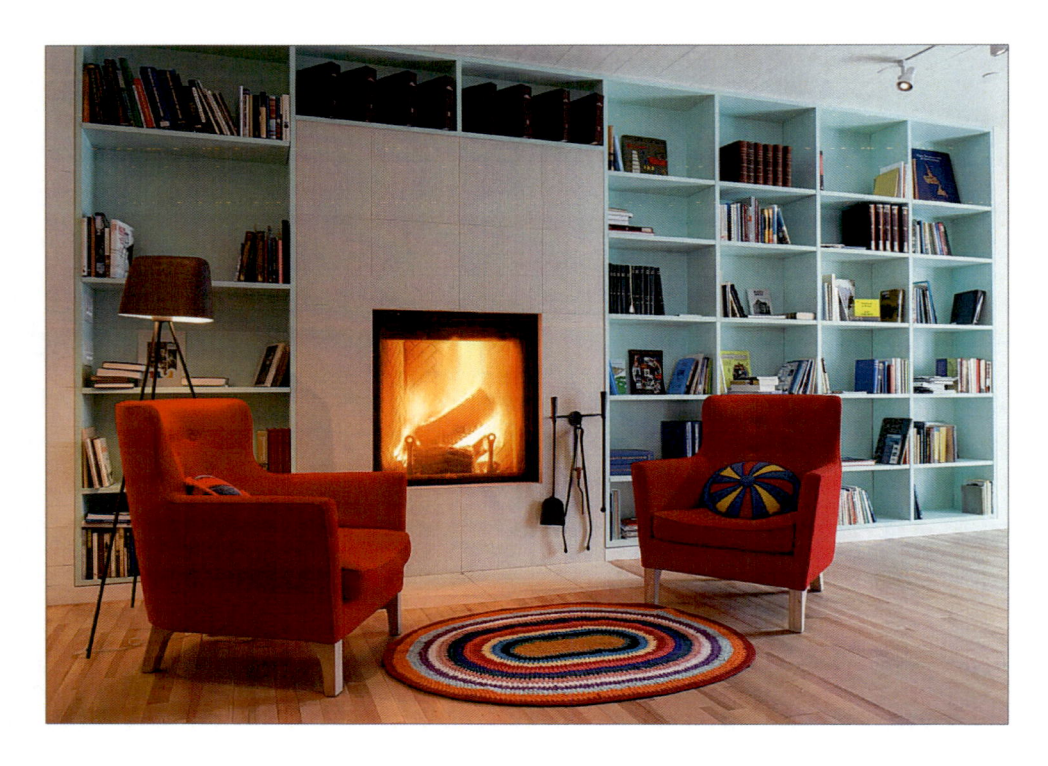

Figure 41. Close-Up of a Mummer in the Fogo Island Inn during the Christmas Season (Photo: Paddy Barry) First mention in text: page 72.

Figure 42. Two Mummers at the Fogo Island Inn at Christmas Time (Photo: Paddy Barry) First mention in text: page 72.

Figure 43. Gordon Slade, Chair and Ocean Advisor of the Shorefast Foundation (Photo: Jamie Lewis) First mention in text: page 80.

Figure 44. Zita Cobb, President and Founder of the Shorefast Foundation (Photo: Luther Caverly) First mention in text: page 83.

Figure 45. Fishers Hauling in the New Cod Pot that Enables Higher Price Points (Photo: Paddy Barry) First mention in text: page 129.

Figure 46. The New Cod Pot on the Deck of the Fishing Boat, it Enables Sustainability (Photo: Paddy Barry) First mention in text: page 129.

Figure 47. A View of the Motor Vessel Ketanja Near an Iceberg (Photo: Alex Fradkin) First mention in text: page 130.

Figure 48. Visitors Taking The Ketanja Boat Tours to See Icebergs, Seabirds and Whales (Photo: Alex Fradkin) First mention in text: page 130.

Figure 49. The Punt Chair was Built by Carpenters with Punt Boat Skills (Photo: Steffen Jaggenberg) First mention in text: page 133.

REFERENCES

Note: The use here of "n.d." or no date signifies that no date was provided by the published Web-based reference. Readers should note further, that this extensive compilation of references should be used and delved into for the origins of the many concepts, methods and cases from the literature and from effective intelligent development practice. Exploring these sources can lead you and your fellow regional and place development stakeholders to additional discoveries that can enrich your local planning and development execution.

Acemoglu, D. and Zilibotti, F. (1999) "Information Accumulation in Development," *Journal of Economic Growth*, 4: 5-38.

Bartlett, S. (2008) *The Grit and the Courage*. St. John's, Newfoundland and Labrador: Creative Publishers.

Bates, P. (October 21, 2103) "Aspects of Fogo Island Initiative May Be Transferable to Cape Breton," *Cape Breton Post*. Online. Available at: http://www.capebretonpost.com/Opinion/Columnists/2013-10-21/article-3434186/Aspects-of-Fogo-Island-initiative-may-be-transferable-to-Cape-Breton/1 (accessed October 28, 2013).

Battle Harbour (n.d.) Online. Available at: http://www.battleharbour.com/ (accessed August, 3, 2014).

Bennis, W. (1976) *The Unconscious Conspiracy: Why Leaders Can't Lead*. New York: AMACOM (A Division of the American Management Association).

Bolster, W.J. (2012) *The Mortal Sea: Fishing the Atlantic in the Age of Sail*. Cambridge, Massachusetts and London, England: The Belknap Press of Harvard University Press.

Bossen, H. and Beck, J.P. (Editors) (2014) *Detroit Resurgent: A Counternarrative of Hope and Vision. East Lansing*: Michigan State University Press.

Bozikovic, A. (July 18, 2013) "Building a Newfoundland for Thirtysomethings," *The Globe and Mail*. Online. Available at: http://www.theglobeandmail.com/arts/art-and-architecture/building-a-newfoundland-for-thirtysomethings/article13296608/ (accessed October 24, 2013).

Briggs, J. (June 19, 2013) E-Mail Correspondence by Author. Interviewee located in Skagit County, Washington State, USA.

Briggs, J. (June 21, 2013) E-Mail Correspondence by Author. Interviewee located in Skagit County, Washington State, USA.

Briggs, J. (June 25, 2013) E-Mail Correspondence by Author. Interviewee located in Skagit County, Washington State, USA.

Briggs, J. (December 16, 2013) E-Mail Correspondence by Author. Interviewee located in Mount Vernon, Washington State, USA.

Business Education (May 6, 2013) "Value Creation, a Sustainable Firm or Venture Philanthropy," *Financial Times, The Canadian Press*, October 24, 2013), page 9.

Canada's Historic Places (n.d.) "Battle Harbor National Historic District National Historic Site of Canada," *Canada's Historic Places*. Online. Available at: http://www.historicplaces.ca/en/rep-reg/place-lieu.aspx?id=3453 (accessed August 9, 2014).

Canada's Historic Places (n.d.) "Tilting Registered Heritage District," *Canada's Historic Places.* Online. Available at: http://www.historicplaces.ca/en/rep-reg/place-lieu.aspx?id=2731 (accessed September 2, 2014).

Candice Does the World (n.d.) "I Went to One of the Four Corners of the World." Online. Available at: http://www.candicedoestheworld.com/2012/09/i-went-to-one-of-the-four-corners-of-the-world/ (accessed October 2, 2013).

CBC News (August 14, 2014) "Cod Pot Fishing Method a Hit with Fogo Island Fishermen, Chefs." Online. Available at: http://www.cbc.ca/news/canada/newfoundland-labrador/cod-pot-fishing-method-a-hit-with-fogo-island-fishermen-chefs-1.2736755 (accessed August 27, 2014).

CBC News (August 23, 2014) "Construction Started on $51M Fogo Island, Change Islands Ferry." Online. Available at: http://www.cbc.ca/news/canada/newfoundland-labrador/construction-started-on-51m-fogo-island-change-islands-ferry-1.2744863 (accessed August 24, 2014).

CBC News (October 14, 2013) "Fogo Island Residents Worried as Winsor Out for Repairs." Online. Available at: http://www.cbc.ca/news/canada/newfoundland-labrador/fogo-island-residents-worried-as-winsor-out-for-repairs-1.2053921 (accessed October 29, 2013).

CBC News (November 13, 2013) "New Ferries Coming for Fogo, Bell Island Runs." Online. Available at: http://www.cbc.ca/news/canada/newfoundland-labrador/new-ferries-coming-for-fogo-bell-island-runs-1.2425076 (accessed July 19, 2014).

Center for Sustainable Destinations (n.d.) "About Geotourism." Washington, D.C.: *National Geographic*. Online. Available at: http://travel.nationalgeographic.com/travel/sustainable/about_geotourism.html (accessed July 17, 2012).

Chan, Y. (2011) *Location Theory and Decision Analysis: Analytics of Spatial Information Technology*. Second Edition. Berlin and Heidelberg: Springer-Verlag.

Clarke, D.J. (2012) *A History of the Isles: Twillingate, New World Island, Fogo Island and Change Islands, Newfoundland and Labrador*. Second Revised Edition. Charleston, South Carolina: CreateSpace Independent Publishing Platform.

Coates, M. (n.d.) "Room to Dream at Fogo Island Inn." PowerPoint Presentation. This presentation was shared with the authors by Melanie Coates, Director, Marketing & Business Development, Fogo Island Inn.

Cobb, A. (August 26, 2014) E-Mail Correspondence by Author. Interviewee is Secretary of the Board of Directors of the Shorefast Foundation located in Joe Batt's Arm, Fogo Island, Newfoundland, Canada.

Cobb, Z. (November 9, 2013) Acceptance Speech, Honorary Degree Presentation, Carlton University, Ottawa, Ontario, Canada.

Cobb, Z. (March 2, 2014) "Commentary: Big Questions of Human Progress Play out in Small Places," *Herald Magazine*. Online. Available at: http://thechronicleherald.ca/heraldmagazine/1189599-commentary-big-questions-of-human-progress-play-out-in-small-places?from=most_read&most_read=1189599 (accessed August 14, 2014).

Cobb, Z. (August 17, 2014) "Converging Futures," Canadian Bar Association Legal Conference, St. John's, Newfoundland. Online. Available at: http://www.cba.org/cba/cbaclc2014/keynote/default.aspx (accessed August 24, 2014).

Cobb, Z. (April 2, 2014) Correspondence to Brett Song.

Cobb, Z. (May 31, 2013) Interview by Authors. Interviewee location Shorefast Foundation headquarters, Highway 334, Building 100, Fogo Island, Newfoundland.

Cobb, Z. (January 28, 2014) "Response: Fogo Island Model for Rural Development." E-mail from Diane Hodgins, Director, Investment Partnerships, Shore Fast Foundation.

Cobb, Z. (February 13, 2014) "Transformation: One Community at a Time." American Fundraising Professionals, AFP – D3 (Debate, Debunk, Delight) Conference. Video Online. Available at: http://afptoronto.org/d3/test-video-gallery-page/ (accessed August 23, 2014).

Cohoe, R. (May 16, 2013) "Memorial and Shorefast Foundation Establish Partnership." Online. Available at: http://today.mun.ca/news.php?id=8458 (accessed October 17, 2013).

Congdon Fors, H. (2014) "Do Island States Have Better Institutions?" *Journal of Comparative Economics*, 42: 34-60.

Connect Michigan and the Antrim County Broadband Committee (January 30, 2013) "Antrim County Technology Action Plan," Connected Community Engagement Program of Connect Michigan. Online. Available at: http://www.connectmi.org/sites/default/files/connected-nation/Michigan/files/antrim_county_mi_technology_plan_final.pdf

Connect Michigan and the Delta County Broadband Committee (May 10, 2013) "Delta County Technology Action Plan," Connected Community Engagement Program of Connect Michigan. Online. Available at: http://www.connectmi.org/sites/default/files/connected-nation/Michigan/files/delta_county_mi_technology_action_plan_final.pdf

Connect Michigan and the Ogemaw County Broadband Committee (September 2013) "Ogemaw County Technology Action Plan," Connected Community Engagement Program of Connect Michigan. Online. Available at: http://www.connectmi.org/sites/default/files/connected-nation/Michigan/files/ogemaw_county_mi_technology_action_plan_final.pdf

Connect Michigan and the St. Clair County Broadband Committee (May 23, 2013) "St. Clair County Technology Action Plan," Connected Community Engagement Program of Connect Michigan. Online. Available at: http://www.connectmi.org/sites/default/files/connected-nation/Michigan/files/st_clair_county_mi_technology_action_plan_final.pdf

Connect Michigan (n.d.) "Home Page." Online. Available at: www.connectmi.org (accessed November 2, 2013).

Connected Nation (Fall 2013) "Beyond the Divide." Washington, D.C.: Connected Nation, Inc. Online. Available at: http://www.connectednation.org/sites/default/files/connected-nation/files/cnctd_fall_final.pdf (accessed November 22, 2013).

Corey, K.E. (1987) "Development in Sri Lanka: A Model for Counterurbanization Policies and Planning?" *Urban Geography*, 8, 6: 520-539.

Corey, K.E. and Wilson, M.I. (2010) "Benchmarking IT Cities," in *Developing Living Cities: From Analysis to Action*. Editors, B. Yuen and K. Seetharam. Singapore: World Scientific Publishing Co. Pte. Ltd.: 127-153.

Corey, K.E. and Wilson, M.I. (2006) *Urban and Regional Technology Planning: Planning Practice in the Global Knowledge Economy*. London and New York: Routledge.

Corey, K.E., Wilson, M.I. and Fan, P. (2015) "Cities, Technologies and Economic Change," Chapter in *Cities and Economic Change: Restructuring and Dislocation in the Global Metropolis*. Editors Paddison, R. and Hutton, T. London and Thousand Oaks, California: Sage Publications: 15-37.

Corey, M. (June 13, 2013) "Understated Luxury," *Trip Advisor. Online*. Available at: http://www.tripadvisor.com/Hotel_Review-g1453896-d4322085-Reviews-or30-Fogo_Island_Inn-Joe_Batt_s_Arm_Fogo_Island_Newfoundland_Newfoundland_and_Labrado.html#REVIEWS accessed October 7, 2013).

Crocker, S. (2008) "Filmmakers and the Politics of Remoteness: The Genesis of the Fogo Process on Fogo Island, Newfoundland," *Shima: The International Journal of Research into Island Cultures*, 2, 1: 59-75.

Dawe, T.V.C. (2006) *Our Own Newfoundland and Labrador*. Teachers on Wheels Inc.

Delbecq, A.L. and Van de Ven, A. (1976) "A Group Process Model for Problem Identification and Program Planning," in *The Planning of Change*. Edited by W.G. Bennis, K.D. Benne, R. Chin and Corey, K.E. Third Edition. New York: Holt, Rinehart and Winston Inc., 1976.

DesignalmiC (n.d.) "Fogo Island Inn/Saunders Architecture." Online. Available at: http://designalmic.com/fogo-island-inn-saunders-architecture/ (accessed October 14, 2013).

Donaldson, Z. (n.d.) "50 Things That Will Make You Say Wow!" Welcome to Oprah. Online. Available at: http://www.oprah.com/spirit/Os-2013-Wow-List-Amazing-Inventions-Cool-Art/2 (accessed October 27, 2013).

Douglas, M. (1986) *How Institutions Think*. Syracuse University: Syracuse University Press.

Duffy, G. (August 27, 2014) E-Mail Correspondence by Author. Interview is Chief Financial Officer of the Shorefast Foundation located in Ottawa, Ontario, Canada.

Editors' Note to Snowden, D. (1998) "Eye See; Ears Hear," in *The First Mile of Connectivity*, Editors Richardson, D. and Paisley, L. Rome: Food and Agriculture Organization of the United Nations: 1-8. Online. Available at: http://www.fao.org/docrep/x0295e/x0295e06.htm (accessed August 25, 2014).

Engel, M. (August 23/August 24, 2014) "Then There Were None," *Financial Times*: 1-2 of the Life & Times section.

Enright, A. (September 25, 2013) "The Most Irish Island in the World," *The Irish Times. Online*. Available at: http://www.irishtimes.com/life-and-style/travel/the-most-irish-island-in-the-world-1.1538579 (accessed November 2, 2013).

Farsani, N.T., Coelho, C. and Costa, C. (2011) "Geotourism and Geoparks as Novel Strategies for Socio-economic Development in Rural Areas," *International Journal of Tourism Research*, 13: 68-81.

Ferreira, G.A. (September 2006) "Participatory Video for Policy Development," *Canadian Journal of Communication*. Online. Available at: http://www.cjc-online.ca/index.php/journal/thesis/view/68 (accessed August 27, 2014).

Feyrer, J. and Sacerdote, B. (2009) "Colonialism and Modern Income: Islands as Natural Experiments," *The Review of Economics and Statistics*, 91, 2: 245-262.

Fischer, S.R. (2012) *Islands: From Atlantis to Zanzibar*. London: Reakion Books Ltd.

Fitzpatrick, J.W. (August 31, 2014) ""Saving Our Birds," *The New York Times*: 1 and 6-7 of the Sunday Review section.

Fogo Island Arts (n.d.) "About Fogo Island Arts." Online. Available at: http://afptoronto.org/d3/test-video-gallery-page/ (accessed August 18, 2014).

Fogo Island Arts (September 27, 2013) "Fogo Island Dialogues: Culture as Destination." Online. Available at: http://fogoislandarts.ca/news/ (accessed October 5, 2013).

Fogo Island Co-operative Society Ltd. (n.d.) "Home Page." Online. Available at: http://www.fogoislandcoop.com/ (accessed September 28, 2013).

Fogo Island Dialogues (n.d.) Fogo Island Dialogues Home Page. Online. Available at: http://fogoislandarts.ca/programs/dialogues/ (accessed August 17, 2014).

Fogo Island Inn (n.d.) "Home Page." Online. Available at: http://www.fogoislandinn.ca/ (accessed October 2, 2013).

Fogo Island Partridgeberry Harvest Festival (n.d.) "Community Report – 5th Annual Festival Oct 6th & 7th 2012." Unpublished report. Three pages.

Frederick, E. (September 24, 2013) Correspondence by Author. Interviewee located in Lansing, Michigan.

Friedmann, J. (June 2010) "Place and Place-Making in Cities: A Global Perspective," *Planning Theory and Practice*, 11 (2): 149-165.

Gappert, G. (Editor) (1987) *The Future of Winter Cities*. Newbury Park, California: Sage Publications.

Geology At The Edge Organization (n.d.) "About." Online. Available at: https://www.facebook.com/GeologyAtTheEdge?hc_location=timeline (accessed July 20, 2014).

Geology At The Edge Organization (October 31, 2012) "Canada's First Community-Based Geology Residency Program is Now Accepting Applications." Online. Available at: https://www.facebook.com/FogoIslandInn/posts/360298210727977 (accessed July 20, 2014).

Goose Cove Retreat (n.d.) "Home Page." Online. Available at: http://www.goosecoveretreat.com/ (accessed October 24, 2013).

Goulet, D. (1983) *Mexico: Development Strategies for the Future*. Notre Dame and London: University of Notre Dame Press.

Grameen Bank (n.d.) "Introduction." Online. Available at: http://www.grameen-info.org/index.php?option=com_content&task=view&id=197&Itemid=197 (accessed August 24, 2014).

Harris, L. (2008) "Life at the Edge of the Sea," *Newfoundland Quarterly*, 101, 1: 10-13 and 36-41.

Hodge, G. (1963) "Use and Mis-Use of Measurement Scales in City Planning," *Journal of the American Institute of Planners*, 29, 2: 112-121.

Hodgins, D. (May 16, 2013) E-Mail Correspondence by Author. Interviewee is Director, Investor Partnerships, of the Shorefast Foundation located in Ottawa, Ontario, Canada.

Hodgins, D. (August 8, 2013) E-Mail Correspondence by Author. Interviewee is Director, Investor Partnerships, of the Shorefast Foundation located in Ottawa, Ontario, Canada.

Hodgins, D. (January 28, 2014) E-Mail Correspondence by Author. Interviewee is Director, Investor Partnerships, of the Shorefast Foundation located in Ottawa, Ontario, Canada.

Hodgins, D. (August 18, 2014) E-Mail Correspondence by Author. Interviewee is Director, Investor Partnerships, of the Shorefast Foundation located in Ottawa, Ontario, Canada.

Hodgins, D. (August 21, 2014) E-Mail Correspondence by Author. Interviewee is Director, Investor Partnerships, of the Shorefast Foundation located in Ottawa, Ontario, Canada.

Hoggart, K. (1979) "Resettlement in Newfoundland," *Geography*, 64, 3: 215-218.

Hose, T.A., Markovic, S.B., Komac, B. and Zorn, M. (2011) "Geotourism – A Short Introduction" *Acta Geographica Slovenica*, 51, 2: 339-342.

International Development Research Centre (n.d.) Home Page. Online. Available at: http://www.idrc.ca/EN/Pages/default.aspx (accessed August 27, 2014).

Jackson, T. (2009) *Prosperity Without Growth: Economics for a Finite Planet*. London and New York: Earthscan.

Johnson GEO CENTRE (November 26, 2013) "Shorelines, Fire and Ice: Geological Stories in the Rocks of Fogo Islands and Change Islands," promotion for Public Lecture at the Johnson GEO CENTRE by Andrew Kerr, St. John's, Newfoundland. Online. Available at: http://www.geocentre.ca/learn/public-lectures/past-lectures/ (accessed August 25, 2014).

JTC Corporation (n.d.) Home Page. Online. Available at: http://www.jtc.gov.sg/Pages/default.aspx (accessed August 16, 2014)

Katz, B. and Bradley, J. (2013) *The Metropolitan Revolution: How Cities and Metros are Fixing Our Broken Politics and Fragile Economy*. Washington, D.C.: Brookings Institution Press.

Kellner, J. (Editor) (2014) *Furniture of the Fogo Island Inn*. Joe Batt's Arm, Fogo Island, Newfoundland: Shorefast Foundation.

Kerr, A. (2013) "The Fogo Process from a Geologist's Perspective: A Discussion of Models and Research Problems," Current Research, Newfoundland and Labrador Department of Natural Resources Geological Survey, Report 13-1: 233-265. Online. Available at: http://www.nr.gov.nl.ca/nr/mines/geoscience/publications/currentresearch/2013/Kerr-Fogo_2013.pdf (accessed August 26, 2014).

Kittiwake Economic Development Corporation and D.W. Knight Associates (July 2008) "Fogo Island-Change Islands Socio-Economic Strategic Plan: A Shared Vision for a Very Special Place." Gander, Newfoundland: Kittiwake Economic Development Corporation.

Kobalenko, J. (April 2008) "Into Battle," *Canadian Geographic Magazine*. Online. Available at: http://www.canadiangeographic.ca/magazine/apr08/explorer.asp (accessed August 9, 2014).

Kunsthalle Wien (May 26, 2013) "Facing Neoliberalism." 1:08.37 Length Video of Zita Cobb and Liam Gillick convened and Moderated by Nicolaus Schafhasen. Online. Available at: http://www.youtube.com/watch?v=pOihyHGg1A4 (accessed October 5, 2013).

Kurlansky, M. (1997) *Cod: A Biography of the Fish That Changed the World*. New York: Penguin Books.

Lachapelle, P. (2008) "A Sense of Ownership in Community Development: Understanding the Potential for Participation in Community Planning Efforts," *Community Development: Journal of the Community Development Society*, 39, 2: 52-59.

Lee, Jr., D.B. (1973) "Requiem for Large-Scale Models," *Journal of the American Institute of Planners*, 39, 3: 163-178.

Linnaeus University (n.d.) "Tourism, Local Foods and Regional Development." Online. Available at: http://lnu.se/about-lnu/conferences/avslutade-konferenser/2013/tourism-local-foods-and-regional-development-30-september--1-october-2013?l=en (accessed October 14, 2013).

Lochnan, K. (2011) *Black Ice: David Blackwood Prints of Newfoundland*. Toronto: Art Gallery of Ontario.

Loeffler, TA (March 15, 2007) "Newfoundland and Labrador: The Rock," *MyEverest*. Online. Available at: http://www.myeverest.com/newfoundland-labrador (accessed August 3, 2014).

Lummus, R.R., Krumwiede, D.W., and Vokurka, R.J. (2001) "The Relationship of Logistics to Supply Chain Management: Developing a Common Industry Definition," 101, 8: 426-431.

Marien, E.J. (February 2003) "SCM & Logistics: What's the Difference?" *Inbound Logistics*. Online. Available at: http://www.inboundlogistics.com/cms/article/scm-and-logistics-whats-the-difference/ (accessed September 21, 2013).

McClelland, S. (June 2014) "Saving Fogo and Change Islands," *Canadian Geographic Magazine*. Online. Available at: http://www.canadiangeographic.ca/magazine/jun14/new-ocean-ethics-project.asp (accessed July 22, 2014).

McDonald, M. (May 30, 2013) Interview by Authors. Interviewee location Fogo Island Inn, Joe Batt's Arm, Fogo Island, Newfoundland.

McGrain, T. (2014) *The Lost Bird Project*. Hanover and London: University Press of New England.

Mellin, R. (2003) *Tilting: House Launching, Slide Hauling, Potato Trenching, and Other Tales from a Newfoundland Fishing Village*. New York: Princeton Architectural Press.

Memorial University of Newfoundland (May 27, 2014) "Geography Alumnus is the Shorefast Foundation's Geologist-in-Residence." Online. Available at: https://www.mun.ca/geog/////////news.php?id=3563 (accessed July 20, 2014).

Menkhoff, T., Chay, Y.W. and Loh, B. (2004) "Notes from an Intelligent Island: Towards Strategic Knowledge Management in Singapore's Small Business Sector." Singapore: Research Collection

Lee Kong Chian School of Business. Online. Available at: http://ink.library.smu.edu.sg/lkcsb_research/1920 (accessed August 16, 2014).

National Film Board of Canada (1968) "The NFB and Fogo Island, Newfoundland: A Continuing Story." Online. Available at: http://www.onf.ca/selections/fogo-island/lecture/ (accessed November 21, 2013).

National Geographic Society (n.d.) "Center for Sustainable Destinations." Online. Available at: http://travel.nationalgeographic.com/travel/sustainable/about_geotourism.html (accessed October 2, 2013).

Neis, B. (1981) "Competitive Merchants and Class Struggle in Newfoundland," *Studies in Political Economy*, 5: 127-143.

Nemtin, B. and Low, C. (May 1968) *Fogo Island Film and Community Development Project*. Unpublished Report. Montreal: National Film Board of Canada, 30 pages.

Newfoundland and Labrador Heritage (n.d.) "Migratory Fishery and Settlement Patterns," Newfoundland and Labrador Heritage. Online. Available at: http://www.heritage.nf.ca/exploration/settlement_patterns.html (accessed August 12, 2014).

Newfoundland and Labrador Heritage (n.d.) "The Truck System," Newfoundland and Labrador Heritage. Online. Available at: http://www.heritage.nf.ca/society/truck_system.html (accessed August 12, 2014).

Newfoundland and Labrador Tourism Board (February 2013) "Tourism Vision Evaluation Annual Report 2012. St. John's: Newfoundland and Labrador Tourism Board, 44 pages.

Newhook. S. (2009) "The Godfathers of Fogo: Donald Snowden, Fred Earle and the Roots of the Fogo Island Films, 1964-1067," Newfoundland and Labrador Studies, 24, 2: 171-197. Online. Available at: http://www.synergiescanada.org/journals/etc/nflds/1131 (accessed August 25, 2014).

NL Interactive (Fall 1998) "The Fishery," The Life and Times of Pre-Confederation Newfoundland. Online. Available at: http://nfinteractive.com/galleries/confederation/fishery.html (accessed August 2014).

Northern Cod Review Panel, and Leslie Harris (1990) *Independent Review of the State of the Northern Cod Stock: Executive Summary and Recommendations*. Ottawa: Communications Directorate, Department of Fisheries and Oceans.

Nova Central School District (November 20, 2013) "Fogo Island Central Academy." Online. Available at: http://www.ncsd.ca/school_profile/fogo_island_central_academy.asp (accessed November 20, 2013).

Ölands Skördefest (n.d.) "Ölands Skördefest - The Story in English." Online. Available at: http://www.skordefest.nu/Eng/se/70/ (accessed October 14, 2013).

Peattie, L. (1970) "Drama and Advocacy," *Journal of the American Institute of Planners*, 36: 405-410.

Robinson, A. (November 19, 2013) "Businessman Says PCs ignore Blue Book Promise with Ferry Contract," NL News Now.Com. Online. Available at: http://www.nlnewsnow.com/News/Local/2013-11-19/article-3486771/Businessman-says-PCs-ignore-Blue-Book-promise-with-ferry-contract/1 (accessed November 21, 2013).

Rogers, E.M. (1976) "Communication and Development: The Passing of the Dominant Paradigm," *Communication Research*, 3: 213-240.

Rogers, E.M. (1962) Diffusion of Innovations. *New York: The Free Press*.

Rose, G.A. (2007) Cod: *The Ecological History of the North Atlantic Fisheries*. St. John's, Newfoundland: Breakwater Books Ltd. CreateSpace Independent Publishing Platform

Roseland, M. (2012) *Toward Sustainable Communities: Solutions for Citizens and their Governments*. 4th Edition. Gabriola Island, BC: New Society Publishers.

Rosenbaum, S. (2011) *Curation Nation, Why the Future of Content is Context: How to Win in a World Where Consumers are Creators*. New York: McGraw Hill.

Rosenberg, M. (n.d.) "William Morris Davis," About.com Geography. Online. Available at: http://geography.about.com/od/historyofgeography/a/williamdavis.htm (accessed October 26, 2013).

Ross, R. (October 3, 2013) "Rural Revival," The Guardian, Newspaper published in Charlottetown, Prince Edward Island. Online. Available at: http://www.theguardian.pe.ca/ (accessed October 4, 2013).

Saeks, D.D. (August 10/August 11, 2013) "Deep Sea Change," *Financial Times*, House and Home Section, page 2.

Senge, P.M. (2006) *The Fifth Discipline: The Art and Practice of the Learning Organization*. New York: Doubleday.

Senge, P.M., et. al. (2008) *The Necessary Revolution: How Individuals and Organizations Are Working Together to Create a Sustainable World*. New York: Doubleday.

Shorefast Foundation (n.d.) "Arts." Online. Available at: http://www.shorefast.org/?page_id=1058 (accessed October 5, 2013)

Shorefast Foundation (n.d.) "Board of Directors." Online. Available at: http://shorefast.org/about-us/board-of-directors/ (accessed August 8, 2014).

Shorefast Foundation (n.d.) "Home Page." Online. Available at: http://www.shorefast.org/?page_id=237# (accessed October 2, 2013).

Shorefast Foundation (n.d.) "New Ocean Ethic." Online. Available at: http://shorefast.org/our-projects/ocean-ethic/ (accessed August 8, 2014).

Shorefast Foundation (2013) "New Ocean Ethic: Creating a Center for Ocean Literacy on Fogo Island and Change Islands. Joe Batt's Arm, Newfoundland: Shorefast Foundation, 5 pages.

Shorefast Foundation (2013 and 2014) "News: Dialogues." Online. Available at: http://fogoislandarts.ca/news/dialogues/ (accessed July 20, 2014).

Shorefast Foundation (n.d.) "Our Foundation." Online. Available at: http://shorefast.org/about-us/overview/ (accessed August 14, 2014).

Shorefast Foundation (July 31, 2014) "Shorefast Controller Position." E-mailed to author from Diane Hodgins, Director, Investment Partnerships, Shorefast Foundation.

Simon Fraser University (n.d.) "Canada Ocean Series." Online. Available at: http://www.sfu.ca/cstudies/science/canadaoceanlecture.php (accessed October 4, 2013).

Singbridge Corporate Pte Ltd (n.d.) Home Page. Online. Available at: http://www.singbridge.sg/ (accessed August 17, 2014).

Sixth Annual Fogo Island Partridgeberry Harvest Festival 2013 (n.d.) "Home Page." Online. Available at: http://www.fogoislandpartridgeberryfestival.com/index.php?option=com_content&view=article&id=47&Itemid=53 (accessed October 13, 2013).

Slade, G. (September 17, 2008) "Remembering Dr. Leslie Harris," The Pilot. Online. Available at: http://www.lportepilot.ca/Opinion/Columnists/2008-09-17/article-1423157/Remembering-Dr.-Leslie-Harris/1 Online. (accessed July 30, 2014).

Slade, G. (June 14, 2013) Telephone Interview by Author. Interviewee is Chair and Ocean Adviser for the Shorefast Foundation located at Mt. Pearl, Newfoundland.

Slade, G. (August 8, 2014) E-Mail Interview by Author. Interviewee is Chair and Ocean Adviser for the Shorefast Foundation located at Mt. Pearl, Newfoundland.

Slade, G. (August 27, 2014) E-Mail Interview by Author. Interviewee is Chair and Ocean Adviser for the Shorefast Foundation located at Mt. Pearl, Newfoundland.

Smithsonian Environmental Research Center (n.d.) "Home Page." Online. Available at: http://www.serc.si.edu (accessed November 2, 2013).

Sopiee, M.N. (2005) From Malayan Union to Singapore Separation: Political Unification in the Malaysia Region 1945-65. Kuala Lumpur: University of Malaya Press.

Story, G.M., Kirwin, W.J. and Widdowson, J.D.A. (Editors) (1990) Dictionary of Newfoundland English. Second Edition with Supplement. Toronto: University of Toronto Press.

Such, P. (1978) *Vanished Peoples: The Archaic Dorset & Boathook People of Newfoundland.* Toronto: NC Press Limited.

Sullivan, J. (October 11, 2010) "He Taught Us 'the Truth Lies in the Rocks'" *The Globe and Mail.* Online. Available at: http://v1.theglobeandmail.com/servlet/story/LAC.20101011.NWOBITHANKATL/BDAStory/BDA/deaths (accessed July 30, 2014).

Sustainable EDGE (n.d.) "Home Page." Online. Available at: http://wp.s-edge.com/ (Accessed September 28, 2013).

Svenska Academien (2013) "Biobibliographical Notes." Online. Available at: http://www.nobelprize.org/nobel_prizes/literature/laureates/2013/bio-bibl.html (accessed August 23, 2014).

Thant, M., Tang, M. and Kakazu, H. (1998) *Growth Triangles in Asia: A New Approach to Regional Economic Cooperation.* Second Edition. Oxford and New York: Oxford University Press.

The Canadian Encyclopedia (January 23, 2014) "Fogo Island," *The Canadian Encyclopedia.* Online. Available at: http://www.thecanadianencyclopedia.ca/en/article/fogo-island/ (accessed August 13, 2014).

The Canadian Press (October 24, 2013) "Food Truck Tops People's Choice List for Canada's Best New Restaurants," Toronto Star. Online. Available at: http://www.thestar.com/entertainment/2013/10/24/food_truck_tops_peoples_choice_list_for_canadas_best_new_restaurants.html (accessed November 2, 2013).

The Compass (October 15, 2013) "Fogo Island Inn Wins Award." Online. Available at: http://www.cbncompass.ca/?controllerName=article&page=1&contextId=3428722&siteId=15&action=changeRating&bizClass=article&bizId=3428722&rateValue= (accessed October 18, 2013).

The Pilot (November 4, 2013) "Twenty Cruiseships Visited Newfoundland Ports in 2013," The Pilot, Online. Available at: http://www.lportepilot.ca/News/Local/2013-11-04/article-3465713/Twenty-cruiseships-visited-Newfoundland-ports-in-2013/1 (accessed November 6, 2013).

Town of Change Islands (n.d.) "Home Page." Online. Available at: http://www.changeislands.ca/ (accessed September 27, 2013).

Town of Fogo Island (2013) "Fogo Island Tourism Guide." Town of Fogo Island, Newfoundland, two pages.

Town of Fogo Island (n.d.) "Home Page." Online. Available at: http://www.townoffogoisland.ca/home/ (accessed September 27, 2013).

University Center for Regional Economic Innovation (n.d.) "2012-13 Student-Led, Faculty-Guided Projects," Center for Community and Economic Development, Michigan State University.

Online. Available at: http://www.reicenter.org/projects/current-projects (accessed October 17, 2013).

University of Guelph (October 26-27, 1998) "Partnerships and Participation in Telecommunications for Rural Development: Exploring What Works and Why," Online. Available at: http://www.loka.org/pages/guelphconf.htm (accessed August 27, 2014).

Van de Ven, A.H. and Koenig, Jr., R. (1976) "A Process Model for Program Planning and Evaluation," *Journal of Economics and Business*, 23, 3: 161-170.

Vettoretto, L., 2009. A Preliminary Critique of the Best and Good Practices Approach in European Spatial Planning and Policy-Making. *European Planning Studies*, 17 (7), pp. 1067-1083.

Wells, K. (October 8, 2013) "Chefs on the Edge, The Pilot, Newspaper published in Lewisporte, Newfoundland. Online. Available at: http://www.lportepilot.ca/Community/2013-10-08/article-3421611/Chefs-on-the-edge/1 (accessed October 12, 2013).

Wells, K. (August 6, 2014) "Citizen Science on the Horizon," The Pilot, Newspaper published in Lewisporte, Newfoundland. Online. Available at: http://www.lportepilot.ca/News/Local/2014-08-06/article-3825431/NEW-OCEAN-ETHIC/1 (accessed August 9, 2014).

Wells, K. (August 21, 2013) "Update (Aug. 21) Stranded Ferry Passengers Cause for Concern," The Pilot, Newspaper published in Lewisporte, Newfoundland. Online. Available at: www.lportepilot.ca

Williams, H. (1964) "The Appalachians in Northeastern Newfoundland, a Two-Sided Symmetrical System," *American Journal of Science*, 262 (10): 1137-1158.

Williamson, T. (1989) "The Fogo Process: Development Support Communications in Canada and the Developing World." In AMIC-NCDC-BHU Seminar on Media and the Environment, Varanasi, February 26-March 1, 1989. Singapore: Asian Mass Communication Research and Information Centre. Online. Available at: http://hdl.handle.net/10220/895 (accessed August 14, 2014).

Wilson, J.T. (1966) "Did the Atlantic Close and then Reopen?" *Nature*, 19 (2): 676-681.

Wilson, M.I. and Corey, K.E. (2008) "The ALERT Model: A Planning-Practice Process for Planning Knowledge-Based Urban and Regional Development," in *Knowledge-Based Urban Development: Planning and Applications in the Information Era*. Editors Yigitcanlar, T., Velibeyoglu, K. and Baum, S. Hershey, Pennsylvania: IGI Global: 82-100.

Wilson, M.I., Kellerman, A. and Corey, K.E. (2013) *The Global Information Society: Technology, Knowledge and Mobility*. Boulder, Colorado: Rowman & Littlefield Publishers, Inc.

INDEX

A Model for Rural Development, 138
Architecture, 43, 44, 54, 70, 73, 85, 91, 97, 108, 139, 151, 202, 206
Arctic, 137, 143, 145
Art Gallery, 70, 209
Asia-Pacific Region, 106, 114
Atlantic Canada, 50, 68, 137
Bacalao Restaurant, 129
Basques, 19
Battle Harbour Historic Site, 79, 80, 109, 137, 168, 202
Beothuk, 19, 20, 52, 108, 146
Bergen, Norway, 54
Best Practice, 10, 15, 59, 102, 120, 138
Big-business, 50
Briggs, Jonathan, 13, 41, 45, 46, 47, 92, 93, 100, 103, 117, 164, 202, 203
Britain, 19, 20, 22, 49, 72, 202, 209
Broadband, 40, 99, 117, 153, 154, 164
Business Assistance Fund, 38, 42, 43, 45, 46, 47, 53, 56, 63, 91, 92, 99, 102, 106, 115, 116, 125, 128, 130, 132, 139, 164
Business Development, 26, 31, 42, 85, 100, 107, 110, 119, 120, 152, 163
Business Model, 118, 161
Business Trust, 55, 78, 126, 127
Cabot, John, 19
Canada Ocean Lecture Series, 67, 68
Caribbean, 49
Carpentry, 59, 80, 155
Change Islands, 4, 9, 10, 12, 13, 15, 19, 20, 31, 33, 37, 39, 40, 41, 42, 43, 45, 46, 47, 49, 54, 55, 56, 63, 64, 65, 66, 68, 69, 71, 79, 84, 85, 90, 91, 93, 94, 95, 96, 98, 102, 104, 105, 106, 107, 108, 109, 110, 112, 113, 114, 116, 117, 118, 119, 120, 125, 126, 128, 130, 131, 134, 135, 136, 139, 144, 145, 146, 159, 163, 164, 169, 175, 203, 208, 209, 212, 213
Charitable Organizations, 31, 32, 55, 56, 78, 80, 139
Charrette, 48, 133
Chefs, 49, 50, 51, 52, 71, 183, 203, 214
Christmas, 49, 72, 73, 195
Cinema, 25, 44, 85, 143
Citizen Science, 214

Civil Society, 10, 96, 103, 104, 111, 131, 134, 135, 137, 138
Cobb, Alan, 31, 32, 81, 131
Cobb, Anthony, 31, 32, 81
Cobb, Zita, 3, 4, 14, 15, 16, 31, 32, 33, 43, 48, 55, 56, 57, 71, 77, 82, 83, 84, 85, 89, 91, 94, 97, 98, 101, 114, 116, 118, 119, 120, 121, 125, 130, 134, 136, 137, 145, 168, 169, 196, 208
Cod, 11, 19, 20, 21, 25, 51, 58, 65, 66, 67, 68, 90, 91, 128, 129, 130, 136, 146, 159, 168, 177, 178, 197, 203, 209, 210, 211
Cod Moratorium, 25, 66, 67, 91, 129, 146
Cod pot, 68, 128, 129, 203
Colonialism, 19, 22, 134, 165, 206
Community Capital, 31, 33, 55, 120
Community Decision Making, 56
Community Host Program, 49, 58
Community Ownership, 13, 32, 38, 53, 55, 56, 83, 94, 96, 103, 105, 126, 163
Community Participation, 55, 56
Comparative Advantage, 12, 43, 73, 163, 164, 166
Connect Michigan, 26, 99, 153, 154, 204, 205
Connectedness, 25, 32, 37, 39, 40, 41, 55
Control, 21, 26, 32, 50, 56, 105, 121, 127, 128, 134, *See* Empowerment, Self Determination, Localization, Self-Reliance
Costa Rica, 84
Counterurbanization, 165
Crafts, 46, 47, 103, 155, 157, 159
Cultural Capital, 47, 53, 55, 56, 57, 65, 68, 73, 85
Davis, William Morris, 90, 211
Definition Process, 12, 32, 43, 138, 151
Demonstration, 64, 101, 140, 141, 142, 143, 144, 145, 163, 164, 166
Design Charrette, 48
Developing countries, 24
Developing Economies, 165
Development - Definition, 32
Development from Tradition, 54
Development Process, 4, 32, 83, 101
Devon, 20

Distant Capitalists, 91
Diversity of Local Economy, 117
Diversity of the Local Economy, 31, 32, 54, 56, 57, 64, 101, 104
Dorset, 20, 213
Drama as Development Metaphor, 77
Eco-dining, 49, 50, 51, 53, 102, 104, 108, 110
Economic Capital, 42, 55, 56, 57, 69, 85, 118
Economic Development, 5, 10, 13, 37, 45, 46, 115, 126, 138, 208, 213
Economies of Scale, 120
Economuseum, 110
Ecosystem, 10, 42, 54, 58, 66, 67
Ecotourism, 46, 48, 139
Electric Power, 39, 40, 164
Empowerment, 3, 38, 53, 56, 104, 111, 118, 121, 139
Entrepreneurial Assets, 106
Entrepreneurship, 32, 51, 54, 110, 118, 144
Ethics, 38, 51, 55, 69, 209
Europe, 19, 20, 43, 64, 70, 91, 95, 106, 114, 151, 214
Evaluation, 55, 81, 82, 94, 101, 102, 113, 126, 132, 138, 142, 153, 163, 169
Experiment, 3, 4, 12, 24, 50, 79, 82, 84, 96, 100, 105, 114, 119, 125, 128, 129, 131, 133, 138, 139, 145, 161, 166, 168
Exports, 3, 5, 10, 48, 83, 116, 165, 166
Factory Fishing, 65, 66
Ferry Service, 39, 40, 41, 49, 53, 85, 95, 98, 99, 108, 111, 117, 131, 164, 203, 211
Fisheries, 19, 20, 21, 67, 68, 129, 203, 210, 211
Fishing Industry, 20, 21, 22, 23, 25, 26, 27, 40, 42, 43, 49, 50, 54, 55, 65, 66, 67, 68, 69, 70, 79, 81, 90, 91, 101, 105, 108, 109, 112, 115, 116, 117, 125, 129, 132, 139, 164, 210
Flake, 155
Flat Earth Society, 58
Fogo Island, 3, 4, 9, 10, 11, 12, 13, 14, 15, 16, 19, 20, 22, 24, 25, 26, 27, 31, 32, 33, 37, 38, 39, 40, 41, 42, 43, 44, 45, 46, 47, 48, 49, 50, 51, 52, 53, 54, 55, 56, 57, 58, 59, 60, 61, 63, 64, 65, 66, 67, 68, 69, 70, 71, 72, 73, 77, 78, 79, 80, 81, 82, 83, 84, 85, 86, 89, 90, 91, 92, 93, 94, 95, 96, 97, 98, 99, 100, 101, 102, 103, 104, 105, 106, 107, 108, 109, 110, 112, 113, 114, 115, 116, 117, 118, 119, 120, 121, 125, 126, 127, 128, 129, 130, 131, 132, 133, 134, 135, 136, 137, 138, 139, 140, 141, 142, 143, 144,145, 146, 147, 155, 156, 157, 159, 161, 163, 164, 165, 166, 167, 168, 169, 170, 175, 176, 177, 179, 180, 181, 182, 183, 184, 185, 186, 191, 192, 194, 195, 202, 203, 204, 205, 206, 207, 208, 209, 210, 212, 213
Fogo Island Airstrip, 40, 98, 99, 117, 164
Fogo Island Arts Program, 38, 42, 43, 44, 45, 49, 53, 56, 63, 64, 65, 78, 91, 93, 94, 98, 105, 106, 115, 117, 125, 128, 130, 132, 161, 164, 167, 206, 211
Fogo Island Co-Operative Society, 26, 27, 46, 127
Fogo Island Dialogues, 38, 44, 56, 63, 64, 65, 66, 94, 102, 106, 114, 116, 117, 130, 133, 161, 166, 206, 207, 212
Fogo Island Inn, 25, 26, 38, 42, 43, 44, 45, 47, 48, 49, 50, 51, 52, 53, 54, 55, 56, 57, 58, 59, 60, 63, 64, 68, 69, 70, 71, 72, 73, 78, 81, 84, 85, 86, 89, 91, 93, 94, 97, 98, 99, 102, 103, 106, 107, 108, 109, 110, 112, 115, 116, 118, 125, 126, 127, 129, 130, 131, 132, 138, 143, 155, 164, 165, 167, 179, 180, 181, 182, 183, 184, 185, 186, 191, 192, 194, 195, 204, 205, 206, 207, 208, 209, 213
Fogo Island Model, 3, 4, 12, 13, 15, 19, 22, 31, 67, 68, 70, 73, 80, 82, 83, 84, 89, 90, 92, 97, 100, 106, 116, 117, 119, 120, 121, 125, 128, 135, 137, 138, 139, 140, 141, 142, 143, 144, 145, 147, 161, 163, 168, 169, 204
Fogo Island Model - Activation, 140, 143, 144, 145
Fogo Island Model - Benchmark, 25, 94, 126, 128, 129, 130, 131
Fogo Process, 17, 19, 22, 23, 24, 25, 26, 27, 41, 60, 132, 135, 140, 143, 144, 145, 168, 205, 208, 214
Food, 49, 50, 51, 102, 145, 182, 183, 206, 213
Food Festivals, 51
Foraging, 59

Framework, 3, 13, 32, 33, 43, 67, 71, 72, 89, 90, 112, 120, 126, 139, 142
France, 19, 20, 49, 117
Friedmann, John, 77, 135, 137, 169, 207
Fuller, Buckminster, 121
Fund Raising, 111, 116
Funk Island, 146
Garden, 50, 146, 184, 185
Geology, 43, 58, 92, 93, 128, 130, 151, 207
Geopark, 151, 152
Geotourism, 10, 13, 38, 42, 43, 45, 46, 49, 50, 51, 52, 53, 54, 56, 58, 59, 66, 69, 70, 71, 72, 73, 80, 84, 85, 89, 91, 92, 93, 94, 99, 102, 103, 104, 106, 107, 108, 109, 110, 114, 115, 116, 117, 128, 130, 132, 133, 138, 139, 151, 203, 210
Global Marketplace, 3, 25, 37, 40, 44, 92, 106, 108, 132, 133
Goose Cove Retreat, 108, 207
Grameen Bank, 45, 141, 207
Grand Banks, 19, 92
Great Auk, 146
Green Design, 48
Greenland, 19
Greeter Dogs, 60, 72
Gros Morne National Park, 109
Harris, Leslie, 9, 25, 40, 60, 70, 136, 194, 207, 210, 212
Hawai'i, 165
Henry VII, 19
Heritage Carpenters, 80
Hospitality, 9, 27, 39, 57, 81, 85, 89, 107, 110, 111, 138, 144
Human Capital, 55, 56, 57, 84, 85, 86, 90, 96, 139, 168
Humber Valley Resorts, 108
Hybrid Organizations, 107
Implementation, 11, 26, 63, 65, 67, 80, 84, 94, 96, 97, 100, 116, 128, 130, 141, 142, 161, 163, 165, 166, 168
Indonesia, 165, 166
Inform Action, 126, 133, 163, 167
Information Accumulation, 101
Information Society, 4, 40, 112, 135, 140, 153, 169
Information Technology, 165

Intelligent Development, 3, 4, 10, 13, 33, 66, 85, 96, 119, 120, 121, 133, 134, 147, 161, 169, 202
Intelligent Island, 165, 209
International Development Research Centre, 144, 208
Internet, 25, 39, 99, 153
Investment Partnerships, 68, 114, 115
Ireland, 20, 46, 72, 73, 206
Islandness, 12, 165
Job Creation, 37, 38, 92, 95, 113, 114
Justice, 38, 84, 98
Kalmar, Sweden, 51, 52
Kerr, Andrew, 93, 208
Knowledge Economy, 31, 40, 112, 132, 135, 153, 169
L'Anse aux Meadows National Historic Site, 19, 109
Land-Grant, 138
Learning Organization, 55, 82
Life Cycle, 3, 4, 89, 90, 92, 102, 106, 115, 118, 119, 120, 128, 132, 139, 141, 166
Linnaeus University, 51, 209
Local Government, 24, 46, 95, 98, 100, 131, 144, 153, 169
Locality, 16, 33, 57, 83, 85, 93, 104, 111, 125, 127, 128, 133, 142, 145, 168
Localization, 14, 27, 42, 49, 51, 52, 65, 83, 109, 111, 113, 125, 133, 141
Logistics, 37, 209
Lost Bird Project, 146, 209
Low, Colin, 140
Majumder, Shaun, 108
Malaysia, 165, 166, 212
Marketing, 38, 43, 53, 68, 70, 71, 72, 73, 80, 94, 103, 107, 114, 115, 116, 133, 155, 164
Massive Open Online Course (MOOC), 113
McDonald, Murray, 49, 50, 51, 52, 71, 183, 209
Measurement, 94, 207
Mellin, Robert, 73, 108, 209
Memorial University, 24, 67, 68, 80, 83, 93, 101, 113, 135, 136, 140, 143, 144, 145, 164, 209
Merchant Credit System, 19, 20, 22
Metaphor, 11, 64, 92, 166
Michigan, 9, 10, 11, 26, 99, 138, 153, 154, 170, 202, 204, 205, 207, 213

Michigan State University, 138
Microfinance, 42, 45, 91
Migration, 91
Mindset, 5, 11, 19, 22, 32, 37, 44, 47, 50, 66, 69, 82, 89, 132, 136, 139, 167
Modeling, 4, 12, 31, 37, 73, 77, 82, 83, 84, 92, 97, 100, 118, 119, 121, 125, 126, 128, 131, 133, 166, 170
Montreal, 63, 83, 210
Mummers, 72, 195
Mummery, 72, 73
Munro, Alice, 14
National Film Board of Canada, 24, 25, 70, 135, 143, 210
National Geographic Society, 42, 151, 210
Natural Capital, 55, 56, 57, 58
Natural Resource Utilization, 3, 20, 23, 43, 53, 66, 69, 79, 80, 105, 111, 119, 126, 129, 139, 147, 151, 164, 167
Natural Resources Utilization, 111
Netherlands, 41
Networks and ICT Connectivity, 4, 25, 31, 38, 39, 40, 64, 65, 68, 69, 83, 93, 99, 102, 103, 106, 108, 109, 110, 111, 112, 113, 116, 118, 130, 132, 140, 141, 145, 151, 153, 155, 164, 168
New Economy, 40, 140, 168
New Ocean Ethic Program, 38, 63, 65, 66, 67, 68, 69, 79, 94, 102, 105, 111, 115, 116, 117, 125, 133, 147, 164, 212
Newfoundland - Burlington, 108
Newfoundland - Deer Lake, 110
Newfoundland - Joe Batt's Arm, 73, 204, 208, 209, 212
Newfoundland - St. John's, 63, 83, 86, 91, 93, 108, 110, 129, 202, 204, 208, 210, 211
Newfoundland - Tilting, 20, 54, 73, 203, 209
Newfoundland - Twillingate, 47, 108, 109, 203
Newfoundland and Labrador, 20, 22, 26, 47, 73, 92, 95, 99, 104, 108, 109, 110, 138, 202, 203, 205, 208, 209, 210
Newfoundland History, 19, 20
Nicole's Café, 50, 129
Nobel Prize, 14
Not-Just-for-Profit., 56
Nouvelle Newfoundland Cuisine, 108
Ocean Advocacy, 112

Ocean Awareness, 56, 66, 112, 115, 116
Ocean Ethic and Literacy Centre, 67, 84, 115, 116
Ocean Network (Education, Research), 112
Ocean Science, 112, 113, 114, 116
Old Economy, 40
Open Systems Planning, 116, 120
Ordinary Folks, 135, 136
Ottawa, 86, 204, 206, 207, 208, 210
Outport, 9, 21, 25, 27, 40, 59, 60, 70, 73, 79, 91, 109, 136, 168
Participatory media (Film, Video), 24, 135
Partridgeberry, 47, 48, 52, 157, 207, 212
Philanthropy, 77, 91, 108, 163
Physical Capital, 55, 56, 57, 58, 90
Pilot, 12, 25, 48, 80, 100, 119, 141, 142, 143, 144, 145, 166
Place-making, 77, 135
Policy, 9, 13, 51, 69, 79, 81, 94, 112, 136, 137, 145, 165
Portugal, 19
Practitioners, 10, 13, 44, 51, 68, 73, 89, 113, 119, 125, 132, 144, 151
Process Improvement, 15, 53, 116
Profitability, 108, 115, 116, 139
Proof-of-concept, 12, 80, 101, 113, 119, 141, 163, 164, 166
Punt, 44, 131
Quebec, 25, 110
Queen Elizabeth I, 19
Random Passage, 109
Red Bay National Historic Site, 9, 109
Regional Development, 3, 4, 5, 10, 12, 13, 22, 25, 41, 43, 51, 54, 77, 79, 81, 83, 84, 85, 89, 92, 100, 101, 102, 104, 107, 119, 120, 125, 135, 137, 161, 163, 165, 166, 167, 168
Regional Economic Development Boards, 5, 13
Regional Planning, 11, 13, 135, 154
Regulatory Issues, 50, 53, 81, 100, 119, 164
Re-purposed Buildings, 58
Resettlement, 22, 23, 24, 25, 26, 27, 80, 132, 134
Residential Program, 105, 116, 144, 190, 209
Restaurants, 38, 48, 49, 50, 51, 57, 70, 71, 108, 109, 129

Return-on-Investment, 115
Revenue Generation, 42, 43, 64, 115, 133, 166
Rockin' Fogo, 51
Rogers, Everett M., 32, 142, 211
Romania, 41, 98
Roseland, Mark, 33, 55, 84, 161, 211
Sacred, 59, 118, 169
Saunders, Todd, 54, 70, 206
Scenarios, 3, 89, 96, 105, 106, 141
Schafhausen, Nicolaus, 64, 106
Scholarship, 114
Self Determination. *See* Empowerment, Localization, Self Reliance
Self-Determination, 44, 103, 111
Senge, Peter, 55, 161, 211
Seven Planning Elements, 31, 37
Seven Seasons of Fogo Island, 159
Sheppard, Kevin, 93
Shorefast Foundation, 3, 10, 11, 12, 14, 15, 19, 22, 25, 27, 29, 31, 32, 33, 37, 38, 40, 41, 43, 44, 45, 46, 47, 48, 50, 52, 55, 56, 57, 58, 63, 64, 65, 66, 67, 68, 69, 71, 75, 77, 78, 79, 80, 81, 82, 83, 84, 85, 86, 89, 90, 91, 92, 93, 94, 96, 97, 98, 99, 100, 101, 102, 103,104, 105, 106, 107, 108, 110, 111, 112, 113, 114, 115, 116, 117, 118, 119, 120, 121, 125, 126, 127, 128, 129, 130, 131, 132, 133, 134, 135, 136, 137, 139, 140, 143, 144, 145, 146, 147, 151, 155, 161, 163, 164, 165, 166, 167, 168, 169, 175, 177, 193, 196, 204, 206, 207, 208, 209, 211, 212
Shorefast Foundation - Board of Directors, 32, 78, 79, 80, 81, 82, 131, 137, 204, 211
Signature Cocktail, 186
Simon Fraser University, 67, 113, 130, 212
Singapore, 12, 51, 114, 165, 166, 205, 209, 212, 214
Slade, Gordon, 32, 67, 69, 79, 80, 136, 168, 196
Smithsonian Environmental Research Center (SERC), 113, 212
Snowden, Donald, 140, 143, 206, 210
Social Business, 3, 26, 100, 102, 118, 131, 139, 161, 166
Social Capital, 26, 55, 56, 57, 64, 84, 85, 101, 132, 168

Social Enterprise, 48, 56, 78, 84, 106, 108
Social Entrepreneurship, 3, 91, 102, 104, 107, 117, 119, 121, 139, 166
Socio-Economic Strategic Plan, 37, 46, 208
Spain, 19, 20
Specificity, 14, 33
Sri Lanka, 165, 205
Strategic Planning, 15, 37, 54, 165, 169
Strategy, 3, 10, 11, 13, 26, 31, 33, 37, 38, 42, 44, 54, 59, 63, 64, 65, 67, 69, 70, 81, 82, 84, 85, 89, 91, 92, 101, 106, 108, 110, 115, 116, 120, 132, 133, 141, 142, 153, 165, 166, 168, 169
Straus, Jozef and Vera, 45
Student-led Faculty Guided Research, 101
Super Lobster Pool Restaurant, 109
Supply Chain Management, 209
Supply Chains, 51, 102, 119
Surplus Allocation, 103, 126
Sustainability, 31, 37, 48, 53, 54, 57, 66, 69, 79, 94, 103, 105, 115, 117, 120, 132, 133, 138, 139, 147, 151, 152, 164, 168, 203, 210
Systems Management, 55, 120
Team, Shorefast Foundation, 3, 14, 15, 77, 79, 81, 82, 86, 94, 120, 125, 137, 139, 161
Technology Action Plan, 153, 204, 205
Test Bed, 141
Thanksgiving, 47, 52, 102, 157
Theory, 31
Toronto, 48, 65, 71, 86, 109, 209, 212, 213
Tourism. *See* Geotourism
Tourtellot, Jonathan, 42, 151
Training, 45, 47, 68, 99, 103, 107, 117, 141, 142, 144
Transparency, 13, 84, 126, 163
Triangles, 49, 166
Truck System, 21
Understanding, 22, 33, 64, 65, 67, 79, 101, 151, 166, 168, 169
University Center for Regional Economic Innovation, 101, 109, 145, 213
University of Guelph, 143, 144, 214
Value Creation, 118, 139
Value-added, 15, 41, 42, 63, 106, 109, 118, 127, 146, 164
Venice, Italy, 19
Vienna, Austria, 63, 64

Volunteers, 31, 86
Ways of Knowing, 37, 57
Wild Forage, 50

Williams, Harold, 92, 136, 214
Yunus, Muhammad, 45